HOSTING STATES AND UNSETTLED GUESTS

WORLDS IN CRISIS: REFUGEES, ASYLUM, AND FORCED MIGRATION

Elizabeth Cullen Dunn and Georgina Ramsay, *editors*

HOSTING STATES AND UNSETTLED GUESTS

*Eritrean Refugees in a Time
of Migration Deterrence*

Jennifer Riggan and Amanda Poole

Indiana University Press

This book is a publication of

Indiana University Press
Office of Scholarly Publishing
Herman B Wells Library 350
1320 East 10th Street
Bloomington, Indiana 47405 USA

iupress.org

Manufactured in the United States of America

First printing 2024

Cataloging information is available from the Library of Congress.

ISBN 978-0-253-06798-2 (hardback)
ISBN 978-0-253-06799-9 (paperback)
ISBN 978-0-253-06800-2 (ebook)

We dedicate this book to all refugees:
past, present, and future.

With love and appreciation for our families,
who supported us on this journey:
G, Zuzu, Griffin, Ermias, Yona, and Sami.

Contents

Preface

WHEN WE STARTED our fieldwork in 2016, the world seemed united in optimism about its capacity to address what had been termed the global refugee crisis. Even though we found many reasons to be critical of the specific policy proposals that undergirded this optimism, we still had hope. Along with many refugees and humanitarian professionals, we hoped that Ethiopia's pledges and the Global Compact on Refugees and the Global Compact for Safe, Orderly, and Regular Migration that followed would provide a platform to leverage even more substantive reforms in Ethiopia and beyond. For refugees in northern Ethiopia, this was not to be the case.

In spring 2020, a year after our last visit to Ethiopia, the COVID-19 pandemic swept across the world, effecting stringent border closures and stranding many already isolated refugee communities. But in Ethiopia, the worst was yet to come.

In November 2020, on the night of the presidential election in the United States and only days after we submitted the complete draft of this manuscript to the press, the Nobel Peace Prize–winning Ethiopian prime minister, Abiy Ahmed, launched a military offensive in the Tigray region of northern Ethiopia in reputed defense against a Tigrayan attack on the government's military base in Tigray (Miller 2022; Mersie et al. 2021). This launched a brutal civil war that has decimated the Tigray region, where the majority of Eritrean refugees resided, as well as the neighboring Amhara and Afar regions. Eritrean forces have played a central and controversial role in the war.

This complex and seemingly intractable civil war stunned even the most battle-scarred of observers with its horrific levels of brutality toward civilians (including refugees) and its tactical deprivations of aid to both civilians and refugees. The Hitsats camp, where we conducted our fieldwork, was destroyed early in the war, as was the Shimelba camp. Two of our other field sites, the Mai Aini and Adi Harush camps, were on the front lines of fighting. We were unable to locate many of our interlocutors. Information blackouts made it impossible to get accurate information.

Given how much has changed and how much instability still persists, a full discussion and analysis of developments after the war began would require turning this into a very different book. For this reason, the primary scope of this book is limited to the initial years of our fieldwork: 2016 through early 2019; however, where we can, we discuss developments beyond 2019. We have also added a brief epilogue noting changes that took place after the war began. The conflict in Tigray raises serious questions about the viability of places like Ethiopia as safe places for refugees to settle long term. The case we discuss here—Ethiopia between 2016 and

2019—is important because it reinforces the need to listen to refugees' concerns about political and policy developments. Refugees always knew that Ethiopia was an unpredictable, uncertain, and potentially unsafe place for them. This book illuminates the effects of policies, which expanded the role of hosting states in the Global South, on unsettled guests who were in search of safety and stability. The guests who appear in these pages became increasingly desperate in the wake of war. As is the case with Eritreans, safety continues to be an elusive goal for increasing numbers of displaced people. We believe that makes this book more relevant than ever.

Acknowledgments

THIS BOOK HAS its origins in Eritrea, a country whose people generously and graciously shared their lives with us, first when we traveled there as Peace Corps volunteers in the 1990s (at separate times and to separate towns), later when we traveled as researchers (at the same time but to separate regions), and during the many times we returned to the country to deepen relationships with friends and, in Jennifer Riggan's case, family. We are currently unable to travel to Eritrea due to the political circumstances that sent many refugees fleeing. Love for Eritrea; a deep concern for the plight of its people, who have been displaced so many times; admiration for their resilience, fortitude, and creativity; and a strong desire to see all of them find a safe haven are at the core of this book.

More than anyone else, we need to thank residents of the Mai Aini, Adi Harush, and Hitsats camps; refugees in Addis Ababa; and refugee university students in various parts of the country, particularly the people we cannot name for reasons of human subjects protections. Many people spent long hours hosting us, talking with us, helping us understand how things worked in the camps, and sharing their worldview with us. We hope we have been able to honor all you have shared with us.

No one writes a book in isolation, particularly one that is as long in coming together as this one. There are many people who have provided support, intellectual guidance, knowledge, insight, and inspiration. Near the top of the list of people we need to acknowledge is Dr. Alebachew Kemisso Haybano, from the Centre for Comparative Education and Policy Studies at Addis Ababa University, who provided all of those things. Other colleagues from Addis Ababa University also provided support during many thought-provoking conversations, including Dr. Temesgen Fereja, Dr. Fekadu Adugna, Dr. Getaneh Mehari, and Mulu Getachew.

It is impossible, when doing research with refugees, to "go it alone." The nature of the work requires a broad network of people who care about your work enough to incorporate you into their networks, explain how permissions are acquired and camps are accessed (a constantly shifting process), and share their wisdom and understanding with you. While we were in Ethiopia, the assistance, advice, insight, and companionship of Dr. Bereket Berhane, Dan Connell, Eyob Awoke, Patrick Phillips, Natalia Paszkiewicz, Tsionawit GebreYohannes, Welai Kidanemariam, and Mulugeta W/Eyesus made this project possible, as did the assistance from other staff who were at the time working for the Danish Refugee Council, the Jesuit Refugee Services, the United Nations High Commissioner for Refugees (UNHCR), Ethiopian Orthodox Tewahedo Church Development and Inter-Church Aid Commission (DICAC), and the Administration for Refugee and Returnee Affairs in Shire, Addis Ababa, and the three camps where we worked. We are particularly thankful to the teachers and school directors who shared insights with us.

Throughout the process of writing this book, we have had intellectual support from many people and institutions. Numerous panels in which we participated at the American Anthropological Association and African Studies Association provided feedback on this work. We are particularly thankful to Samer Abboud and Ben Muller for inviting us to their workshop on International Interventions and Local (In)Security and the subsequent panel at the International Studies Association meeting. We would like to thank Abigail Adams, Laura Bisaillon, Sally Bonet, Lauren Carruth, Cati Coe, Hilary Parsons Dick, Daniel Mains, Marit Ostebo, Terje Ostebo, Trish Redecker Hepner, Susan Shepler, Lahra Smith, Megan Styles, Stephen Thomas, Magnus Treiber, Awet Weldemichael, Mike Woldemariam, and many others for important conversations at conferences, on panels, and elsewhere throughout the course of writing this book. All of the participants at the Georg Arnhold 2019 symposium contributed exceptional work of their own and also provided brilliant support for our initial ideas. We owe a particular debt of gratitude to Thea Abu El-Haj for coorganizing the symposium and for being a stalwart intellectual companion on this and many other projects.

Numerous research assistants at Arcadia University and Indiana University of Pennsylvania (IUP) worked on this manuscript at various stages. We are thankful to Sabrina Calazans, Tamara White, Taylor Mailly, Tessa Kilcourse, Kassidy Brown, Camille Bauerle, Alessandra Sabba, Rachel Kuria, and Rania Rashid.

Riggan is particularly grateful to the intrepid members of her COVID-19 writing group who not only provided a space to write in quiet companionship several times a week but also had undying enthusiasm for this project: Thea Abu El-Haj, Sally Bonet, Beth Rubin, Reva Jaffe-Walter, Elen Skilton, and Karishma Desai.

Riggan received funding and support from the following sources during various phases of the project: Fulbright IIE, the Georg Arnhold program at the Georg Eckert Institute, the Wolf Humanities Forum at the University of Pennsylvania, and the Steinbrucker Endowed Chair at Arcadia University.

Amanda Poole received funding and support from the following sources: a PASSHE Professional Development Grant, the IUP University Senate Research Committee, and the IUP College of Humanities and Social Sciences.

We are deeply thankful to the wonderful editors at Indiana University Press—Allison Chaplin, Elizabeth Dunn, and Georgina Ramsay—as well as the anonymous reviewers, without whom this book would not exist.

Finally, a book does not get written without someone to make sure that the members of your household are fed, go to bed on time, get their homework done, and are generally cared for, and for that we are thankful to our partners, Gerald Smith and Ermias Zemichael, and our extended family members, including Dana, Kelly, Jeannie, Lee, John, Ann, Matt, Erin, Cis, and Kim. More than anything, we are thankful to our children, Griffin, Zuzu, Yona, and Sami, who also sacrificed, albeit unwittingly, while we were traveling to Ethiopia and spent long hours away from them while writing.

HOSTING STATES AND UNSETTLED GUESTS

Introduction

Precarity, Time-Making, and the Case of Eritrean Refugees in Ethiopia

"My Dream Is So Many Things"

Sitting on a low concrete bed in the tent issued by the United Nations High Commissioner for Refugees (UNHCR) that he shared with seven other young men in the Hitsats refugee camp, Habtom told us that he had a hard choice to make.[1] Ethiopia was supposed to have been a way station as he followed his two younger siblings from Eritrea to Europe. When he set out on this journey, he knew the risks of northward migration could include torture, slavery, death, or winding up as a refugee back in this camp or an asylum seeker in another country for an indefinite period of detention.[2] In the camp, to his surprise, he was drawn into government- and international non-governmental organization (INGO) sponsored programs designed to slow onward movement; he was hired to do work for a small amount of incentive pay with an aid organization, volunteered as a teacher with young children, and successfully passed the matriculation exam with the help of an INGO tutoring program, earning him a scholarship to attend a university in Ethiopia.[3] And yet, despite his relative success and his excitement about the possibility of university education, Habtom was haunted by the specter of falling into nothingness in the camp: "Simply sleeping and eating is boring to me. We are like animals." Habtom was so terrified of being stuck in a temporality that he equated to being "like animals" that he was not willing to abandon his goal of northward migration. When we first interviewed him, he surprised us at the end of the interview by asking us to advise him about which possible future to choose: "My dream is so many things! What should I do?" Several months later, Habtom had migrated onward.

Habtom's story is far from unique. His dilemma is particularly striking when we consider that it occurred against the backdrop of a wave of policies put in place to deter migration. Spurred by target countries in the wealthier parts of the world, approaches to migration management increasingly seek to block the flow of migrants and refugees moving northward through offshore asylum processing, detention of migrants and refugees on arrival, or by failing to ensure humane crossings over borders and seas (Collyer 2019; Andersson 2016b). Meanwhile, in the Global South, policies that merge humanitarianism, security, and development function as a form of migration deterrence by encouraging migrants to stay in their home or transit countries.[4] Thus, as literal and figurative walls are thrown up in an effort to deter migration to wealthy countries in the Global North, there are corollary efforts to deter migration in the Global South that are oriented around emphasizing long-term hosting and local integration as the most promising of the three "durable solutions" for refugees.[5]

Despite programs designed to stem onward movement and a widespread awareness of the horrors that migrants face at every step along their journey, Eritrean refugees make up one of the largest groups of migrants attempting to reach Europe, and many of them pass through Ethiopia. At first glance, Habtom appeared to be a poster child for the success of programs aimed at deterring migration by offering opportunities in Ethiopia; he was planful, ambitious, determined, hardworking, and intelligent. His aspirations to continue his education aligned with the goals of educational programs offered to refugees. Significantly, opportunities to study at the university level and work in the camps made Habtom pause and consider remaining in Ethiopia, yet in the end, he migrated. Why would someone take such a risk when they were offered a safe place to stay?

After several years of research in camps and urban settings in Ethiopia, variations on Habtom's story became a familiar refrain. We realized that refugees are motivated not only by place but also by time. Although the camp was a safe place, Habtom said that living there relegated him to a time that was dehumanizing. It was just as important to Habtom to have a future oriented toward what he regarded as progress as it was to have a safe place to live.

What is this notion of progress, and why is it worth the risk of death? Why was the offer of progress in Ethiopia not enough for refugees? To answer this question, it is important to move beyond the idea that all refugees need is a safe place. Our work joins a growing literature that demonstrates that a focus on temporality is essential to understanding both the lived experience of refugees and the discrepancies between how refugees enact temporal agency and the temporal assumptions embedded in humanitarian and migration management policies and practices (Brun 2016; Çağlar 2016; Dunn 2017; Hoffstaedter 2019; Feldman 2018; Horst and Grabska 2015; Jacobsen et al. 2021; Ramsay 2019). One of the premises of our book is that the fundamentally spatial orientation of global approaches to migration deterrence clashes with refugees' fundamentally temporal orientation. While these new policy paradigms look promising for an international community eager to find humane solutions to the so-called migrant crisis, they ultimately misread the needs and motivations of refugees, mistaking their participation in programs or attendance at a university as a desire to settle permanently in Ethiopia and making assumptions about how they think about both the present and the future.

New policy paradigms aimed at local integration are teleological. They are oriented toward an end. This emphasis on a singular end posits a binary between staying and leaving. Not only is this binary problematic, but it also contains a key temporal paradox: policies intend to encourage refugees to *stay*, but discourses, practices, and policies related to hosting refugees (not to mention the material conditions of political instability and violence) continue to promote a sense of *temporariness*. This sense of permanent (or indefinitely extended) temporariness causes refugees to experience the present as protracted and discontinuous with a hopeful future; we refer to this as *temporal suffering*. The juxtaposition of an end point with this condition of permanent temporariness results in a particular form of temporal suffering that we call *teleological violence*. Temporal suffering and teleological violence ensue when refugees work hard to succeed but face structural and symbolic barriers that prevent them from moving forward. These barriers include, but are not limited to, the legal prohibition of refugees' working in the formal sector in Ethiopia and their inability to continue their education at the graduate level. Educational programs, which are often a key component of initiatives to stem migration, play a particular role in teleological violence; they not only promise progress, they also orient people toward it, and yet, the harder refugees work to achieve this promised progress, the more painful temporal suffering and teleological violence become.

New efforts to encourage refugees to stay offer powerful alternatives that refugees take seriously, knowing the perils of irregular migration. Yet the sense of impermanence in the host state and the pain of interminable waiting for opportunities for legal migration are a source of suffering for refugees. This is at the heart of Habtom's choice and of the choices that many refugees are faced with.

Time in Unstable Places[6]

"There are always 30,000 people in the camps, but never the same 30,000 people," a camp official told us when we struggled to comprehend the unchanging nature of population data in the face of camp spaces that were constantly in flux. We returned to the camps in northern Ethiopia every few months between summer 2016 and summer 2018. On each return visit, we found businesses, shops, and restaurants that had previously been open closed, and others that had been closed were open. Some of our interlocutors opened and closed a different business every few months. A young woman who we got to know, the daughter of one of our interlocutors, was engaged in something different every time we came—school one time, then school and a dance group, then just the dance group, then nothing. School directors in the camps constantly bemoaned the fact that they could not hang on to refugee teaching staff because they quit. This everyday instability was often blamed on "onward movement." However, we knew that many who had quit businesses, jobs, or activities had not gone anywhere. They were moving on but without moving out.

We might think of these shifts as attempts at effecting temporal movement. Spatially, camps are spaces of waiting and containment, but temporally, they are spaces of flux and change. Refugees moved from activity to activity, like opening and closing shops and restaurants, hoping that something would yield progress, but it seldom did. As we will detail further, the economy of the camp could not sustain the abundance of small businesses, and refugees were legally prohibited from working or owning businesses outside the camp. The fact that these changes never led anywhere can illuminate our understanding of the relationship between structural violence and agency.

This account of fluidity and flux in the camp is indicative of broader realities of refugees' lives. And yet, refugees are often characterized by their separation from past lives, land, and culture while simultaneously being analytically and physically separated from host country nationals. Until fairly recently, the emphasis on place and place-making neglected the temporal dimensions of migration.[7] One of the reasons migration is regarded as a spatial rather than a temporal process derives from what anthropologists have termed the "sedentarist bias," which asserts that the "natural" condition for humans is to be settled in one place and that each human being has a natural place in their country of origin (Malkki 1995a, 1995b).

The sedentarist bias is problematic because it leads to the assumption that migrants and refugees are supposed to be attached to a particular place, but it also contains within it a linear, teleological narrative. Displacement is supposed to have a beginning, a middle, and a settled end point. Refugees are thought of and think of themselves normatively as being on a linear, teleological trajectory away from a "bad" place and toward a better one (Ramsay 2019). Embedded in these characterizations are assumptions that forced migration is fundamentally spatial rather than temporal, and if time is considered, it is construed as linear and unidirectional. These limited perspectives deny the multimodal, multifaceted, and temporal nature of displacement, which may begin long before people leave their home and continue long after they reach a destination.

As anthropological work on displacement and precarity has begun to more closely examine time, scholars have begun to understand that people are not only uprooted from place; they are uprooted from daily temporal rhythms that order and provide coherence to social life (Ramsay 2019).[8] They are "dis*timed*" (Jansen 2008). This temporal displacement operates on multiple registers. Displacement ruptures incremental time (the rhythm of the day, week, year, etc.) and the coherence of daily routines as people are displaced from habitual routines of thought and action. It also ruptures the life course, operating on an existential level, obliterating expected futures. As Georgina Ramsay observes, displacement involves the loss of the sense of permanence of place and time, "forcing people to radically rethink themselves in relation to a new, uncertain, and often disconcerting projection of the world and future possibilities within it" (Ramsay 2019, 17).

Eritreans are a case in point of the temporal nature of mass displacement, or "distimement" (Jansen 2008). The Eritrea where we lived in the mid-1990s (shortly after Eritrea's independence from Ethiopia) through the mid-2000s (long after the border war had ruptured the postindependence benevolence between the two countries) no longer exists. The places that we inhabited are still there, physically. Some, like the capital city, Asmara, seem frozen in time—it contains a menagerie of Italianate modernist architecture and was declared a World Heritage Site in 2017. But the social relationships that made these spaces into places have profoundly shifted as people fled and families fractured. Long before Eritreans flee the country, they experience both temporal and spatial displacement.

Displacement in Eritrea happens in the context of a temporal incarceration that ruptures both everyday rhythms and a sense of time moving forward. The Eritrean state radically controls people's time in intimate ways. Eritrea is governed as a military encampment that surveils and commandeers human lives and futures. Mandatory national service for all adults in Eritrea extends indefinitely and often involves military service in harsh conditions far from home and the rural and urban livelihoods that depend on them. National service workers receive meager stipends and face extreme restrictions on work and travel that curtail their ability to start or support families. Indeed, some Eritreans we met in the refugee camps noted that the austere political control of life in Eritrea inhibits conception, as husbands may rarely get the chance to visit their wives. The lack of a rule of law and the severe punishments for perceived acts of political disloyalty (like attending a prayer meeting for a religious group outside of the few state-sanctioned religions, attempting to evade national service, or criticizing the single-party state) displace people from a sense that their world is predictable. People may be arrested arbitrarily and detained indefinitely. Asmara may look like a museum in United Nations Educational, Scientific, and Cultural Organization (UNESCO) catalogs, but for many Eritreans, life there entails both being cut off from a planful future and being displaced from the temporal rhythms of daily life at individual and collective levels as people flee, hide, are detained, and disappear. Thus, Eritrean refugees do not become displaced when they flee, but before. Fleeing is their first act of temporal agency. The temporality of displacement begins long before migrants move from place to place. While the temporality of displacement does not begin with fleeing the country, it also doesn't end with asylum in Ethiopia – the bureaucratic temporalities of humanitarian policy profoundly shape time for refugees in ways that continue to be destabilizing.

Speed Bumps and the Slow Temporalities of Humanitarian Policy

We met Habtom for the first time in September 2016, the same month that Ethiopia was taking center stage as a cohost of Barak Obama's Leader's Summit on Refugees, which immediately followed the United Nations Summit for Refugees and Migrants. The United Nations General Assembly had called for the summit of world leaders to encourage global coordination around refugee and migration management. To this end, the 2016 Refugee Summit and subsequent Global Compacts on Refugees and Migration placed a strong emphasis on migration management through changing the nature of refugee hosting in the south with support from wealthy northern countries. The Global Compact joined an emerging series of global policy efforts, like the Khartoum Process and the Rabat Process, to stem the flow of migration, in part by making southern states better hosts. Ethiopia, host to 883,546 refugees at the end of September 2017 (UNHCR 2018a), played a key role in these efforts. Initiatives like the university scholarship program that attracted Habtom are seen as models of good refugee hosting, as is the out-of-camp program (OCP), which has allowed a limited number of Eritrean refugees to reside outside of camps if they can show they have an Ethiopian sponsor.

At the 2016 New York Summit, Ethiopia made nine pledges, many of which were oriented toward ending camp-based care by promoting local integration with the goal of making life for refugees in Ethiopia more viable. These pledges included expanding the OCP to 10 percent of the refugee population; making work permits available to some refugees; creating a hundred thousand jobs in industrial parks, one-third of which would go to refugees; making land available to a hundred thousand refugees; and enabling local integration for refugees who have been in Ethiopia for more than twenty years (UNHCR 2019). There were also pledges to enhance social services, particularly education, and provide documentation, such as birth and marriage certificates, drivers' licenses, and bank account information, to refugees.

The New York Declaration itself came on the heels of the Khartoum Process, which was initiated in 2014 and proposed to coordinate countries along the Horn-Europe migration route to address the dangers of irregular migration. Each of these policy initiatives reflects a major shift in global refugee management paradigms by emphasizing local integration, rather than repatriation and resettlement, as a durable solution for refugees. Refugee studies scholars Alexander Betts and Paul Collier detail the rationale for this policy shift as an economic solution to a failing system of global refugee management, one that would restore "refugees' autonomy through jobs and education" (2017, 10) by incentivizing investment from wealthy nations and corporations into "haven" countries like Ethiopia, where refugees could be incorporated as economic actors, laborers, and entrepreneurs.

Although praise has been given to Ethiopia for its role in refugee hosting, the relationship between the host country and its restless guests is a fraught one. Refugees' perspectives on these emergent migration management paradigms were shaped by their experiences with the tremendously slow rollout of new policies, their awareness of the curtailment of legal migration options, and their knowledge of the increased dangers of irregular migration. While donations immediately began flooding in following Ethiopia's pledges in fall 2016, the developmentalist focus of these pledges met with a great deal of skepticism on the ground. Donors pledged to mobilize $500 million for two industrial parks provided that one-third of the jobs go to refugees, but refugees and INGO aid workers alike wondered who would be willing to move out of the camp and possibly forgo rations and free, if inadequate, housing to work for a dollar a day in industrial parks. Despite the disbelief that providing refugees with work in industrial parks could be an effective strategy, talk about this continued among Ethiopian government officials of the Administration for Refugee and Returnee Affairs (ARRA), the INGO community, and refugees themselves. Yet there was no specificity about the important details, including which of the many camps in the periphery of Ethiopia would provide refugee labor and whether refugees would be given work permits and asked to apply for these and other jobs or be assigned to them. After many months of asking about the status of this pledge, we collected several rumors, all shared in off-the-record conversations, that the move to provide industrial park jobs to refugees was the brainchild of public-private partnerships (not ARRA) and was driven by the goal of attracting funding for industrial parks rather than helping refugees. The link to refugees appeared to be a loose, perhaps only rhetorical, coupling.

As we detail in the next chapter, INGO, and government actors continued meeting to develop plans to implement Ethiopia's new approach to refugee management. Refugees, meanwhile, were told of these pledges in large meetings and reminded of them any time they asked for needed changes to rations or pass permits or for opportunities for higher education or employment. But the new refugee proclamation sat for years, waiting for parliamentary approval. Refugees waited, growing more cynical as the months and years wore on. They had no means to gather information about the status of the pledges, the proclamation, or the implementation of any of these changes. Reminding refugees of the pledges operated as a sort of antipolitics machine; the pledges were a mechanism to keep refugees waiting hopefully instead of pressing for resources that might make their lives in Ethiopia more viable.[9]

On one of our last visits to the camps in summer 2018, we sipped Cokes with Fitsum at a bar along the road that passes through the Mai Aini refugee camp, one of four camps that host Eritrean refugees in northern Ethiopia. As a refugee community leader who had lived in the camp for nearly a decade, Fitsum offered a perspective on change in the camp that was always valuable, even though he typically spent a good deal of time telling us how nothing had changed since our last visit. His analysis of what constituted *nothing* was always incisive.

Refugees in the camp had been waiting for two years for "the pledges" to be implemented into law. Torn between hope and cynicism, they were eager to know what change this promised law might bring but skeptical about whether anything would really improve. As we wrapped up our conversation about the sluggish process of implementing these changes, Fitsum gestured to the busy road in front of us and said with a smile, "One thing has changed. Do you notice anything different?" A large bus, used for long-distance travel along this major transportation route, lumbered over an enormous speed bump in the road, while a smaller minivan and an SUV with an INGO logo on its door slowed to a stop to wait its turn.

"Of course!" we answered. How could we have missed the speed bumps? Only moments before, our own vehicle had made the slow climb over the speed bumps spaced along the crowded road that divided refugee housing, restaurants, and bars from key service providers, such as schools, the UNHCR office, and clinics.

Fitsum told us about his efforts to get speed bumps installed. "We'd been asking for speed bumps for a long time, and they did nothing. Then a child got killed," he said flatly. "It was really a terrible accident."

The speed bumps are emblematic of the slow temporalities of policy. At once a lifesaving triumph and the result of death, they are a persistent reminder that those who create and implement policy designed to protect refugees in their day-to-day lives often remain oblivious to the real needs of refugees—and that people die as a result. The speed bumps were the result of a project that refugee leadership invested in to improve the safety of the camp residents. They are a pointed example of refugees' ongoing and intensive struggles to insert themselves and their needs into the conversation about things that affect them but also a reminder that their efforts may be neglected, even if disaster strikes and people die.

The incident related to the speed bumps calls our attention to temporality in a variety of ways. First, it highlights the sluggishness of humanitarian time. Second, it points to the everyday prioritization of a humanitarian policy that is responsive to procedures set elsewhere. It stresses the fact that refugees probably will not be able to insert their own sense of urgency into those priorities. Finally, it reveals the knowledge refugees gain from living in the time and space of the camp, where attention is often focused on the community and the quotidian dangers and stresses faced by its members. Fitsum's story about the speed bumps thus reveals the disjunctures between the temporalities of humanitarian policy and practice on one hand and refugees' everyday time on the other.

The stalled pledges, which promised progress, provided further evidence that camps were a place where time did not move forward. Refugees waited for years for the rollout of this series of policy reforms that they were repeatedly told would radically improve their prospects. However, a redrafted refugee proclamation, which included provisions for greater freedom of movement, expanded access to education, and delimited rights to work, run businesses, get land, and even attain citizenship, was only voted into law shortly after the conclusion of our fieldwork in January 2019. Furthermore, most components of the revised proclamation, including those that were poised to help refugees the most (for example, the provision of work permits), were not worked out. Refugees in Ethiopia also could not work or open a business legally, nor could they pursue a graduate degree. Their status as noncitizens clearly placed them in subordinate positions. As time passed, refugees felt the potential for each initiative waning.

Ethiopia's 2019 refugee law and the pledges that preceded it were part of a bold experiment in global migration management that encompasses and intersects with a number of initiatives oriented toward stemming onward migration from the Horn of Africa, including the Khartoum Process and the New York Declaration. Viewed from the perspective of migration-deterrence initiatives that seek to secure the borders of Europe while attempting to adhere to humanitarian principles, these new trends suggest a shift in border maintenance southward—or, in other words, an off-offshoring of border management—transforming what has been called a humanitarian-security nexus into a humanitarian-security-*development* nexus, something we discuss in detail in chapter 1. In other words, these policy paradigms sought to merge the management of humanitarian emergencies with migration deterrence through a new emphasis on local integration in large refugee-hosting states in the south.

Given the stalled rollout of new policies, why were Ethiopia's pledges and the Global Compact hailed with such hopes? Why was it thought that these promises would actually make things better for refugees and for the global "refugee crisis"? We would argue that this has little to do with the demonstrated efficacy of such policies and more to do with the underlying assumptions of these policy paradigms. On one hand, these assumptions are teleological; they seek to assign an end point to the trajectory of refugee flight. On the other hand, these policies, as with many refugee policies, contain within them a sedentarist bias that fixates on place rather than temporal notions such as progress, waiting, and being stuck. Taken together, these two assumptions work to locate the end point for refugees in large hosting states in the Global South, such as Ethiopia. We develop both of these points later in this chapter. However, to understand why it is problematic to consider a place like Ethiopia as an appropriate end point for refugees, it is important to recognize Ethiopia as a place of chronic instability with an ever-changing stance toward Eritrea and Eritreans.

Instability in the Hosting State: The Case of Ethiopia

The first time we met with Berihu, a young refugee who would become one of our closest interlocutors, we sat with him on a hotel balcony in the small town adjacent to the camp where he was living. "People always talk about their problems—their pain and their pressure," he mused, "but I want to talk about my hopes." Berihu's talk of the future, however, was threaded with stories of his past. As a young boy, he had witnessed the border war when his town was attacked by Ethiopian forces: "I've seen people shot in front of me, it was terrible. I've seen terrible things during the war. Loud noises still disturb me." His memory of conflict and his fear of violence from the Eritrean government contributed to his overall sense of precarity in the camp, which was too close to the border for comfort. Being there gave him an interminable sense of stagnation and of anxiety for his safety. At one point during our conversation, a truck bed abruptly dropped to the ground with a loud bang that made all of us jump. We looked quickly to Berihu and found him shaken but holding himself together. "It's OK," he told us. "This is daylight, and we are outside."

Berihu's concerns were shared by many Eritrean refugees hosted in Ethiopia, a country that had forcibly expelled people of Eritrean descent just a few decades ago. The concerns of Eritrean refugees like Berihu focused not only on the past but also on their long-term safety in the region. They raised critical questions about the meaning of hosting and hospitality in contexts of instability. And they reminded us that policies related to stricter migration controls and the rollback of refugee protections might be global but are always shaped by (and are themselves a form of) regional politics. The formation of the camps to house Eritrean refugees in Ethiopia and the development of policies specifically focused on Eritrean refugees are constituted by a complex history between the two countries. This history, in turn, shapes the experiences of refugees in Ethiopia. Regional politics are the grounds on which the biographies of people and policy intersect.

Because of the complex history between Ethiopia and the large numbers of Eritreans attempting to migrate to Europe, Eritrean refugees have been at the vanguard of many of Ethiopia's integrative policy initiatives. Eritrea gained its independence from Ethiopia in the early 1990s after thirty years of guerrilla warfare. Prior to Eritrea's 1993 independence from Ethiopia, Eritreans were considered Ethiopian citizens. Following the outbreak of a border war between the two countries in 1998, an estimated seventy-five thousand Eritreans, suddenly recategorized as foreigners, were forcibly deported from Ethiopia to a country that many had never been to. In the early 2000s, after fighting ended and a long state of no war, no peace had begun, Ethiopia started to welcome Eritrean refugees.

In 2004, Ethiopia instituted an open-door policy to Eritrean refugees, ensuring rights of asylum to any who crossed the border. Ethiopia established Shimelba camp in 2004 to house the continuous influx of Eritrean refugees fleeing the country and to provide safer accommodation for the thousands who had been living in Waala Nihibi, a temporary camp located on former battle grounds close to the border (Treiber 2019). Since then, four camps were established in the Tigray region and two camps in the Afar region.

Tens of thousands of Eritreans fled into neighboring Ethiopia, which officially hosted over a hundred and seventy thousand Eritrean refugees in 2018, many of whom resided in six camps along the border (UNHCR 2018b). Some of our interlocutors had been born and raised in Ethiopia, were deported to Eritrea, and then fled back to Ethiopia as refugees. For many Eritreans, however, Ethiopia is a stop on a longer journey that involves extremely dangerous and costly attempts to reach a final site of asylum. In 2015, UNHCR reported that eighty-one thousand registered Eritrean refugees were missing from the camps and were suspected of moving on through irregular channels (UNHCR 2016, 2017a, 2017b).[10]

At the time of our fieldwork, Ethiopia granted prima facie recognition to most asylum seekers from surrounding countries, a practice that was framed by government officials as a form of regional grassroots diplomacy and "people-to-people relations." Eritrean refugees were a particular target of these strategies of grassroots diplomacy. As such, they were perceived as being singled out for special policies that gave them more mobility and privilege than other refugees. For example, in

2010, citing historical and cultural linkages with Eritreans, Ethiopia created the out-of-camp program (OCP), which allowed Eritrean refugees who had a sponsoring family member in Ethiopia to forgo refugee assistance in exchange for living out of camp. Similarly, a college scholarship program was formed to enable refugees who pass a matriculation exam to attend college in Ethiopia. These policies enabled a certain amount of mobility for Eritrean refugees, with limits. The OCP was restricted to Eritreans with family in Ethiopia who may support them, and as work permits were not provided to refugees, many were unable to afford life in urban areas with precarious and low-paid positions in the informal economy. Also, college scholarships were limited in number and accessible only to those with the education level to pass the exam.

Even though Eritrean refugees were the focus of these pilot policies, the process of changing policies to move toward greater local integration was slow and failed to benefit Eritrean refugees. Although Ethiopia declared that it was moving away from a policy of encampment, this long-standing approach to refugee hosting persisted. Eritrean refugees continued to be subject to prohibitions on work in the formal economy and stringent restrictions on mobility. The pledges, and later the new refugee law, promised economic and educational opportunities that never materialized. For Eritreans, the possibility of belonging in Ethiopia was complicated by their refugee status, but also by the political history between the two countries, which we discuss in chapter 2. Thus, Eritrean refugees who had fled an indefinite national service program that commandeered their everyday lives, goals, and future while forcibly containing them in space, then found themselves in Ethiopia, where their refugee status and internment in the camps did the same.

Berihu's fear points to the salience of regional politics but also to the discordant temporalities of hospitality and precarity. There is a rich and growing literature on the concept of hospitality and hosting refugees (Agier 2021; Dikeç et al. 2009; Friese 2010; Rozakou 2012). Much of this literature astutely details the specific culturally contingent political logics and power dynamics involved in guest-host relations, including examinations of how culture in host states and even national identity can form around the act of being a good host (Agier 2021; Appadurai 2019). However, very little of this work explores the notion of hospitality in countries in the Global South. What are the temporalities of hospitality in highly unstable places? How do they engage with the temporalities of local integration, migration, and encampment to shape the relationship between refugees and the hosting state?

We contend that there is a massive disjuncture between the ostensibly permanent nature of integration, which is proffered as an end point, and the impermanent nature of hosting and hospitality. A guest, by definition, is temporary. Furthermore, hospitality may be rendered unstable by the broader political and security situation. The welcome extended to the guest can be revoked. Refugees' status can change. This has certainly been the case in Ethiopia. Policies that posited Ethiopia as a viable long-term hosting state contained within them both a sedentarist bias and teleological assumptions about the ends of refugee flight; however, with the slowness of the policy rollout and the instability of Ethiopia itself, it seemed impossible to imagine that Ethiopia would ever be a place that could provide that end.

Teleological Violence

One of our goals in this book is to explore the intersecting and often clashing nature of different temporalities, the violence of dominant temporalities, and the opportunities that exist for temporal agency (Mathur 2014; Stubbs 2018).[11] We have already noted several different temporalities in refugee and migration management policy—the slowness of humanitarian bureaucracy, the sense of crisis, and the sedentarist teleology inherent in identifying a safe place at the end of refugees' journeys. Teleological time and teleological notions of progress are important to examine because of their dominance in the early twenty-first century. Teleological notions of progress can be thought of as a "hegemonic temporality" (Filippini 2017; Stubbs 2018).[12] Hegemonic temporality, according to Paul Stubbs, "is a force which prevails over other temporalities . . . whilst never managing to assimilate other temporalities completely" (2018, 27). Drawing on Stubbs, we argue that teleological time is hegemonic, not only in refugee policy, but in refugees' temporal imaginaries, even as it is interwoven with other temporalities.

In its broadest terms, teleology is concerned with ends and movement toward an end point. In anthropology and elsewhere, teleology is often equated with modernist notions of progress and viewed through a critical lens (e.g., see Ferguson 1999). Dating back to the Enlightenment, the belief in progress became a conceptual underpinning of the Industrial Revolution, where time was money—an equation that worked to produce a temporally disciplined population and an incessant movement toward "the open horizon of the future" (Nowotny 2018, 48). Recent scholarship in anthropology has reconceptualized teleology in a more general, open-ended sense as the daily experience of working toward certain ends that may be disrupted by conflict, displacement, or loss of agency (Bryant and Knight 2019; Ramsay and Askland 2020).

One might think of modernist conceptions of teleology as distinct from more open-ended notions, but we see them as intertwined and interdependent. The former equates notions of teleological ends to modernist notions of progress, evolution, and the belief in the capacity (or inevitability) of humanity to move forward in a positive direction. The latter focuses more broadly on ends, acknowledging that we are all moving forward toward multiple ends through our ordinary everyday activities. While our focus on the developmentalist underpinnings of local integration policies (especially schooling) leads us to emphasize teleology as progress, we suggest that it is always difficult to disentangle these more open-ended notions of teleology from those of progress. Indeed, putting these different notions of teleology in conversation with each other allows us to raise questions about temporal power and exclusion: Whose teleologies benefit whom?

For example, in some parts of the world, notions of progress may seem obsolete;[13] however, not everyone has the privilege to leave them behind. This is particularly the case when "ends" are pursued in the context of daily life by people who face profound social and economic marginalization. For marginalized people such as refugees, progress is not thought of as a luxury or an option; it is necessary to survive. But even if progress is essential for refugees, it is also elusive, if not impossible to achieve. The necessity of progress coupled with the elusivity or impossibility of actually progressing constitutes teleological violence.

The concept of teleological violence sheds light on how and why policies and projects that seem so aligned with refugee aspirations, such as education and work opportunities, may not only fail to meet intended outcomes but also put refugees in harm's way. In the sections and chapters that follow, we introduce refugees' accounts of the lived experience of teleological violence and how they navigated its painful and vexing contradictions.

Teleological time becomes violent when people believe that hard work, discipline, having a plan, and attaching that plan to broader developmental goals will lead to personal and collective progress and prosperity but also know they will face very specific impediments that will stall their progress and aspirations. In other words, teleological violence ensues when refugees feel beholden to temporalities that promise the rewards of a bright future but also know that that future is out of reach, a condition Elizabeth Cullen Dunn notes in her work on "nothingness" in refugee camps (2017). Teleological violence results from the temporal contradictions produced when disadvantaged populations have experiences that lead them to believe that they can and must overcome limitations that are impossible to overcome.

Time without Telos: The Violence of Waiting and Stuckness

The camp in particular and Ethiopia in general are purgatorial spaces of suffering. Time in camps thickens and becomes weighty and sluggish in no small part because of how narratives of migration and progress position the camp as an unmoving space of stuckness and waiting. It is a way station, not an end point. Refugees are not just incarcerated spatially in camps and detention centers but temporally as well; they are mired in a state of liminality that cuts them off from the future (Brun 2016; Dunn 2017; El-Shaarawi 2015). Long periods of waiting are a component of what we call *temporal suffering*. Temporal suffering refers to how structures that constrain refugees physically also act temporally. One example of temporal suffering is when refugees are forced to endure the "chronic present" when they are relegated to the refugee camp (Dunn 2017). Refugees suffer because there is too much time but also because time lacks meaning. And most of all, they suffer because they have a desire for a future that they cannot control or act in meaningful ways to bring into being.

The problem of waiting is emblematic of both the structural control over refugees' time and the violence of teleological time.[14] Waiting is a key means through which power works through the body in time and space. Pierre Bourdieu discusses the problem of waiting for a future that is "too slow in coming" (Bourdieu 2000, 209). This is not only painful; it is also an expression of power that produces dependency and vulnerability as marginalized groups are made to wait by those who control time and whose time is deemed more valuable. Waiting is also tethered to teleological time for displaced peoples. They are left to wait for an end point of integration or resettlement into a nation-state (Drangsland 2020) in which the present—and the refugees or displaced peoples inhabiting the present—are always incomplete, behind, and lacking (Khosravi 2021). The problem of waiting is not limited to refugees; it also applies to other forms of marginalization and failure to progress (Auyero 2012; Brun 2015; Janeja and Bandak 2018; Jeffrey 2010; Khosravi 2017). However, the constant pressure of teleological time on refugees makes waiting and stuckness particularly acute.

We might think of enforced stuckness as time without telos (empty time, time that stands still, the future that lacks an end point). Time without telos is not inherently painful, but the hegemony of teleological temporalities that normalize progress makes time that does not progress seem like a failure and thus a source of suffering. Teleologies produce particular notions of "ends" and end points that frame assumptions about wants, needs, and a sense of what one deserves (see Olwig 2021 for a discussion of how this plays out in asylum processes). They organize time through a staged, linear sequence oriented toward progress while also assuming the inevitability of progress.

Schooling and the Violence of the Unknowable Future

Teleological violence leaves refugees stuck in an extended period of waithood where time is stripped of telos, while also foreclosing on the future that is promised by teleologies. Many studies of education in refugee camps have pointed out the dilemma of an "unknowable" (Dryden-Peterson 2017) or profoundly precarious future for refugees (Bellino 2018; Dryden-Peterson et al. 2019; Pherali and Moghli 2021; Stevenson and Baker 2018). Cindy Horst and Katarzyna Grabska (2015) refer to this as a condition of "protracted uncertainty." By exploring the problem of the future for refugees, these studies pave the way for us to understand the gravity of the situation that emerges for refugees when they lack a future but desperately need and want one. They do not have the ability to actualize meaningful movement toward an end point, something Ramsay and Hedda Haugen Askland (2020) think of as "teleological rupture."

We can find an example of these violent temporalities in Habtom's story. Habtom was well aware that a university education in Ethiopia might feel like progress in the short term, but because refugees are not permitted to work legally or continue with their education at the graduate level, he knew he would likely wind up overeducated and stuck back in the camp with no prospects for progress. There were plenty of other refugees who had traveled that path, many of whom expressed bitter regret.

Formal schooling is often looked to as a way to fix the problem of the unknowable future and provide a sense of certainty. Indeed, refugees would agree that opportunities for further education are essential. However, making formal schooling available without providing opportunities to use that education is a form of teleological violence that deserves particular attention.

Formal schooling experiences—and success at schooling in particular—produce an orientation toward the future and present that is rooted in both individual ambition and a sense of duty to help society develop. Schools are factories of modernist teleology and a key part of the machinery that has made it so ubiquitous. Furthermore, temporality in schools has been theorized as disciplined; it is ordered incrementally to work toward this teleological end (Foucault 1978). Present and future are ordered in a linear sequence in which one step builds on the previous and leads toward the next. This linear ordering inherently disciplines its subjects, leading them to believe that their actions in the present will shape their future (Foucault 1978). The refugee condition, however, entails structural constraints that prevent refugees from actualizing ambitions installed by the temporal machinery of schooling. Formal education results in teleological violence not only because formal schooling fails to enable refugees to progress but also because it creates expectations.[15]

Teleological violence acts both by blocking the possibility of actualizing certain timelines and holding open other—often more risky and always more painful—timelines. As such, it operates symbolically and structurally but can lead to actual physical violence either through neglect, while refugees wait for promised opportunities, as we saw in the case of the speed bumps, or when refugees give up on waiting and instead actualize their ambitions by making the risky decision to migrate.

The growing literature on temporal precarity among refugees and particularly the notion of the "unknowable future" (Dryden-Peterson 2017) orients us toward thinking about the dilemma of time for refugees, particularly refugee students, but we fill in an important gap in this literature by asking what people *do* in the face of this unknowable future. Our exploration of the interplay of time without telos and different manifestations of teleological time extends and specifies these discussions about the pain caused by the unknowable future.

In contexts in which change is radical and constant, forms of temporal violence, such as waiting, stuckness, and the foreclosing of the future, are complicated by other embodied experiences of time that are at once less linear and more agentive, pushing us to consider a theory of practice that is adapted to understand situations of radical precarity. As Katerina Rozakou (2020) points out, there is a lot of attention paid to the condition of waiting and other forms of temporal suffering for migrants and refugees, but there has been far less focus on "struggles over time." Here, we develop the concept of time-making to explore how refugees fill empty time with meaningful activities that are palliative but also take agency by making their own future. However, even with these highly agentive forms of time-making, refugees never fully escape the pain of time without telos or teleological violence.

From Having Time to Making Time

The Meskel holiday of 2016 was celebrated on a hot September day in communities across the Tigray region of northern Ethiopia, including the four Eritrean refugee camps there. In the Mai Aini camp, the two top Ethiopian administrators were positioned alongside leaders of the Orthodox Church on plastic chairs under ornate umbrellas to witness the five-hour drama recounting and celebrating the discovery of the true cross. Hours later, the bonfire was set ablaze, and people danced and sang in a wide ring around the fire until, much to the crowd's relief, the cross in the center fell heavily to the south, indicating peace for the year to come. In the ceremony, the religious calendar points to a year that should be marked by something different from the last. And indeed, a degree of uncertainty undergirded life in the camps, along a contested border, even for those who had lived there since the first camp for Eritrean refugees opened in Ethiopia in 2004. In everyday life, though, people in Mai Aini were stuck waiting in a sort of timeless space. One of the administrators explained the length of the ceremony that hot day, leaning over to us under the shade of umbrellas held by children, whose arms must have been exhausted by that point: "They are refugees! They have a lot of time."

This statement—that refugees have a lot of time—is misleading. While *having* time calls our attention to an abundance of time that seemed to permeate the refugee camp, the experience of having time was juxtaposed with the experience of being controlled by time. Refugees had little control over how much time they had, when events occurred, or how time was allocated, let alone how resettlement processes unfolded in ways that were experienced as obscure and nonlinear. The assumption that refugees *have* a lot of time, particularly in the present, often accompanies depictions of their lives as empty, vacant, and unmoving. As we noted earlier, these concepts are central to teleological violence. However, failing to acknowledge that refugees also have temporal agency can result in an emphasis on their victimhood and therefore miss the temporal dimensions of decisions that they make.

How do we make sense of temporal agency in the context of displacement and humanitarian containment? Mustafa Emirbayer and Ann Mische define temporal agency as "a temporally embedded process of social engagement, informed by the past . . . but also oriented toward the future" (1998, 962); it is the capacity to imagine alternative possibilities and operate practically in the present in relation to an evaluation of past and future. This definition was developed to avoid linearity and is useful in terms of thinking through how people draw from the past and future to act in the present, but we find that it does not fully escape the idea of a unidirectional movement of time. Indeed, we found that refugees often engaged with time in ways that reflected their rejection of the idea of past as behind, future as in front, and present as sandwiched in between. Instead, they practiced stretching and shrinking different units of time by making them meaningful or altering their meaning.

Focusing on disruption complicates these ideas about the relationship between past, present, and future (Kallio et al. 2021).[16] Sami Hermez's notion of "in the meanwhile" calls attention to how the present and future are put in a nonlinear relationship with each other, selectively decoupled and recoupled (2017). In between bouts of conflict in Lebanon, Hermez's interlocutors created a sense of normalcy while anticipating the possibility of new waves of conflict breaking out at any time. Refugees' orientation toward the present is similarly bracketed by the anticipation of unforeseeable yet expected events in the future and a need to find meaning in the present despite concerns about the future. Similarly, Kirsi Kallio, Isabel Meier, and Jouni Häkli's notion of "radical hope" explores how displaced people find meaning in the present and future and in the relationship between them. Radical hope "involves an active orientation toward the present along with dissociation from the facts of anticipated futurity that constantly threaten to thwart people's agency" (Kallio et al. 2021, 4008). These perspectives on temporal agency are critical because they push back against the dehumanizing forms of temporal violence that leave people waiting, steal their time, and render them perpetually backward or as not belonging to modern times and places (Khosravi 2021). We explore particular mechanisms of temporal agency that become ways in which refugees seek solace in their efforts to improve the present and insist that a desired future be possible.

What we call *time-making* is an agentive response to the pain brought on by temporal suffering and teleological violence. In colloquial speech, *making time* is a saying suggesting that amid a chronic shortage of time, we can make more time—which is, of course, impossible. The phrase *I'll make time* evokes a spatial imagery of squeezing things in or moving large objects. What we are really doing when we claim to make time is prioritizing, giving precedence to certain activities or events over others; for example, rest or time with family and friends gets pushed to the side to make time for work, or a passion project gets delayed when someone of higher rank tells us to focus on what they want us to focus on. When we say we will make time, we are saying that certain things warrant more time or are better suited to certain specific times than others. In other words, making time is an act of ascribing meaning to events within time. Although refugees do not often suffer from a scarcity of time (although they sometimes do), given the abundance of temporal pressures that they face, they still prioritize how to use their time and engage in acts that make time meaningful, and many resent when their ability to make time is taken from them.[17]

To understand how time is made meaningful, we draw, in part, on theories of place-making. Through processes of place-making, people engage in symbolic practices and rituals that endow space with social meanings. More than just serving as a neutral background for social action, place involves social processes and practices that are shaped within particular environmental, historical, and political conditions (Altman and Low 2012; Gupta and Ferguson 1997; Raffles 2014). As a result, everyday spaces become meaningful places, but they also attach themselves to longer-term time as it punctuates the life cycle and cosmological time as it attaches a lifetime with a broader set of meanings. Just as refugees ascribe place with meaning (Lems 2016), they also engage in temporal strategies that make time meaningful. Indeed, for people who are forcibly displaced and then forcibly contained as a result, having agency over making time meaningful may be more important than making place meaningful and also may be an integral part of coping with precarity, permanent temporariness, and living in undesirable places. If place-making is about endowing physical space with meaning through a variety of social and relational processes and thereby turning it into place, then similarly, time-making endows particular points in time with meaning through sociality and relationships.

Time-Making and Teleological Violence

In the vignette that began this introduction, Habtom spoke of the pain of living in the camp. Time in the camps has been described both in the literature and by refugees themselves as "nothingness" (Dunn 2017) or "empty time"—what we also think of as time emptied of telos. Research in camp settings explores how this temporality is fraught with uncertainty and suffering, as refugees are unable to work meaningfully toward a desired future (Brun 2016; Dunn 2017; El-Shaarawi 2015) and are stuck waiting in conditions of protracted containment (El-Shaarawi 2015). We might say that Habtom had lost what Arjun Appadurai calls the "capacity to aspire" (Appadurai 2004). And yet, he continued to aspire, clinging to "radical hope" (Kallio et al. 2021).

One of our objectives here is to understand how temporal agency manifests among a population suffering under one of the most repressive sets of structural constraints. We shift focus to supple, multitemporal connections between actions and aspirations, the imagination of alternate futures that lack connective tissue to the present, and alternate relations to the present that are not just about waiting but also about care. We argue that temporal agency in conditions of displacement exists in a symbiotic relationship with teleological violence. Temporal agency manifests in the presence of stuckness and spatial constraint, especially given that stuckness renders the present unstable and the future out of control.

We take up several questions as we theorize the symbiosis of temporal agency and teleological violence among refugees: How does temporal agency work in conditions of displacement, where the temporality of suffering is openly acknowledged and teleologies are simultaneously desired and acknowledged as a source of suffering? What kinds of temporal practices reflect the phenomenology of the unstable present and out-of-reach future? How does taking agency over time—what we call *time-making*—enable refugees to cope with enforced stuckness while waiting for a future that may or may not come? How do refugees take control over a future that has been all but foreclosed?

Time-making calls our attention to the materiality and phenomenology of lived everyday experience as they are embedded in and exert pressure on the broader imaginaries and narratives of time, progress, and stuckness. Borrowing from approaches to phenomenology that place phenomenological perspectives alongside an analysis of social structure and political economy (Desjarlais and Throop 2011), our concept of time-making seeks to place the temporality of refugee experiences alongside both imaginaries of progress and structural constraints to achieving progress.[18] This resonates with practice theory, which explores the dialectical relationship between structure and agency, as humans are shaped by social, economic, and political structures but are simultaneously participating in and altering the ways in which these structures shape them, along with the structures themselves (Ortner 2006).[19] Bourdieu's theory of practice is also foundational to understanding the temporal operation of power and structural violence (1977). Bourdieu understands the actor to formulate a relationship to the near and distant future while rooted in present experiences. Through bodily action and rhythm within particular social spaces, the body forms a relationship to space and to time. Lines of difference and power operate within the context of this spatiotemporal habitus.

We explore three distinct strategies by which refugees make time. The first includes a strategic embrace of the telos of education—particularly higher education—that recognizes and pushes back against barriers faced by refugees. The second strategy involves caretaking, a form of time-making that is concerned with the present and involves warding off stuckness, imposed waiting, and the purgatorial suffering of empty time. Finally, a critical form of time-making involves prophetic future-making. Distinct from the linear and incremental expectations of planning, prophetic future-making attaches to a point in the distant future (Guyer 2007) and disciplines the present in accordance with that distant future that may not ever come.

Refugees engaged with education as a form of time-making that embraces teleological time, in spite of its contradictions. Teleological time is both a source of suffering and extremely important to refugees. Refugees often described education as a counterpoint to the empty time in the camp because it was a medium that should connect the present to a hopeful future if one is willing to work hard enough. Education not only produces an imaginary of progress, but through processes of schooling, it also disciplines people such that they order and organize their daily lives in service to that notion of progress. Habtom noted, "People [will] work for development in general. You need quality of life. That is why I'll take any education—in order to bring progress, to grow up." But, as we detailed earlier, these notions of teleological progress also hurt refugees because they shifted the focus away from the structural impediments to progress toward refugees' use (or misuse) of time. Despite the pain caused by education, refugees wanted—and felt that they deserved—progress. This is why many refugees sought out educational opportunities, and even in light of the failure of education to produce a viable future, they advocated for more. In order to make formal education arrive at its promised end, educated refugees organized and advocated for refugees to have the same future opportunities as Ethiopians; they engaged in teleological time-making.

Caretaking involves efforts to fill the present in meaningful ways. The concept of temporal caretaking that we develop in chapter 4 focuses our attention on how certain habits, rituals, and practices geared toward the present play an important role in supporting mental health and community building. Refugees' efforts to improve their communities are palliative forms of time-making by which they heal from temporal harm, even as it is constantly unfolding. Caretaking wards off the suffering caused by waiting, stuckness, and enforced presentism by making a temporary place more livable. Caretaking often involves a focus on community, such as grassroots centers to care for the mentally ill, small businesses, and youth tutoring programs. At the same time, caretaking rejects the teleological orientation of policies that posit Ethiopia as a permanent end point—a place of settlement.

The third time-making strategy we explore is prophetic future-making. Given the precarity of teleological time, how do refugees make the future? The problem of the future for refugees and other marginalized people has been well theorized. Ghassan Hage (2016) discusses the importance of a future in which you can expect to have expectations. Appadurai theorizes people as inherent future-makers. Relatedly, a rich literature on hope notes its particular temporal structuration (Miyazaki 2006; Brun 2016; Jansen 2016). We contend that hope is an essential temporal concept, but it needs to be understood for its phenomenology, its material effects, and its particular relationship to the future. When Berihu recounted the traumas of war and the strains of living as a refugee in Ethiopia, he introduced his comments by saying, "I want to talk about my hopes." Hope, as we discuss in chapter 5, is not a luxury; it is an essential strategy of prophetic future-making.

Caught between the specters of traumatic, empty time and the violence of teleological time, refugees turn to various incarnations of future-making that are oriented toward what Jane I. Guyer calls prophetic time (2007). Prophetic time is a temporality that abandons the near future and a sense of incremental planning, focusing instead on the distant future. Prophetic time enables an escape from the drudgery of empty time, arguably making the emptiness of the present bearable. It also leaps over the incremental steps of teleological time. Prophetic time-making is not simply imaginative; it leads to decision-making that has material consequences as planfulness and caution are abandoned and risky actions, including but not limited to secondary migration, come to seem like the only option. Future-making based on prophetic notions of time is a way of conceptualizing the future in a manner that rejects the logics of linear teleologies and instead moves toward a future that is out of reach, distant, and does not have clear steps to reach it. In this dispensation, the dream of the future is actualized in the present through a series of daily disciplined actions with no direct connection to the aspirational future. It is based on faith that that future will come to pass. Prophetic future-making correlates with caretaking because it abandons the near future and any prospect of planning for or controlling it.

Although refugees are faced with certain structural constraints and temporal violence, they are not without agency. When we first visited the camps, we were struck by what appeared to be an abundance of time and how slowly things seemed to move. As we spent more time in the camps, it became clear that the slow pace did not indicate a lack of urgency or forward thinking. This was not a vacuum where time—or forward-moving time—did not exist; it was a space of clashing temporalities. In chapters 3, 4, and 5, we explore these strategies in more detail, noting that refugees make time through acts of caretaking, their advocacy for making teleological time work for them despite their wariness of it, and the selection of distant- over near-future-making. These stories help us appreciate how, although people suffer tremendously because of time and telos, they are not passive.

Methodology

Our research took place between 2016 and 2019 and involved six periods of fieldwork in three Eritrean refugee camps in the Tigray region and longer-term research in Addis with urban refugees and policy makers over the course of a year (2016–2017). We have focused on education as the crucible in which refugees come to position themselves in relation to their home and host state, craft their aspirations, and understand belonging in local and global communities. As such, we observed classrooms and interviewed school directors, teachers, students, and former students of the primary and secondary schools that refugees attended. We conducted focus groups and individual interviews with students in various stages of participating in Ethiopia's refugee college scholarship program, from those preparing for the matriculation exam, to enrolled students, to graduates. We also interviewed NGO workers and administrators involved with vocational training programs, psychosocial support programs, and community theater programs geared toward limiting secondary migration. In addition to face-to-face interviews with Eritrean refugees living in and out of camps, we have used social media to connect with focal participants, some of whom have left the country, matriculated to distant university campuses, relocated to urban areas, or returned to camps. Our research draws heavily from interviews with young men, who make up most of the camp populations and the population of refugees involved with the college scholarship program. As a multisited project, this is not an ethnography of the refugee camp as such.

Rather, we focus on the overlapping temporal and spatial realities facing refugees who live in or move through Ethiopia.

This research focuses on three of the camps in Tigray—Mai Aini, Hitsats, and Adi Harush—as well as on refugees in Addis Ababa and at various universities. Mai Aini was formed in 2008 and was the site of intensive programming related to the care and education of youth and minors. In addition to the Ethiopian and transnational organizations operating in Mai Aini, there were nine camp-based organizations that formed to assess and address refugee needs, including a youth association and children's parliament (UNHCR 2018c). A short distance from Mai Aini, Adi Harush was established in 2010, bringing a population of refugees to the camp and attracting local Ethiopians to the adjacent village of Mai Tsebri, which grew into a town with a bustling market and a secondary school filled with Ethiopian and Eritrean students. Opened in 2013, Hitsats was the newest camp and was the only camp in Tigray not connected to the national power grid. Hitsats was more isolated, located farther north at the end of a gravel road in a depression that creates a hotter climate. Despite its resource issues, the most rapid expansion of infrastructure was occurring at Hitsats during our fieldwork, and the largest number of new arrivals were being sent there. Also, Hitsats had a reputation for being the camp to which refugees were sent when it was suspected they may attempt to leave the country. We also held regular focus groups with Axum University students and were in touch with refugee university students and graduates in Addis Ababa.

Throughout the course of our research, we attempted to balance ongoing relationships with breadth. We connected with people who were particularly insightful—both refugees and INGO employees—across time and sometimes space. One of the biggest challenges with multisited research is not having enough time to allow relationships to develop organically. For this reason, having an intentional focus was essential. While we did make efforts to connect with a variety of people, education served as a fulcrum for this work, and we made extra efforts to seek out those who were attending or had attended a university; our visits to the camps were ordered with visits to the schools and other facilities that were providing educational programming. However, we also made sure to conduct focus groups with out-of-school youth, recent arrivals, and dropouts and to converse with people we met on meandering walks through the camps, although wandering through the camps was often challenging.

Research across time and space reveals excruciating inequalities and disjunctures. We often had to work at a frenetic pace to conduct research with people who were stuck in place and had a lot of time. In contrast, we never had enough time. Our own schedules and the demands of being hosted in the camps meant that we were often rushed. And yet we valued any time we could find to just "hang out," the most tried and true of ethnographic methods. Perhaps not surprisingly, some of our most useful research relationships have emerged in the electronic sphere, in the space between visits to "the field."

All of our research encounters were overshadowed by the pressing question of the meaning of research. One of our interlocutors, on our first meeting, stated, "You keep coming back and asking us questions, and nothing changes." At first, we were confused. We had never met this individual before, but his comment spoke to the perceived futility of research on and with refugees. In contrast, another interlocutor regularly implored us to "be a big microphone" and to find a way to broadcast refugee concerns to the world. We close with the words of one of our interlocutors, who emailed us as we were drafting this introduction: "If it is too late for me, it is not too late for my son. You must tell the story that we are not free to tell. The world must know about our struggles." The assumption here is that those who hear these struggles are not already aware of them and will care to change them. We write this in the hopes that this is true.

Overview of the Book

Teleological time is part of the processes that generate displacement and the cruelties of temporal and spatial confinement. It produces particular notions of "ends" and end points that frame assumptions about what refugees need or want. Teleological violence forms a through line for this book. Chapters 1 and 2 focus on how policies and bureaucracies produce these forms of violence. Chapter 1 explores a new wave of policies emphasizing local integration as a form of teleological violence brought into being in response to a perceived migrant crisis in Europe and the requisite mandate that the crisis be addressed by stemming migration in home, host, and corridor countries in the south. Chapter 2 specifies the case of Ethiopia and demonstrates that despite Ethiopia's being positioned as a stable country and a viable end point, the long history of animosity (particularly toward Eritrea and Eritreans) and the always-temporary nature of hospitality explain why refugees regard it as a transit country rather than a viable end.

Chapters 3 through 5 turn to forms of refugee agency, exploring the interplay of temporal violence and distinct strategies of time-making. Through projects of time-making, refugees strategize toward different kinds of future *and* engage temporally with particular spaces. Each chapter takes up a different form of time-making among refugees and examines its intersection with temporal violence. Chapter 3 takes up the paradox of teleological time, which refugees both covet and understand as causing them tremendous suffering. Chapter 4 looks at the interplay of *camp time*, which is structured by the politics of waiting and the bureaucratic-legal limitations faced by refugees (even outside of refugee camps), and caretaking, a form of time-making concerned with making the present more livable, even in a temporary place. Chapter 5 turns to the future and considers the ways that refugees function as future-makers even amid extremely constrained—and perhaps impossible—options.

Notes

1. All names used throughout this book are pseudonyms.
2. Throughout this book, we use the term *refugee*, rather than *asylum seeker* or *migrant*. We do this for several reasons. First, we set out to study refugees and the policies, laws, and practices of refugee management in Ethiopia. The majority of our interlocutors were legally refugees in Ethiopia; all identified as refugees. Second, we believe that the term *refugee* is more specific than migrant in an important way: it refers to people who understand themselves as having fled from a life that was untenable due to war, natural disaster (including climate change–related disasters), political persecution, or a broad swathe of other circumstances that put them in danger. We do not use the term as a means to draw arbitrary, legal distinctions between refugees, asylum seekers, or migrants or to privilege the refugee category. Indeed, the individuals we are writing about would likely be labeled asylum seekers or migrants if they chose to leave Ethiopia and migrate elsewhere. The term *refugee* is an important one because it emphasizes those in need of refuge; however, the current, increasingly restrictive laws, legal systems, and legal processes around the world are not capable of determining who is and is not a refugee. The legal terminology, therefore, is reductive. Around the world, there are exponentially more people who merit refugee status than receive it, including many Eritrean refugees in Ethiopia who make the journey northward.
3. Refugees who live in camps are not legally allowed to work, but they can receive a small amount of incentive pay, which amounts to pocket money for work done. Incentive workers often perform vital functions in the camp, and the lack of payment for these services is something that is noted as problematic. Incentive pay, at the time of our fieldwork, was approximately one dollar per day.
4. We adopt Catherine L. Besteman's (2019) framework of the Global North and Global South to describe migration management paradigms, pointing to the bifurcation of the world into zones of resource extraction that have made daily life unsustainable and zones of wealth accumulation (namely the United States, Canada, Europe, Australia, New Zealand, Russia, the Gulf States, and East Asia).
5. The three durable solutions are local integration, resettlement, and repatriation. In light of protracted conditions of war and political violence around the world, repatriation is increasingly seen as a very limited durable solution. More recently, with the drying up of resettlement opportunities due to policy shifts in the United States and elsewhere, local integration in countries of first asylum is often posited as the most viable option.
6. Our thinking here is inspired by Carol J. Greenhouse, Elizabeth Mertz, and Kay B. Warren's work (2002) on ethnography in unstable places.
7. Even initial attempts to focus on time and temporality in humanitarianism have had a spatial focus, emphasizing being stuck in place as a precarious liminal condition. We draw on and contribute to a growing body of literature that shows being "stuck" is a complex, nonlinear temporal condition (Brun 2016; Dunn 2017; Ramsay 2019; Horst 2006).
8. Traditional analyses of time in anthropology have not adequately accounted for situations where things are simultaneously in almost constant flux and in stasis. Time is often thought of as instrumental on one hand and linear on the other. Earlier anthropological approaches were particularly interested in two elements of temporality: first, understanding how time was organized and coordinated incrementally in the short term (hour, day, week, year), and second, understanding the processes of meaning-making vis-à-vis the much longer passage of time (lineage, descent, heredity, cosmology). Émile Durkheim observed that time

provides a frame to organize common human experience and divide experience into categories ([1912] 1965). Bronislaw Malinowski focused on time as a measuring and coordinating device (1927). Time is also a way to produce and reproduce common meanings. Edward Evan Evans-Pritchard introduced a dual/concurrent notion of time as divided into ecological time, which refers to everyday temporal rhythms, and structural time, which points to structures that allow for the long passage of time—in his case, intergenerational descent (1939). Building on Evans-Pritchard's assertion that time is not only a means through which to unify, organize, and coordinate, but also embedded in the lived, social experience of the everyday, the field of anthropology has continued along this trajectory, detailing and exploring the ways multiple temporalities coexist and intersect. These same framings are helpful to understand what happens when time is ruptured.

9. These policies can be seen within the conceptual framework developed by Tricia Redeker Hepner and Magnus Treiber (2017, 2020) to consider how refugees are depoliticized by contemporary migration management policies.

10. According to UNHCR's end-of-year reporting on numbers of Eritrean refugees in Ethiopia at the end of 2016, there were 165,300 Eritrean refugees in Ethiopia (2016). During 2016–2017, data collection including biometric verification was improved. In 2017, UNHCR reports two different sets of numbers of Eritrean refugees in Ethiopia. End-of-year reports indicate that there were 164,700 Eritrean refugees in Ethiopia (2017a). However, the UNHCR website on Eritrean refugees and asylum seekers from Eritrea to Ethiopia notes significantly different numbers: "By the end of 2017, UNHCR, in partnership with the government of Ethiopia, partners, and the donor community provided protection and humanitarian assistance to 75,074 Eritrean refugees hosted in 6 camps in the Tigray (38,064) and Afar (37,010) regions" (2017b). In conversations with NGO officials, ARRA staff, and camp administration, it was commonly noted that some eighty thousand to ninety thousand refugees had been "lost." There were various theories for this, including data collection errors, a large amount of onward movement between 2016 and 2017, and undocumented refugees living in urban areas.

11. Nayanika Mathur (2014) notes the multiplicity of forms of temporality and discusses the intersection of several different ones, bureaucratic and nonbureaucratic. She argues that bureaucratic time mediates between conflicting temporalities. We take our cue from Mathur's work in our understanding of the relationship between different temporalities but focus less on bureaucracy and instead examine how notions of teleology show up in different temporalities.

12. It is useful here to think about how Stubbs brings together notions of heterotemporalities (or multiple temporalities) and hegemonic temporality. According to Stubbs, "Taken together these concepts allow us to address 'temporal plurality' without ignoring dominant power structures which tend to unification" (2018, 3).

13. Helga Nowotny argues that the concept of progress has aged in recent decades, overcome by planned obsolescence, waste products, environmental crisis, and war, leading her to question how people claim temporal agency when the present begins to "devour the future" and "the horizon remains flat and motionless" (2018, 49). While this is an important observation, we also note that the concept of progress still holds sway in many parts of the world and among marginalized, precariously situated populations who still need to progress (or at least to believe in progress) to survive.

14. Waiting has become a popular topic in the anthropology of time, particularly among anthropologists interested in the condition of marginality and displacement. Craig Jeffrey, Patricia Jeffery, and Roger Jeffery (2008) note that waiting may be an existential condition, as people wait for a future that conditions of marginality have held at bay, a situation that is particularly painful for educated people who have done all the "right" things and failed to

succeed. Vincent Crapanzano theorizes "waiting as a de-realization of the present" and further elaborates that "waiting . . . is directed towards the future—not an expansive future, however, but a constructed one that closes in on the present. . . . Its only meaning lies in the future—in the arrival or non-arrival of the object of waiting" (1985, 44).

15. In contexts where there is overeducation, the wrong kind of education, and/or mass youth underemployment, education can also produce false hopes and lead to despair (O'Neill 2014; Mains 2011; Jeffrey 2010; Jeffrey et al. 2005; Derluguian 2005). This notion of a future that is inaccessible or out of reach due to structural barriers provides the foundation for much work on youth unemployment, structural barriers, and precarity. For example, in the context of urban youth in Iran, Shahram Khosravi explores how keeping people waiting without losing hope has "been part of the mechanism of domination" (2017, 79)—a technique of statecraft that produces dependent subjects, or what Javier Auyero refers to as "patients of the state" (2012). Waiting and boredom are also key attributes of unemployed educated Ethiopian youths' sense that they have been betrayed by the future (Mains 2011). Unemployed educated youth embody a set of habits and practices that reflect this complex relationship with a future that they still want to have hope in, despite the visceral evidence of it having failed them. As they fill the time with chewing khat and other activities, they remake social worlds around the precarity of the future. In a similar vein, Jeffrey's (2010) work on Indian unemployed youth explores an array of similar practices, referred to as "timepass."

16. Kallio, Meier, and Häkli draw on Emirbayer and Mische's (1998) Meadian conceptualization of the three temporal facets of agency related to past conditioning, problematizing the present, and responding to possible future uncertainties (Kallio et al. 2021). But their emphasis on disruption allows them to move beyond the predetermined sense of how the past, present, and future influence each other that is part of the Meadian formulation.

17. In some respects, this is similar to the concept of "time tricking," which refers to the "different ways in which people individually and collectively attempt to modify, mangle, bend, distort, speed up or slow down or structure times they are living in" (Moroşanu and Ringel 2016, 14). Roxana Moroşanu and Felix Ringel argue that time tricking has two manifestations— changing perceptions of time and changing the contents of time's succession. Less emphasized in the concept of time tricking is the present, particularly the phenomenological present that is lived in a state of stuckness or waiting and the relationship of the present with the making of the future that serves as a logical response to the foreclosure on teleological notions of progress.

18. Robert Desjarlais and C. Jason Throop (2011) argue that phenomenology often has been misunderstood based on simplistic understandings of consciousness and a flawed belief that phenomenological approaches did not acknowledge the presence of politics, structures, or discourses. The variant of phenomenology that we draw on is similar to practice theory in that both look at the dialectical relationship between structure and agency.

19. Temporalities of practice theory are often more concerned with historical time. Sherry B. Ortner (2006) notes that things change slowly, so attending to historicity matters. Thus, for practice theory, a turn to historicity was important to make other imperceptible changes perceivable over time. However, we need to raise questions about this for a couple of reasons: First, how is this assumption of change as slow and hard to perceive without attending to the long *durée* relevant to contexts where change is radical and constant? What does it mean to bring theories of temporal power into phenomenological discussions of temporal agency?

1 Migration Deterrence and the Nexus of Humanitarianism, Development, and Security

"In Ten Years, We Will Not Have Refugee Camps"

When we first heard the above words spoken by a midlevel administrator at the Ethiopian Administration for Refugee and Returnee Affairs (ARRA), we thought it sounded fantastical. Up until this point, Ethiopia had maintained a fairly strict encampment policy, placing the vast majority of nearly nine hundred thousand refugees in camps constructed along the perimeter of the country. But then we heard the same thought repeated almost word for word by ARRA's deputy director. Soon, the phrase started appearing on television, in various media sources, and in policy documents. Clearly, Ethiopia's refugee policies were on the move, even if their end goal was to ensure that refugees would not be. What was going on here? Although depicted in Ethiopia as a component of the country's distinct strategy of being a generous host of refugees, something we take up in chapter 2, this shift away from encampment and toward local integration also reflects global changes in the humanitarian policy apparatus and in migration management.

There are long-standing and well-developed critiques of the humanitarian policy apparatus. While all these critiques acknowledge the inability of the humanitarian regime to properly care for or protect refugees due to lack of funding or political will, many focus on the problem of the so-called durable solutions.[1] Durable solutions are based on a sedentarist teleology; they are focused on getting refugees to a safe *place* and as such are teleological, or oriented toward a particular end. This emphasis on place inherent in durable solutions fails to recognize that the problem of refugees is not only physical (locating bodies in places) but also political and thereby neglects refugees' elusive quest for rights, which are denied in no small part because refugees do not fit into the "national order of things" (Malkki 1995b). We would extend this argument to say that the problem of the humanitarian apparatus is also a temporal—and a teleological—paradox. While the humanitarian policy apparatus has a mandate to come up with a settled end point for refugees, it inevitably fails to do so. Indeed, local integration has been critiqued for creating a class of people deemed settled but without full citizenship rights (Hovil 2014).[2] Meanwhile, refugees have their own teleological orientation and desire for progress, which illuminate the teleological violence of both durable solutions and the policy paradigms introduced to replace them.

Several suggestions to address the failure of durable solutions have been proposed. Katy Long (2014) notes the need to exchange the settled ends promised by durable solutions for more open-ended and long-term processes of development and peace building. She also argues for thinking about more open migration as a trajectory apart from durable solutions. Indeed, a growing literature argues that migration is a key strategy of development, and the fact that the Global Compacts on Refugees and Migration were created in tandem and are often referenced together seems to recognize the importance of considering the linkages between the two phenomena.[3] However, in contrast, migration management paradigms in Europe and elsewhere have only grown more restrictive. Migration management has been in transition for several decades, with a clear trend: following the oil shocks in the 1970s, it has steadily become increasingly difficult for economic migrants to access legal pathways for migration northward (Andersson 2016a) and for asylum seekers to access legal channels to migrate and claim asylum.

Alexander Betts and Paul Collier propose a different approach to the refugee crisis (2017). They detail the political and economic fallout that they believe would ensue from guaranteeing the right to migration. They also challenge the current ethics that underpin the refugee regime, questioning the extent to which it is the international community's responsibility to protect and provide safe havens for refugees. The concept they develop that has been most resonant with policy, however, is that of the win-win solution: creating greater economic opportunity for host countries through emphasizing refugees as economic actors.[4] This raises a critical question about whether this new emphasis on development is supplanting traditional notions of protection.

The emphasis on development over protection is found in an array of initiatives, some of which had been in place for several years, and others that were coming online at the time of our fieldwork. The Khartoum Process and the Global Compact on Refugees—the former intergovernmental and regional and the latter intragovernmental and global—are different from each other in many respects; however, they converge around the common notion that development will stem irregular migration and facilitate economic opportunities for both refugees and hosts.

This developmental approach to refugee management has often been paired with initiatives that sought to limit migration. The Rabat and Khartoum processes in 2005 and 2014, the Valletta Summit and subsequent development of the European Trust Fund for Africa in 2015, and more recently the Global Compacts, have led to an increasingly securitized form of migration management. These recent processes have not only solidified the long-term trend of securing northern borders but also have extended this border protection southward into countries like Ethiopia with a new suite of policies focused on encouraging migrants to remain in their region of origin (Andersson 2016a; Collyer 2019; Chandler 2018).

A key question that needs to be raised is whether these economic development approaches to refugee management are something new or are another form of local integration stripped of the humanitarian promises of an end point, a safe place, and protection. When viewed from the perspective of refugees who continue to languish in camps, initiatives such as the Khartoum Process and the Global Compacts seem to be the latter, as they fail to bring about the promised sea change in refugee management; however, they have been effective in shifting discourse on migration management and refugee hosting at the global and regional levels. The underlying assumptions about time and place inherent in these developmental initiatives still relegate refugees to a particular place—the Global South—and delimit progress and ambition to what can be accomplished in that settled place. These assumptions also reflect two different teleologies. The first is the teleology of durable solutions, which posits that the international community has a responsibility to ensure an end to refugee flight in a particular place; this approach does not always consider the differences between how refugees and the humanitarian apparatus view that end point. The second is the inherent teleology of development, which posits that development and developmental approaches bring about a better future for refugees.

These paradigms not only rest on shaky assumptions about the temporal and spatial nature of development and integration, they also rest on other fault lines. The same ARRA official who first told us about the end of camps also noted that open borders in Ethiopia are tied to stronger walls around Europe. Indeed, these global policy shifts have implications for countries all along the migration routes, albeit in different ways for refugee- and migrant-producing countries, transit countries, and target countries. Migrant-producing and transit countries like Ethiopia are the particular focus of development initiatives aimed at encouraging migrants and refugees to stay, but these initiatives are also paired with funding for security and border management. At the same time, these global management regimes espouse the humanitarian goal of preventing death and suffering proliferated by illegal secondary migration.

These goals crystallize in what we call the *humanitarian-dvelopment-security nexus*, which is the fusion of the humanitarian-development nexus and the humanitarian-security nexus. The humanitarian-*development* nexus is a concept that has received more focus in recent years to bridge the disjuncture between short-term, typically postconflict relief and long-term development. It can be defined as "transition or overlap between the delivery of humanitarian assistance and the provision of long-term development assistance" (Strand 2020, 104).[5] This term—the *humanitarian-development nexus*—is used in the applied literature to explore an integrated service delivery model. Because of this emphasis on the pragmatics of policy implementation, the nexus is not particularly focused on the question of whether vulnerable populations are adequately protected, leaving some scholars with concerns about the incommensurability of development practices with humanitarian ideals (Lie 2020). Understanding the humanitarian-development nexus is important to our discussion of locally integrating refugees, as it undergirds efforts in Ethiopia and elsewhere to host refugees long term; however, the term we develop below—the *humanitarian-development-security nexus*—has a different genealogy. It emphasizes not only the fusion of development and humanitarianism but also the preoccupation with the security of northern borders.

The Emergence of the Humanitarian-Development-Security Nexus

What has been called the humanitarian-security nexus has emerged in recent years in response to the perceived "migrant crisis" in Europe (Andersson 2017; Jones et al. 2017). Building on work on migration and border management, scholars theorized a humanitarian-security nexus in which the mandates of securing borders through policing and being humanitarians (often through saving lives) become intermingled (Andersson 2017; Jones et al. 2017). We explore the function of the humanitarian-security nexus at the borders of Europe and argue that the humanitarian-development nexus in places like Ethiopia effectively extends the humanitarian-security nexus southward, externalizing processes of borderwork and humanizing it through the auspices of this new convergence of development and humanitarianism.

Because the humanitarian-security nexus is rooted in a response to the so-called migrant crisis, it is important to look at this crisis a bit more closely. Ruben Andersson argues that the increase in *illegal* migration was produced by the long-term erosion of channels for *legal* migration (2016a, 2016b). Andersson's work details the history of migration policy and demonstrates that while there were many pathways for legal migration from Africa to Europe prior to the 1970s, since then, these have been consistently eroded. Thus, while media representation and public perception presents 2014–2015 as a moment of "crisis" requiring a security response, the numbers of migrants and refugees entering Europe through irregular channels had been steadily rising for several years. Additionally, a security response to these increased flows had already been in place for some time (Andersson 2016a). The so-called migrant crisis is thus much more a crisis of European borders than one of movement.

Subsequent policy responses have appeared to address the vulnerabilities of asylum seekers while actually foregrounding the concerns of European countries. Over the past few years, a growing literature has attended to "the emergence of a transnational discourse of compassionate border security that fuses humanitarian and militarized logics" (Little and Vaughn-Williams 2016). This literature explores phenomena such as the offshoring of border protection through migration deterrence, the interplay of duties and mandates between humanitarian actors and border patrol, and the overall linkage of humanitarianism with border security (Pallister-Wilkins 2015, 2017; Andersson 2016b; Little and Vaughn-Williams 2016). Similar to borderwork more broadly, "humanitarian borderwork" is conceptualized as an effort to "govern mobility" (Rumford 2008). However, humanitarian—or compassionate—borderwork attempts to govern mobility and guard borders while supposedly "alleviating the worst excesses of violence that take shape around sovereign borders" (Jones et al. 2017, 59). In this process, actors charged with protecting borders also wind up attempting to fulfill a humanitarian mandate—preventing migration but also preventing people from dying while migrating (Pallister-Wilkins 2017). Although we see these practices of humanitarian borderwork most acutely in search and rescue operations in the Mediterranean, they have other manifestations as well. For example, an array of partnerships between countries in the north and south result in the offshoring of border controls to countries on the southern side of the Mediterranean, often in exchange for development funds (Andersson 2016b). Efforts of countries in the Global South to retain refugees can be seen as a form of "humanitarian borderwork," as they keep refugees away from the borders of countries in the Global North but do so in ways that ostensibly improve the lives and safeguard the humanity of refugees.

Conceptualizing the borderwork on the southern/Mediterranean borders of Europe as humanitarian or compassionate illuminates a key paradox: securing a porous border across which many people would flee from desperate circumstances is, inherently, a violent process. It cannot be done compassionately. Each new attempt to humanely secure the Mediterranean border of Europe renders the entire region more violent and inhumane. We suggest that as it becomes increasingly clear that the paradox of humanitarian bordering is unresolvable, the quest to be humanitarian while protecting European borders shifts southward, focusing away from border management and fixating on the root causes of migration. This shift is generally depoliticized in that it focuses on poverty, rather than political violence, as a key driver of migration, and it also focuses on development, rather than political reform, as the solution.

Not only does the humanitarian-development-security nexus depoliticize the conditions that produce forced migration, it also deepens the vulnerability of migrants. According to Adrian Little and Nick Vaughn-Williams, "Compassionate borderwork enacts worlds, creates and delimits political and ethical possibilities, and has concrete and often contradictory—if no less violent—effects on the lives of targeted populations produced as 'irregular'" (2016, 3). Indeed, increased securitization of the migrant "crisis" has transformed migration from illegal to criminal (Chandler 2018; Hovil and Oette 2017). Smugglers are criminalized ostensibly to *protect* migrants. In the process, however, migrants themselves are increasingly treated like criminals through the auspices of increased detention and violence. The criminalization of smuggling might be seen as one of many facets of humanitarian borderwork, while the criminalization of migration is anti-humanitarian borderwork.

As the humanitarian rationale of these north-south partnerships wobbles, it reveals a political economy of amplified risk and reward—what Andersson calls an "illegality industry" (2016a). Because smuggling is demand-driven and the demand does not cease when states on both sides of the Mediterranean cooperate to limit migration, increased security around migration means that migrants are forced to utilize more dangerous pathways. If this illegality industry was brought into being by earlier reforms that limited legal migration, then the criminalization of migration and smuggling has made this industry even more risky and therefore lucrative for smugglers. Limitations on legal migration enact and enable a thriving illicit industry but also a particularly symbiotic relationship between countries in the north and south.

While scholars have noted the presence of a *migration*-development-security nexus (Andersson 2016a) and the increased usage of development funding to enhance the capacity (and will) of states bordering Europe to curtail the numbers of migrants, less attention has focused on the similar usage of development funding further south in large refugee-hosting states such as Ethiopia. It is important to examine this because increasingly, through the auspices of regional intergovernmental migration management initiatives, such as the Khartoum Process and the Global Compacts on Refugees and Migrants, new emphasis is placed on development. A closer look at how the humanitarian-development-security nexus is produced in these global migration management initiatives in the south further illuminates the contradictory landscape that blurs humanitarianism and development—and, in doing so, erodes the security and well-being of migrants.

The Humanitarian-Development-Security Nexus in the Khartoum Process and the Global Compact on Refugees

Generated thousands of miles away from each other and drawing together very different kinds of actors, the Global Compact on Refugees and the Khartoum Process have spawned initiatives that share an emphasis on funding development in large refugee-hosting states. In the case of the Khartoum Process, there is an express language of addressing root causes of migration through sustainable development, while in the case of the Global Compact on Refugees, the emphasis on development is couched in terms of alleviating strains on host communities and increasing resilience among refugees. Both initiatives share a focus on local integration and development assistance for both host communities and refugee communities in large hosting states in the Global South, such as Ethiopia.

The Khartoum Process, otherwise known as the Horn of Africa Migration Route Initiative, was modeled after the Rabat Process, launched in 2005. Both processes are an initiative of the European Union's (EU's) Global Approach on Migration and Mobility. Although the express goal is to reduce the dangers associated with illegal/irregular migration, the more important implicit goal is radically slowing migration to Europe, often doing so through the twin processes of connecting migration to development (and thereby addressing the assumed root cause of migration) and securing borders (Stern 2015). Importantly, unlike the Rabat Process, the Khartoum Process has included little emphasis on legal migration, safe passage, or humanitarian corridors. Funding available through the auspices of the Khartoum Process is focused almost exclusively on border security and local integration/development initiatives.

Following the Valletta Summit, the Valletta Action Plan outlined goals for the Khartoum Process and allocated resources through the auspices of the European Union Trust Fund for Africa (EUTF). The 2015 Valletta Summit Action Plan identifies five "priority domains" and sixteen "priority initiatives." The priority domains relate to development benefits of migration and addressing root causes of irregular migration and forced displacement; legal migration and mobility; protection and asylum; prevention of irregular migration, smuggling, and trafficking; and return, readmission, and reintegration. Of these, the first and third are almost exclusively focused on development. The first priority concentrates on various facets of development, including alleviating poverty, building resilience, facilitating sustainable livelihoods, and attracting investment and creating jobs in Africa. Similarly, the third goal focuses on asylum largely in the country of first asylum and frames protection as an issue of alleviating strain on the host community. The Regional Development and Protection Program (RDPP), which funds development projects for refugee and host communities, is housed under the third priority area as a protection measure (Valletta Summit Action Plan 2015). Michael Collyer's analysis demonstrates that 95 percent of financial commitments for the Valletta plan went to initiatives oriented toward development-focused priority areas (70 percent was specifically allocated to the first priority area). However, these goals were also coupled with a focus on security, and there is a political expectation that these development projects will reduce irregular migration (Collyer 2019; Chandler 2018).

The Khartoum Process is based on a "problematic political economy," as Lucy Hovil and Lutz Oette detail (2017). It entails a political asymmetry that elevates the need for European states to secure their borders over the varied needs of origin or transit states. In doing so, it assumes that migrants make it to Europe due to the technical incapacity of states along the migration route rather than the fact that refugees cannot or do not want to stay in origin or transit countries for an array of reasons (see also Stern 2015). This configuration puts European states in the role of generous donor, neglecting the fact that states in the south are already bearing most of the burden for refugees. It also casts migration as economically motivated, ignoring the reality that many refugees in the Horn of Africa are fleeing political persecution (Hovil and Oette 2017). Indeed, the Khartoum Process has often been criticized for bringing the governments from which refugees are fleeing to the table and, in the name of providing technical support, funding militias, particularly in Sudan. The Khartoum Process also configures a relationship in which transit or origin states along the migration route are coopted into a system of externalized management of European borders (Andersson 2016b), effectively pushing the defense of

European borders not just offshore but also far offshore (Hovil and Oette 2017). This externalized management of European borders involves offering both international legitimacy and resources—in the form of development funds—to countries that are stable enough (or perceived as stable enough) to stanch migration to Europe (Stern 2015). In this process, migration is depoliticized and recast as a development problem, and the emphasis on curbing the onward migration of refugees is addressed through the durable solution of local integration.

Following on the heels of the Valletta Summit and the launch of the EUTF, in September 2016, the United Nations Summit for Refugees and Migrants produced the New York Declaration, which later spawned the Global Compact on Refugees. This nonbinding compact resulted in UN member states making specific pledges regarding their role in managing flows of refugees globally. The Khartoum Process and the Global Compact are different in that the former is regional and intergovernmental while the latter is global and intragovernmental, but there are similarities.

Like the Khartoum Process and the RDPP, the Global Compact on Refugees placed programmatic emphasis on development. The Comprehensive Refugee Response Framework (CRRF) emerged as the blueprint for addressing refugee needs. It has four goals: to ease the pressure on host countries, to enhance refugee self-reliance, to expand access to third-country solutions, and to ensure safe and dignified returns to countries of origin (UNHCR 2018d). In practice, three of these four goals are oriented toward refugee hosting in countries in the south. Only the third goal, which focuses on third-country solutions, requires any commitment from northern or target states. Unlike the Khartoum Process, which focuses on development as a root cause of migration, the Global Compact focuses on development as "easing pressure on host communities" and enhancing the "self-reliance" of refugees. However, the assumption that refugees will remain in the south is the same, as is the assumption that development will stop migration. In addition to stemming the flow of refugees and migrants, this approach hopes to simultaneously reduce dependency on dwindling international assistance and integrate refugees into the labor market (Lenner and Turner 2018; Bardelli 2018). A 2018 UNHCR report on progress made toward the compact is particularly telling. While there is an abundance of funding that has streamed to countries like Ethiopia for these local development initiatives, there is far less commitment to third-country solutions. Indeed, there are fewer resettlement placements available than when the New York Summit took place (UNHCR 2018d).

In an array of conferences, publications, reports, and popular writings, the three durable solutions for refugees (repatriation, resettlement, and local integration) are increasingly reduced to only one truly viable solution—local integration (Betts and Collier 2017; Papademetriou and Fratzke 2016). Since safe and voluntary repatriation is highly unlikely to many of the countries from which refugees come and there is little hope that the supply of resettlement opportunities will match the need, local integration is increasingly seen as the remaining solution. This merger of development and humanitarianism is thus held up as a panacea for many problems—migration toward Europe, dwindling funding for UNHCR and the refugees, and the challenge of finding durable solutions. The new focus on development assumes that if the root causes of migration are addressed, the countries that people migrate from (or in some cases transit through, such as Ethiopia) will become places where people will want to stay.

This assumption is deeply flawed and, we would argue, is a key component of what Catherine Besteman has termed a system of "militarized global apartheid" (2019). The assertion that underdevelopment is one of the root causes of migration casts migration as a symptom of poverty. Collyer analyzed longitudinal data and concluded that not only does development not curtail migration but it also often leads to higher rates of migration because it tends to integrate people into global patterns of travel, education, work, and commerce (2019). In contrast, the global migration compacts discussed above proffer a vision of development for Africa that is peculiarly containerized, severing African countries from global socioeconomic mobility. In doing so, it relies on a sedentarist teleology that refuses to see mobility as something all humans do, tethers progress to places, and relegates would-be migrants to places that are close to their home countries. It not only depoliticizes refugees' movement but also ultimately pathologizes the movement of racialized bodies (Besteman 2019) and creates a structure to keep them in the places from which they come.

There is a great deal of concern about the mismatch between the goals of migration management (to stop illegal migration) and the goals of development funding (poverty alleviation). Drawing on Ana López-Sala's notion of three forms of migration dissuasion—preventive, coercive, and repressive—Collyer argues that these new forms of migration management blur the lines between these forms of dissuasion. Development, which is typically considered preventive dissuasion, is merged with coercive dissuasion, which includes border controls and other forms of interception, and repressive dissuasion, which includes detention and police and military action against migrants (Collyer 2019; López-Sala 2015). Although using development to deter migration is not new, the increased fusion of development with security and migration management may obscure a "hidden agenda" of what we might see as coercive or repressive dissuasion (de Haas 2012, cited in Collyer 2019) and may undermine public support for both migration and development.

Another critique is that development funding is being rerouted toward security measures to curtail irregular migration rather than focusing on poverty alleviation. At one level, it appears that funding for development projects is opening up. The EUTF has given €2.5 billion across Africa since 2015. The EUTF derived 70 percent of its funding from the European Development Fund. However, despite the fact that the resources allocated for migration management come from development funding, much of it goes to border security. These funds are increasingly channeled to what is effectively migration management. In Ethiopia, a large portion of these funds went into the RDPP earmarked for addressing root causes of migration. A related critique is that the effectiveness of development programs is being assessed on the basis of their success at slowing migration rather than alleviating poverty (Oxfam 2017).

The fusion of humanitarianism and development also effectively depoliticizes refugee protection (Bardelli 2018). Humanitarianism creates categories of giver-receiver and protector-protected (Feldman and Ticktin 2010). Although these categorizations are clearly problematic and have been roundly critiqued, they render the refugee as a particular kind of rights-bearing subject. Indeed, refugees derive any rights they may have from their protected status (Pallister-Wilkins 2017). Although this protected status often falls short of its stated objectives, leaving refugees bereft of adequate food, shelter, and protection from violence, it is a status they may use to advocate for what they should have. Protection and humanitarian relief, unlike development, are mandated to be equally allocated to all refugees, whereas development inevitably marginalizes some while it helps others (Bardelli 2018). Even if the on-the-ground implementation of protection falls short, protected status for refugees is the only way refugees can claim any rights at all. For example, although refugee status often binds refugees to the camp, casts them as victims in need of aid, and proffers aid that is often insufficient, it at least ensures they have the right to some basic protections. Protected status also guarantees refugees the possibility of resettlement, distant and unlikely as that may be.

Like humanitarianism, developmentalism is depoliticizing, but in a different way (Ferguson 1994). One might say that this blurring of development with humanitarianism under the auspices of securing European borders is erasing the category of the refugee itself. Extending James Ferguson's conceptualization of development as an "anti-politics machine," Tricia Redeker Hepner and Magnus Treiber argue that refugee management and asylum processes around the world are increasingly a depoliticizing "anti-refugee machine" that strips refugees of their political status and threatens their right to claim protection under international law (Hepner and Treiber 2017, 2021). Even if refugees are not officially stripped of their protected status, their subjectivity under developmental rather than humanitarian regimes is configured around the assumption that they are motivated more by a desire to improve their livelihoods than by a desire to be safe from political violence. Under the humanitarian-development-security regime, the political subjectivity of refugees is effectively sidelined. Being a refugee involves reliance on a political designation, but subjects of development interventions have no such protected status. Developmental subjects, particularly in light of the neoliberal turn in the development industry, are expected to be entrepreneurial hustlers, not cared-for subjects. Although the reality is that refugees cannot rely on assistance and aid alone and are constantly hustling for additional income, their status as protected is essential to their survival.

What is conveniently forgotten in this new configuration of humanitarianism and development is the history of development. Many development initiatives are arguably ineffective at best, inhumane at worst, and more concerned with making profit for economic elites than viable livelihoods for the vulnerable (Lenner and Turner 2018). Ironically, there is also a long history of development-induced displacement in the Global South, including in Ethiopia, where notorious development schemes have uprooted millions (Scott 1998). One need not look back as far as villagization in the 1980s to find such displacement in Ethiopia (Pankhurst and Piguet 2009). Indeed, contemporary dislocations caused by rampant urban development in Addis Ababa have uprooted entire neighborhoods (Megento 2013; Yntiso 2008), and agricultural development has displaced others (Lavers 2012; Makki 2012).

We offer another critique of the utility of development to stem migration that has not been addressed in the literature. The new policy configurations that promoted local integration by merging it with development initiatives made temporal assumptions about what would make refugees stay in a place like Ethiopia. They assumed that development, with all its failures, would bring about hope for a brighter future and that this would be enough to get refugees and other would-be migrants to wait for it. We pick up on our analysis of temporal and spatial assumptions in these new policy paradigms in the last section, but first it is important to provide some context for Ethiopia's particular role in these initiatives.

Ethiopia and the Humanitarian-Development-Security Nexus

As European countries continue to seek solutions to the so-called refugee crisis by attempting to prevent refugees from arriving on their borders, host countries in the Global South, such as Ethiopia, acquire global significance, financial support, and diplomatic standing. While Ethiopia is able to firm up and leverage its status as a host country in international and regional spheres, the unfolding of refugee policy on the ground also reflects the contradictory nature of the humanitarian-development-security nexus.

Although Ethiopia does receive funding for security and migration management (Mengiste 2019), the majority of its funding through the auspices of the Khartoum Process is allocated toward development projects.[6] A 2017 Oxfam report found that unlike transit countries further north in the Sahel and North African regions, Ethiopia earmarked 79 percent of EUTF funding for development projects focused on providing basic services such as education and health care but allocated only 15 percent to migration management and 5 percent to security and peace building (Oxfam 2017). The RDPP provided particular support for Ethiopia's hosting of Eritrean (and Somali refugees) and has resulted in thirty million Euros for Ethiopia to implement projects that focus on integrated service delivery, development, and capacity building for refugees and host communities.

In refugee camps in Ethiopia, there was little evidence of the Khartoum Process, which is telling. What was much more prevalent during the time of our fieldwork (beginning in summer 2016) was talk about Ethiopia's pledges, and later the Global Compacts and the subsequent initiatives, such as the CRRF. The nine pledges Ethiopia made at the 2016 Summit were oriented toward greater local integration and improving the livelihoods of refugees. Ethiopia pledged to expand its out-of-camp program (OCP) to 10 percent of the refugee population; make work permits available to some refugees; create one hundred thousand jobs in industrial parks, one-third of which would go to refugees; make land available to one hundred thousand refugees; and enable local integration and a possible path to citizenship for refugees who had been in Ethiopia for more than twenty years. The country also promised to enhance social services, particularly education, and provide documentation, such as birth certificates, drivers' licenses, marriage certificates, and bank account information, to refugees. Donations for Ethiopia's increased efforts around refugee management began flooding in immediately following the country's pledges in fall 2016. Additionally, as a focus country for the CRRF, Ethiopia took up the global effort to engage in a whole society approach to improve refugee hosting while easing pressure on host countries.

In moving toward local integration and away from long-standing policies of encampment, Ethiopia joined other countries, such as Jordan and Uganda, in viewing refugees as potential economic assets. The proposed policy changes promised to give larger numbers of refugees access to education, the right to work, and the right to reside outside of camps. Overall, these policies were aimed at shifting refugees away from dependence on humanitarian aid (Brooks 2017; Mallett et al. 2017). Policies that promised to give refugees work permits and to provide jobs in new industrial parks recast refugees as economic actors. They also attracted funding (*BBC News* 2016). The World Bank pledged funding for development projects for refugees and host communities (Ethiopian News Agency 2016) and praised Ethiopia for linking socioeconomic opportunities for refugees to its broader plan for rapid industrialization. They joined an array of funders providing financial support for industrial parks with the hopes that they would bring economic benefits to both Ethiopia and refugees (World Bank 2018). The pledges attracted $500 million in donations from the United Kingdom, European Union, and World Bank (Igunza 2017). Even though industrial jobs have failed to bring economic benefits to refugees or to stem onward movement, linking industrial development with stopping onward movement has seemed to be an effective fundraising strategy for Ethiopia.

These projects of humanitarianism not only garnered financial resources for Ethiopia but became a critical component of Ethiopia's international reputation as a stabilizing force in an unstable region (Riggan and Poole 2019). Despite authoritarianism and human rights abuses among its own citizenry, Ethiopia gained a seat on the UN Security Council for a two-year term beginning in 2017. A former Ethiopian foreign minister was appointed head of the World Health Organization (WHO). Dr. Tedros Adhanom declared his appointment to be an indication that Ethiopia had "won the respect and trust of the world" through its diplomatic role in peacekeeping efforts and pointed to "addressing illegal migration" as one of two major goals (along with combating terrorism) during its term on the council (Tesfa-Alem 2016). Indeed, Adhanom's appointment as Director General of the WHO should be seen in a similar light as Ethiopia's critical role in hosting refugees; both raised Ethiopia's international stature.

Ethiopia's willingness to host refugees was also politically strategic at a regional level—a topic we take up in more depth in the next chapter. Ethiopia appeared to be situating itself as a generous host, rather than a beleaguered host country, in part to recalibrate relations with people displaced from neighboring states and to assert a leadership role as regional peace builder. As the Ethiopian state governed subjects who are not its citizens, it extended its reach across borders.

However, the situation on the ground in places like Ethiopia has been complex and shifting. These policies seem to have done more for the country's reputation than they have to stem the flow of refugees from Ethiopia. Even though it has been roundly critiqued for its human rights record, generates its own refugees, and had one of the largest populations of internally displaced people on the planet in 2018 (IOM 2018), Ethiopia remained a popular testing ground for these new policies.

While the intended outcomes of these policies rest on shaky grounds, there are also unintended outcomes. Participation in these broad global migration management initiatives has yielded different results for different actors within Ethiopia, and not all state agencies seem to benefit equally. Just after Ethiopia's pledges were voted into law, ARRA was reorganized, supposedly to play a more limited technical role. Despite the fact that ARRA took the lead in advocating for the pledges and was often heard making a hard sale for Ethiopia's capacity to host refugees in exchange for resources in the wake of the New York Summit, it seemed to be left out in the cold as local integration funneled funds to the Ministry of Finance and other line ministries.

Pledged funds seemed extremely slow to arrive. Interlocutors at ARRA informed us in June 2018 that the World Bank withheld funding for industrial parks as leverage to ensure that Ethiopia passed its new refugee proclamation. What had appeared to be a seamless merger between funding for industrial parks and the pledges in 2016 had yielded little two years later. Most of the parks had not gotten off the ground, and we heard of no refugees working in them. Additionally, it did not seem that much thought had been put into how and why refugees would work in industrial parks. The ends of both developmental efforts and local integration were elusive. Meanwhile, reality in the camps was completely untouched by these policies.

Spatial and Temporal Disjunctures: The View from the Camp

The emergence of a humanitarian-development-security nexus that places greater impetus on large refugee-hosting states in the south and has the potential to make new resources available to them may be a political and financial boon to countries like Ethiopia, but how will it affect refugees themselves? We argue that the insertion of development into new paradigms of migration management relies on a particular spatiotemporal imaginary that is asynchronous with the way refugees think about time, space, and movement through them. Consequently, it is more likely to deepen the vulnerability of refugees than to meet their short- or long-term needs. The spatiotemporal imaginary of policies orchestrated from within the humanitarian-development-security nexus is not only at odds with refugee experiences and aspirations; it is also at odds with the actual spatiotemporality of both humanitarian protection and development aid, which appeared grindingly slow, unpredictable, and, in the words of one refugee, "completely planless!"

Humanitarianism has a particular temporality that is distinct from that of development. In reports and commentary on these new initiatives, particularly on the Khartoum Process, it is noted that "long-term" development goals differ greatly from "short-term" humanitarian goals and that this is likely to become a challenge (Hovil and Oette 2017; UNHCR 2017c, 2017d). However, while the connotation of humanitarianism is that life in a condition of emergency is urgently oriented around the short term—the now—the reality is that living in the humanitarian condition requires lengthy, prolonged, passive waiting (Dunn 2017). Indeed, from the viewpoint of the camp, the stalled pledges fit firmly within a temporality of humanitarian aid, which, in situations of protracted emergency care, cuts off refugees from a planful future and consigns them to the position of waiting in an indefinite present (Brun 2016). If we embrace the notion that humanitarianism, like development, is long term, what is similar and different about the temporality of humanitarianism and development?

Although both humanitarian and developmental temporalities are long, development is intentionally so, while humanitarianism is unintentionally so. The crisis-oriented temporality of humanitarianism conceptualizes a beginning and an end to that crisis (even if that is a fiction). Humanitarianism always promises certain rights and possibilities, including the right to be cared for, even if that care is insufficient, and the possibility of resettlement, even if a minuscule proportion of refugees ever see that possibility. Humanitarianism thus attaches refugees to an international system and the possibilities of life elsewhere, however nebulous that attachment may be. Development holds out no such possibilities; it promises a process, but one that is located in a particular place, a place that is "developing."

The time-space of development also departs from that of humanitarianism because it posits a very different subject position for refugees, one that makes them responsible for the outcome of that process. Developmental subjects are charged with maintaining their survival. While one can *be* protected through the auspices of humanitarian aid and lay claim to certain rights through protection, development requires doing something—and doing something that you can fail at, often with dire consequences and through no fault of your own. When refugees suffer, the responsibility for alleviating their suffering rests with institutions of humanitarian protection, and even though this does not work very well, refugees can and do utilize their protected status to lay claim to rights and resources. When subjects of developmental interventions suffer, no one is responsible for alleviating their suffering, and furthermore, they are thought of as responsible for their success or failure. Another way to think of this is that each paradigm—humanitarianism and developmentalism—gives rise to a different form of temporal violence. While the humanitarian apparatus keeps refugees waiting, stuck, and in stasis due to its failure to bring about any kind of durable solution, development has no better track record. Development holds out a promised end but takes no responsibility for removing the structural barriers that impede reaching that end (Ferguson 1994). Both humanitarian and developmental teleologies relegate refugees to a time that is "belated" or behind other parts of the world—particularly the parts of the world that refugees are trying to reach when they migrate (Khosravi 2021).

When asked why this shift to development was important, the EU's ambassador to Sudan, interviewed by Caitlin L. Chandler, noted the importance of giving long-term hope to refugees: "The real question is: Do you offer hope to these people or not? If they have no hope they will move. You have to offer hope and that can only be relatively long term . . . there are no quick fix solutions." There are two problems with tethering hope to the temporality of development and its long-term vision of progress. First, personal aspirations for development differ from regional or countrywide aspirations. Personal aspirations involve social, spatial, and temporal mobility. They may lead people out of Ethiopia and toward places that are already developed. Second, replacing the short-term humanitarian notion of protection with the nebulous idea of hope is met with a great amount of justified concern by refugees who have been making use of these protections in critical and creative ways.

Ethiopia's pledges were greeted with concern about what the realities of a move from humanitarian aid to a developmental model would look like. This shift suggested a need for refugees to transform from passive recipients of aid to self-sufficient economic actors. However refugees were already economic actors. In fact, the insufficiency of aid required that they be economically savvy. For example, refugees commonly sold rations in the local market and worked as day laborers in the camp and seasonally on agricultural schemes out of the camp. Despite this, the aid refugees received was essential because it was integrated into their economic activity. Refugees' economic acumen amidst scarcity was reflected in their opinions about a proposed scheme to change the provision of aid from rations to cash. No one could live on assistance alone, which was why many sold their rations for cash on the market, and yet many refugees were critical of the proposal that they receive cash instead of rations. Although administrators envisioned this shift as one toward development and away from humanitarian aid, refugees viewed the provision of rations rather than cash as one of the ways that they were protected.

They believed that cash would leave them vulnerable to the potential for graft on one hand and to the vicissitudes of markets on the other. Many feared that this shift would take away economic agency rather than making them more self-sufficient.

There was similar skepticism about industrial park jobs, one of the cornerstones of the Ethiopia's pledges. While the European Union, the United Kingdom, and others pledged hundreds of thousands of euros for the development of industrial park jobs with the caveat that 30 percent of the positions would go to refugees, refugees were skeptical that this model would produce jobs that were stable, pay decent wages, and provide opportunity for advancement. One refugee remarked, "Especially for refugees who settle in Tigray, they are told to get job opportunities around Mekelle in industrial parks. They promised like that. This is a promise." He suspected that refugees would fill the lower positions: "If I expect to be a manager, it doesn't happen. I expect some mothers will work as cleaners, and some refugees will be drivers." Indeed, there was broader debate about industrial parks in Ethiopia and the likelihood that low pay and challenging work conditions would lead to difficulties retaining labor, as has been the case in Ethiopia's textile industry (Hardy and Hauge 2019). Additionally, the parks were not planned for locations that were close to refugee camps, which would mean that refugees would need to relocate away from the camps, leaving them with neither aid nor sufficient wages to support themselves. Seen from the vantage point of refugees, industrial parks and the hope for economic self-sufficiency were a strange pairing.

Refugees described vocational education and small business development programs as almost equally futile. Our interlocutors told us that because they could not work in the formal economy, they had limited opportunities to use vocational skills. They described vocational education as a way to fill their time and develop skills that could help them once they made it to another country. Those who used their skills to open businesses also faced problems. Outside of the camps, refugees were not allowed to own a business without an Ethiopian partner, making them vulnerable to exploitation and theft. Inside the camps, the market was saturated, and it was hard to pay back the loans they took out based on the limited number of customers and resources. Thus, existing efforts to make refugees into viable economic actors were thwarted by legal limitations on work and business ownership. Many refugees held out hope for work permits, another of Ethiopia's pledges, but it was unclear if these would ever materialize, and if they did, how many permits would actually be distributed and what kind of work or procedures would be involved.

Another experimental approach was getting refugees out of camps through the auspices of the OCP. The OCP reversed decades of encampment policies by allowing a limited number of Eritrean refugees to forgo assistance and live out of the camp provided they had a relative in Ethiopia who would sponsor them. The expansion of the OCP was viewed optimistically as an early move away from the strict encampment policy. But the OCP clashed with material realities. Refugees who left the camps could not work formally, leaving them with no legal means to support themselves. While most refugees said this was a good program and very much wanted the option of living out of camp, they noted the large number of people who wound up back in the camp after taking advantage of this program because they could not support themselves financially without assistance.

Embedded in these policies and programs are assumptions that attach refugees temporally and spatially to Ethiopia. Policies intended to promote local integration through development rely on a sedentarist bias and a linear temporality that assumes that refugees are just looking for a place to settle down and will travel a straight path until they find such an end point. Development efforts are intended to constitute particular locations—in this case Ethiopia—as a place where refugees can stop moving and end their journey. However, it is important to question how and for whom Ethiopia could become an end point. Laura Hammond argues in her influential ethnography of the repatriation of a group of Ethiopian refugees from Sudan that repatriation is not an end point, rather, it is the beginning of a new process with a new set of vulnerabilities (Hammond 2004). Georgina Ramsay's (2019) ethnography of refugee resettlement in Australia makes a similar point about resettlement processes. Why would we think local integration for refugees in Ethiopia would be any different? For whom is local integration an end point? Certainly not refugees, who, as we demonstrate in subsequent chapters, think about time and space in more strategic and multifaceted ways. Perhaps local integration, like repatriation or resettlement, is an end point for humanitarian organizations. As one of the three durable solutions, it remains to be seen how durable local integration will be.

Ethiopia's pledges were intended to make refugees feel like they could stay, but they fell short. Refugees were aware of the content of the pledges years before the process of voting them into law and implementing them began, leading to disappointment and frustration. The pledges were announced formally at the World Refugee Day celebrations in the camps in 2017 and generated expectations that things would change. The slow rollout of the pledges revealed a disconnect between refugees' urgency and policy makers' sluggishness. One refugee remarked wryly that after the passage of so much time, "I am taking this as a long-term plan." The pledges came to feel like an instrumental attempt at luring refugees to stay in Ethiopia, while they amounted to empty promises of legal work that never materialized. One refugee, who graduated from college in Ethiopia and was back in the camps collecting rations, explained how much hope he felt when he first heard about the pledges: "I was happy for one month. I was feeling like a man! A fresh man." He added that when the implementation of the pledges was delayed, "I can say it was like cheating."

In summer 2019, almost three years after the New York Summit, refugees were still waiting for the implementation of the pledges. When we started this research, we envisioned that we would track the rollout of these policies, laws, and programs over the years of our fieldwork—from 2016 until 2019—but instead we wound up doing an ethnography of waiting. Refugees were told that big changes were coming but were kept in the dark about the details. The new refugee proclamation, which sat before parliament for well over a year, was not be passed until January 2019, and even then, the logistics of its implementation have yet to be determined at the time of this writing. As policy promises failed to materialize, one pledge that actualized early in 2018—vital events registration—did provide some hope to refugees that the remaining pledges might someday become a reality. But most in the humanitarian community acknowledged that the pledges that had the potential to be most meaningful to refugees—namely the expansion of the out-of-camp program and the provision of work permits—were politically sensitive. The details of these pledges were unlikely to be agreed on any time soon. From the perspective of those in the camp, the plans that circulate in New York, Rome, Geneva, and even Addis Ababa often look like no plan at all. And the hope that these planless plans are supposed to engender is no hope at all.

The Teleological Violence of Local Integration

Local integration as a durable solution has received criticism. While resettlement and repatriation remain elusive, local integration is more complex. As Lucy Hovil notes, efforts to locally integrate refugees are always partial and, in many cases, occur in the margins of the law creating a class of people deemed settled but without full citizenship (Hovil 2014). Thus, attempts to locally integrate refugees are often represented as moving toward a settled endpoint, but instead they result in an extended limbo for refugees. We would suggest that promising refugees an endpoint that is really nothing of the sort is a form of teleological violence.

A key question that needs to be raised is whether these new economic development approaches to refugee management are actually new, or just another form of partial local integration stripped of the humanitarian promise of an end point, a safe place, and protection. When viewed from the perspective of refugees who continue to languish in camps, initiatives such as the Khartoum Process, The RDPP, the Global Compact, and the CRRF, seem to be the latter, as they fail to bring about the promised sea change. However, these initiatives have succeeded in effectively shifting the discourse on migration management and refugee hosting at the global and regional levels.

There are underlying assumptions about time and place inherent in these developmental measures. These initiatives relegate refugees to a particular place—the Global South—and delimit progress and ambition to what can be accomplished in that place. They effectively normalize stasis, leaving refugees in a place where development is behind and progress moves slowly. They rest on teleological assumptions that reveal a disjuncture between the perspectives of refugees and those embedded in the policy apparatus, but they also illuminate the internal contradictions of the policies themselves. As we noted earlier, durable solutions rest on a sedentarist teleology that posits that the end point of the refugees' journey is to be in a *settled* place (at which point the responsibility of the humanitarian apparatus also ends). This spatiotemporal relegation of refugees to host states in the Global South makes a number of problematic assumptions about the nature of belonging and who belongs where. Containing refugees in countries close to their point of origin reflects and reinforces a racial segregation of the world (Besteman 2019; Khosravi 2021).

The telos of development is also problematic; it is utopian and hopeful, belying the experience of precarity, marginality, and insecurity. Policies that posit development-oriented solutions to somehow stem the flow of migrants northward seem to have amnesia about the previous failures of these measures. The utopian, teleological ends of development exist in an indeterminate horizon, yet refugees and other would-be migrants are expected to wait hopefully for it.

Notes

1. Repatriation is often impossible due to the protracted and uncertain nature of political and conflict situations that produce refugees. Meanwhile, resettlement relies on the generosity of host states, and the demand always far outpaces the availability of resettlement opportunities. An estimated 1 percent of refugees worldwide are resettled.

2. Hovil (2014) differentiates between *de facto* and *de jure* local integration, noting that there are many "locally based," informal forms of integration as people move to settle in host countries, while *de jure* local integration requires citizenship or some form of permanent belonging, which is elusive.

3. Since the early 2000s, the literature on migration and development has exploded, moving far beyond a simplistic debate about whether migration is bad for development through processes of brain drain or good for development by increasing household revenues. Rather, newer work on remittances, cultural aspects of labor migration (Dick 2018), and more complex theoretical models to make sense of this relationship (De Haas 2019) have emerged.

4. Betts and Collier (2017) draw heavily on discussions of the Jordan compact, as well as the economic activity present in the Zataari camp in Jordan. They also hold up Uganda as a model of the type of activity they advocate for. For a more critical perspective on the Uganda model, see Hovil (2016).

5. It sometimes integrates peace into a "triple nexus," referencing a "humanitarian-development-peace" nexus (Barakat and Milton 2020).

6. There has been little comprehensive analysis of Ethiopia's specific role in the Khartoum Process, but from existing analyses of funding streams coming out of the Valletta Summit, we can surmise that the majority of funding from the EUTF to Ethiopia is for development rather than migration management or border security.

2   Paradoxes of Hospitality

"A Shining Example of African Hospitality"

In June 2017, during the first celebration of World Refugee Day since the Global Summit, United Nations High Commissioner for Refugees (UNHCR) Filippo Grandi was visiting a refugee camp in the Gambella region in Ethiopia. Grandi announced, "We must help Ethiopia to carry out this heavy responsibility and also be inspired by Ethiopia because it is a very shining example of *African hospitality and international hospitality*" (Xinhua 2017, emphasis added). UNHCR's selection of Ethiopia for its 2017 World Refugee Day celebrations was surely not accidental. Ethiopia is often held up as a model of refugee management. As European countries continue to seek solutions to the refugee crisis by attempting to prevent migrants from arriving on their borders, the hospitality of countries like Ethiopia is intertwined with the emergent political economy of the global humanitarian-security-development nexus.

Hospitality shapes the relationship between refugees and the hosting state on micro and macro levels, from the daily encounters with teachers and aid workers to the discursive framing of Ethiopia's participation in global migration compacts. The first of three key principles in Ethiopia's practical application of the Comprehensive Refugee Response Framework (CRRF) is "to maintain its longstanding history of hospitality in hosting refugees" (UNHCR 2018d, 4). Thus, at the very moment that walls went up around countries of the Global North, Ethiopian hospitality was celebrated and rewarded. Indeed, it seemed to stand in sharp contrast to the inhospitable ways that asylum seekers, refugees, and other migrants were (and still are) treated in Europe and the United States. Yet the hospitality of hosting states in the Global South arguably operates within this larger system that offshores borderwork and stalls refugees in places that cut them off from meaningful livelihoods and hopeful futures. As such, we consider hospitality here not only as the cultural form through which individuals and groups come to engage with and manage difference but also as a tool for social analysis, "a framework for teasing out the significance of geographies of confinement and imprisonment" (Lynch et al. 2011).

A rich literature explores this paradox of (in)hospitality toward asylum seekers and migrants in Europe (Agier 2021; Dikeç et al. 2009; Friese 2010; Rozakou 2012), where hospitality appears at the heart of debates about multiculturalism, and immigration and has been refashioned "as an ethico-political framework for analyzing the worldly realities of living amongst diverse others" (Dikeç et al. 2009). Far less attention has been paid to discourses and practices of hospitality toward asylum seekers and refugees in the Global South, in the context of "humanitarian bordering." What does hospitality mean in a place like Ethiopia, which gains status as a generous host yet is experienced and perceived as a way station by refugees?

Hospitality is always a constraining condition in which the guest and host are engaged in a dance of etiquette; the host is responsible for making sure that the guest is comfortable, and in return, the guest is responsible for being courteous, well-mannered, and thankful. In other words, guests are not to make too many demands or make the host feel they are not hosting well. They are certainly not to make waves. The strain that this dance between guest and host places on both parties is one of the reasons the condition of hospitality is usually temporary. Can people be hosted as guests indefinitely, given that the very nature of hospitality is supposed to be temporary or at least impermanent? In Ethiopia, this paradox is further complicated by a twining of hospitality with security discourse in the context of turbulent regional politics, which has made the long-term likelihood of local integration even less certain.

Focusing on Ethiopia's role as host state, we illuminate the paradox of hospitality by exploring the cultural and political context of being an Eritrean guest in Ethiopia. Anthropological theories related to hospitality and gifting illuminate cultural etiquette and ritual performances around being a guest and host but also expose the performativity of both roles. Ethiopia benefits from being perceived in the international community as a good host, but this role is more complicated at the regional level. There is a complex history of Eritrean belonging and identity in Ethiopia—a history in which the legal status of Eritreans in Ethiopia has changed several times since Eritrea gained its independence—and, depending on the political circumstances, their insider/outsider status has been inflected with an array of mutable attributes.

The lived everyday experiences of refugees in Ethiopia further illuminate tensions and pressures in the host-guest relationship. The sluggishness of bureaucratic time makes refugees feel that their immediate needs do not matter. In other words, they feel less than well hosted but unable to complain, in part due to cultural patterns that expect that a guest will be thankful (and not call attention to their needs) and in part due to political histories in which Eritreans have been violently unwelcomed in Ethiopia in the past. The temporality of hospitality in this context is also one framed by their precarity, as "guests;" Eritreans were once citizens, then enemy aliens, then refugees, and may once more face renewed conflict and dangerous recalibrations of belonging and exclusion.

By exploring the cultural and political contradictions inherent in the performance and practice of hospitality, we ultimately argue that hospitality, which posits temporary and partial belonging, is the antithesis of local integration, which posits permanent and full belonging. The very act of hosting and welcoming refugees as guests thus complicates the binary of staying and going. If the array of policies discussed in the last chapter are indeed intended to support Ethiopia's "shining example of African hospitality" (McDubus 2017) and if hospitality is, by definition, the antithesis of belonging, do those policies not inevitably strain the guest-host relationship and impede local integration?

Hospitality and Refugees: The Tyranny of the Gift

We were both introduced to Eritrean hospitality for the first time when we arrived in the country in the mid-1990s as Peace Corps volunteers. Amanda's Peace Corps group arrived in 1997 and, on stepping off the plane, was warmly welcomed on the tarmac by women wearing *zuríya*—traditional white dresses edged in colorful embroidery. They stood to each side with large smiles, ululating and tossing popcorn in the path of their arriving guests. Toward the end of Jennifer's Peace Corps term, Hillary Clinton paid a state visit to Eritrea and was greeted with a similar ritual. The hospitality in Eritrea extended far beyond staged diplomatic performances on the tarmac or at the US embassy. People stood to insist that we take seats on crowded public buses, saying "you are our *gasha* [guest]." When Amanda left her ID card behind on a trip to visit friends many hours away from her town, it made its way back to her, passing from stranger to stranger until someone dropped it at the school where the American guest was teaching. The performances of hospitality that surfaced in so many places in Eritrea in the early postindependence years were deeply rooted in cultural values surrounding the guest-host relationship and in concepts of home and sociality. Indeed, hospitality is fundamental to how people identify and relate to each other across culture groups in Eritrea and Ethiopia.

The guest-host relationship also challenged the preconceived ideas that one might have about the role of American volunteers traveling to Africa to aid those ostensibly in need. If it hadn't been obvious prior to our arrival, we would have both quickly realized that we, alone and lacking the experience that Eritrean teachers had in the classroom, were the ones in need of care and aid. Hospitality shifted the axis of gratitude. As Peace Corps volunteers, we learned to perform the role of a *gasha*, accepting food appreciatively, welcoming the smell of roasting coffee beans in the coffee ceremony, never asking for anything until it was offered, and bringing a small gift of biscuits, coffee beans, or *áreqí* (anise alcohol) to people's homes. Being a good guest included letting people host us and feed us (sometimes way too much). The role of *gasha* also involved expressing gratitude by participating in community events or working hard to fill teaching responsibilities. Learning to be hosted and perform one's role as guest properly was essential to deepening professional and personal relationships. *Gasha* was a complex and sometimes delicate performative role, and hospitality was the relational framework that carried principles and practices of hosting from the intimacy of the home into the public sphere. Returning as ethnographers to the region at various times has also meant navigating hospitality as the unavoidable condition that makes ethnography possible. Anthropology itself is "inhabited by the paradoxes of hospitality" (Candea and da Col 2012, 3); anthropologists are guests and later hosts of stories and experiences.[1]

As a relational framework with deep cultural resonance, hospitality is a "shared language of human interaction that can move from local to transregional frames of analysis" (Shryock 2012), but it also draws from local practices and values related to kinship, food sharing, and the symbolic substance of home and connection to land (Tesfay 2016). Sába Tesfay describes the centrality of gifting, food provision, and social calls in Eritrean Tigrigna culture as part of a complex of hospitality through which people reinforce social relations, obligations, and belonging. This cultural form, she argues, is supple and extends over space to involve diaspora communities. Through phone calls, visits, cash remittances, and marriages, diasporas remain integrated in a diffuse mechanism of social reproduction. These exchanges also shore up the rank and prestige of particular families, reproducing differences in status and social capital. The larger the feast hosted to celebrate a wedding or significant event, the higher the status of the event, which also creates a broader web of reciprocity toward the hosts.

Sharing food is central to local practices of hospitality and consequently to crafting relationships. Norms around gifting, particularly food provision, provide a way to redistribute resources in the absence of a labor market or public health services (Habtom and Ruys 2007). As a Peace Corps volunteer, Amanda remembers journeying back to her town early one morning. Waiting for the bus to leave, she pulled out a large piece of flatbread to eat for breakfast. Thinking it would be rude not to share with the man sitting next to her, she pulled off a piece for him, but instead of eating it, he took only a crumb for himself before passing the bread up to the next person. The bread passed from person to person on the bus, until everyone had a small piece. This act of sharing effectively extended generosity beyond its original recipient, not only distributing the gift to a larger number of people but also enabling the original recipient to play the role of medium between the giver and a broader group of beneficiaries. Ritually, this sharing binds people together in the collective experience of giving and receiving, which is routinely reproduced in coffee ceremonies and shared meals. Children are taught from a young age to share and serve others and therefore to not be proprietary with food.

These exchanges go far beyond an economic calculation or even immediate sustenance. As Lisa Cliggett argues in the context of economic instability in Zambia, maintaining relations through small, seemingly insignificant gifts is also about maintaining a right to belong and access future support (Cliggett 2003). Similarly, in multiethnic cash-cropping areas in the Ethiopian highlands, performances of hospitality entail a critical redistribution of food and resources and involve emotional registers through which relationships and senses of mutual obligation with nonkin are reinforced (Matsumura 2008). Hospitality and sharing resources are thus deeply rooted in cultural values that are perceived as timeless and traditional yet adapt to provide a form of social reproduction even in the face of economic and political insecurity, migration, and displacement. Additionally, complex power dynamics undergird these exchanges.

Anthropologists have long been inspired by Marcel Mauss's germinal work focusing on the gift to explore relations of power and sociality that undergird acts of exchange (1990). Acts of exchange, or reciprocity, are the mechanisms through which social roles and relations are made solid. Exchanges are moral transactions that maintain relationships, and gifts demand reciprocation in material or symbolic ways.[2] Hospitality is deeply entwined with theories of the gift; both "hold the incomplete and partial function of grasping the complexity of situations that relate the self to the other" (Kawano 2020, 512). Hospitality, however, raises complex questions about issues of sovereignty, alterity, and belonging. It operates as an ambivalent regulatory mechanism and a way to produce moral subjects in the context of social change. Consequently, exchanges made in the framework of hospitality shape social relations in a particular way. As Andrew Shryock argues in the context of Jordan, hosting becomes a test of sovereignty—being "able to feed others, project an honorable and enviable reputation, and protect guests from harm" (Shryock 2012, 20). At the same time, the guest-host relationship is asymmetrical; guests are prisoners of the host, dependent on them for protection and respect until they leave, at which point the guest has the power to shape the host's reputation.

The guest-host relationship reinforces the subordinate and liminal status of refugees. For example, Katerina Rozakou (2012) investigates hospitality as an asymmetrical relation of power in Greece's hosting of refugees and asylum seekers. Asylum seekers must conform to particular ideals of behavior to remain welcomed as "worthy guests"—apolitical bodies dependent on the humanitarian gifts of the host. Similarly, Barbara Harrell-Bond points out that norms of exchange undergird refugee food provision in ways that tend to remove accountability for the adequacy and appropriateness of the "gift" to refugees from donors but reinforce notions that refugees themselves should be held accountable for using food aid in ways that donors feel is most appropriate (Harrell-Bond et al. 1992). Consequently, in many places, refugees have been criticized for selling rations to diversify their diets, even if this is what is necessary for survival.

The guest-host relationship, as we explore here, is also mediated by regional politics, culture, and history, which becomes clear through an examination of the micropolitics of hospitality toward refugees in northern Ethiopia. The role of the host is to provide for the guest, an act of gifting that creates lopsided relations of status, power, and obligation. The role of the guest is to be appreciative but also deferential. As an act of exchange, hospitality is also an act of power and a tool of social control. Although hospitality toward refugees is rooted in humanitarian principles of assisting those in need, exchange is never simply altruistic. And in the context of humanitarianism, the power of the guest to return the favor is indefinitely deferred. This is particularly interesting to think about in terms of how Association for Refugee and Returnee Affairs (ARRA) representatives used the language and framework of hospitality. The narrative of Ethiopia as a good host of refugees was ubiquitous in news and policy documents and framed the ways in which ARRA officials described their work. One of the officials we met with in Addis Ababa described the essential role of Ethiopia as a good host to refugees: If treated well, he reasoned, refugees would contribute to long-term regional peace, becoming ambassadors on return to their countries. If treated poorly, he asserted, "they would not forget." But the ultimate give-and-take of hospitality is suspended when refugees are made to wait indefinitely.

These dynamics play out across scales, including at the micro level. During homestays throughout both of our Peace Corps trainings, we quickly learned the delicate etiquette around meals that required allowing one's host to perform extensive generosity by insisting that guests eat more than they could, then drink a few more beverages, and then eat some more. Meanwhile, the guest was not simply expected to eat and appreciate the food but also to show appropriate reserve, shyness, and deference, a concept that does not translate easily into English but is captured in the Tigrigna word *qeliálem*. After pushing more food and drink on the guest, the host would often insist that the guest should not have *qeliálem* and therefore should feel free to eat and drink without hesitation. And, when the guest was truly ready to stop eating, they often declared, "*Tsegibe, bízey qeliálem*" (I'm full, really, without *qeliálem*). Generosity and *qeliálem* coproduce the performativity of the guest-host interaction.

This complex interplay of over-the-top generosity and *qeliálem* is a kind of dance of etiquette that is central to understanding guest-host relationships in Eritrea and Ethiopia and also illuminates refugee-host relations. *Qeliálem* refers to a demeanor of shyness, hesitation, and deference that is simultaneously idealized and eschewed. Although *qeliálem* is seldom described as a virtue, in the broader cultural context of highland Eritrea and Ethiopia, an absence of it—manifested, for example, by stating one's needs too boldly—would be off-putting and disconcerting. For newcomers to Eritrea culture, failing to grasp this delicate dance between performances of generosity and *qeliálem* could have problematic results. At best, a guest could wind up with an uncomfortably full stomach. At worst, the guest might deplete the host's scarce resources, as the host might likely feel compelled to offer what they could not afford. If performed correctly, *qeliálem* allows the host to magnanimously perform generosity that may be beyond their means without actually depleting their resources. It thus creates a symbiosis between host and guest that simultaneously equalizes relations and reinforces power differentials. It equalizes because it places guest and host on the same footing vis-à-vis their wealth, allowing the host to display abundance through generosity, even if the guest is wealthier than the host or if the host is quite poor. It reinforces power differentials by compelling deference in the guest. While the guest appears to be the one positioned to refuse or accept the gift, in reality, this etiquette empowers the host because it inhibits the ability of the guests to state their needs. The guest is expected to anticipate and attend to the host's feelings. In Ethiopian highland (Amhara) culture, the concepts of *yulugnta* and *megderder* function similarly. *Megderder* is used to refuse food, while *yulugnta* refers to a general disposition of deference and can have political implications. In her work on citizenship in Ethiopia, Lahra Smith (2013) notes the power of *yulugnta* in limiting political participation and leading to performances of deference among disgruntled youth.

Although the word itself was not used, the concept of *qelíálem* showed up repeatedly in Eritrean refugees' commentary on being guests in Ethiopia. Expectations of proper deference framed guest-host relations between refugees and their hosts and had the potential to obscure refugees' needs. The power differentials that are created through gifting take on a particular temporal and spatial dynamic when the gift involves hosting the Other. As Rozakou explains, "As a form of gift, hospitality includes the stranger in the social world of the host, though it is a temporary and conditional inclusion in which the host holds the monopoly on agency" (2012, 565). Hospitality folds strangers into a hierarchical sociopolitical schema while containing the possible danger that they represent. This framework can help illuminate how refugees in Ethiopia are positioned at the intersection of security and hospitality and how Ethiopia's role as a refugee host is deeply intertwined with its diplomatic performativity regionally and internationally.

Hospitality, Refugee Hosting, and International Relations

In a region that has faced protracted conflict and political upheaval, Ethiopia has a long history of both producing and hosting refugees. Hospitality toward refugees has been a remarkably consistent feature of Ethiopian statecraft across this history, dating from the era of anticolonial struggle, when the country welcomed leaders of African independence movements (Reno 2011). Across successive governments and regime types, Ethiopia has adhered to international protocols and standards where refugees are concerned, including the 1951 UN Convention of Refugees, the 1967 Protocol Relating to the Status of Refugees, and the Organization of African Unity (OAU) 1973 Convention. Thus, it is perhaps no surprise that Ethiopia continues to position itself at the front lines of changing global refugee/migration management paradigms. Making countries like Ethiopia a central player in an array of global migration management initiatives is appealing not only because the country houses a large number of refugees (over nine hundred thousand registered refugees and asylum seekers from more than nineteen countries) but also because it has been seen as a stable and cooperative partner (World Bank 2018). Thus, Ethiopian hospitality toward refugees shapes the relationship between refugees and the state and operates as a relational framework between actors in domestic and international spheres.

Ethiopia's refugee management practice arguably is framed by the twin poles of hospitality and security, making it an ideal international partner under the emergent paradigm of the humanitarian-security-development nexus we discussed in the last chapter. Since the 1960s, Ethiopia's refugee hosting has been attached to the country's security apparatus, as Alebachew Kemisso Haybano notes in his detailed history of refugee hosting in Ethiopia (2016). As Haybano tells us, ARRA was created by the communist Derg regime in 1988 and attached to the security apparatus under the Ministry of Internal Affairs. When the Ministry of Internal Affairs was disbanded, a new security entity—the Security, Immigration and Refugee Affairs Authority (SIRAA)—was created, and ARRA became a semiautonomous entity under SIRAA. In 2013, SIRAA was repealed, and ARRA was placed under the newly created National Intelligence and Security Services. While ARRA itself has always remained a semiautonomous unit responsible for refugee and returnee affairs, its linkage with the security apparatus has remained unchanged (Haybano 2016).

Paired with security, the regional politics of hospitality have also been central to Ethiopian refugee hosting. Ethiopia has always had an open-door policy toward refugees; however, despite the country's lack of securitized borders, the relative openness of the door is always calibrated by politics. What this means is that while Ethiopia is expressly open to all refugees from all places, historically the freedom to move and work has been limited, and most refugees are still housed in camps (Haybano 2016). Ethiopia's approach to refugee hosting has thus always been situated at the intersection of humanitarianism, security, and regional politics. What is new(er) in Ethiopia is the country's use of its status as a large refugee-hosting state to position itself as a global player and, in following the initiatives discussed earlier, its increased emphasis on local integration and development.

At the same time, people-to-people relations have always been a core component of Ethiopia's refugee hosting. Ethiopia expressly describes refugee hosting as a form of grassroots diplomacy, whereby it will create better relationships with its neighbors down the road by being hospitable to refugees. In the twenty-year period of frozen conflict that existed between Eritrea and Ethiopia up until June 2018, Ethiopia adopted a prima facie policy toward accepting Eritrean refugees, and in the absence of normalized relations between the countries, Ethiopia arguably established a relationship of hospitality with Eritrean citizens in an attempt to win over the "hearts and minds" of its neighbors (Connell 2012). Representatives from ARRA consistently described refugees as future "ambassadors" who would ultimately return to their country of origin with positive and familial-like ties formed with the Ethiopian state. In Ethiopian government media publications, explicit connections have been made between policies intent on welcoming Eritrean refugees and peace building (Abebe 2017; Gebru 2017).

We can better understand Ethiopia's participation in initiatives such as the Khartoum Process and the Global Compacts when we appreciate how the relationship between the Ethiopian state and its refugees (Eritrean refugees in particular) is determined by Ethiopia's wish to position itself globally as an important refugee-hosting state, its desire to perform regionally as a generous host, and its ongoing emphasis on security. The Khartoum Process, which we discussed in more detail in chapter 1, positions Ethiopia as a state that can benefit from development funding to encourage refugees and migrants to stay but also provides some financial support for security. Similarly, the pledges made during the 2016 Refugee Summit placed Ethiopian hospitality at the center of the world stage at a politically opportune moment.

As Ethiopia was cohosting the summit in New York, the state was facing widespread domestic unrest at home, and its crackdown on political dissent led to highly visible critiques leveraged by Ethiopian émigrés and refugees (Human Rights Watch 2016). While the regime change in 2018 promised democratic reforms and a loosening of state control over political opposition and media, domestic politics continue to be fraught with conflict and internal displacement. Ethiopia produces its own refugees and internally displaced persons (IDPs) in numbers that, at times, have constituted a humanitarian crisis. In 2019, over three million people were displaced by conflict, making Ethiopia the global leader in IDPs. Since then, war in the Tigray region brought violence, hunger, and death to refugees and local Ethiopians—something that we take up in the conclusion. For a country that asserts itself as the only peaceful place in a turbulent region, this raised concerns about whether Ethiopia is the benevolent and stabilizing force that its allies have long imagined it to be (Gettleman 2016). A spokesperson for Refugee International, a nonprofit based in Washington, DC, responded to the news that Ethiopia was forcibly returning citizens who had been displaced by ethnic conflict in the southern Gedeo Zone by saying, "The irony is that the Ethiopian government has been receiving international praise—deservedly so—for its increasingly progressive policies toward refugees, including promoting their right to work and access national services. But the way it's treating its own displaced citizens is not only shameful, it's inhumane" (Refugees International 2019). While these forced returns garnered criticism, the open-door policy toward hosting over nine hundred thousand refugees from surrounding countries garnered praise and furthered the assumption among the international community that Ethiopia was a reliable partner in humanitarian and migration management initiatives. Thus, Ethiopia's role as host exerted and consolidated its status as a stable actor capable of providing security to those in need. This can help to explain why, throughout a time of profound political transition, Ethiopia's policy toward refugees remained remarkably consistent. During a period of domestic turmoil, Ethiopia claimed international political legitimacy through these projects of humanitarianism.

Ethiopia's recently expanded role as host under new migration management paradigms functioned as a performance of hospitality that simultaneously promoted Ethiopia's international reputation, garnered resources, asserted the country's centrality to regional peace building, and attached it all to the security apparatus enabling it to simultaneously welcome and control "outsiders." At first glance, the combination of security and hospitality might seem fraught, but arguably, security is integral to the host-guest relationship. Hospitality is frequently mobilized as an ideal, one that communicates a notion of sacred duty or obligation toward protecting and caring for the stranger, but it is also deeply associated with notions that that stranger could be a threat. Jacques Derrida's model of pure or unconditional hospitality involves "the exposure to the demands of the Other that comes to serve as an ideal against which the worldly politics of territorial inclusions and exclusions can be evaluated and judged" (Dikeç et al. 2009). Consequently, the ideal of hospitality potentially serves as an ethical framework to expand asylum provision and include refugees in social services, such as public education systems, where they may otherwise face discrimination (Perumal 2015). However, Derrida also describes how two figures of hospitality—unconditional and conditional—exist together, and in between these two figures are the grounds of debate about immigration (Derrida 2005). Indeed, hospitality derives from the Greek term *hospes*, which means both friend and enemy (Lynch et al. 2011). As a cultural form involving the management of difference embodied in the figure of the Other, hospitality pushes us to consider both inclusion and exclusion, welcome and hostility, order and disorder. It pushes us to "reflect on broader questions about citizenship, rights, and the ethical treatment of strangers" (Lynch et al. 2011).

Practices of hospitality shore up the power of the state by setting boundaries between insiders and outsiders and exerting sovereignty over the stranger. Rather than unconditionally including the stranger in the political system, hospitality reinforces state power by producing and controlling the stranger as temporary guest. The positionality of the guest is vulnerable, particularly against the backdrop of volatile political transformations. This is aptly illustrated by the changing position of Eritreans in Ethiopia, which we now turn to.

From Citizens to Guests: Eritreans in Ethiopia

What it means to be Eritrean in Ethiopia has undergone profound transformations. Understanding these shifts is essential to being able to grasp the particular political configuration and the vulnerability of being an Eritrean refugee-guest in Ethiopia. Many Ethiopians still imagine Eritrea and Eritreans to be a part of Ethiopia, but this imaginary has historically led to confusion, ambiguity, anger, and violence around the question of Eritrean belonging. Eritreans have been, and continue to be, configured alternately as insiders, outsiders, enemies, special friends, and guests. This configuration plays out through shifting categories of legal citizenship but also in the gray area between the written law and the use of force on behalf of the state.

The number of Eritreans and people of Eritrean descent in Ethiopia has always been hard to pin down due to migration, intermarriage, and a porous border throughout much of the Tigrigna-speaking regions spanning the two countries. This was particularly so before Eritrea became independent while under Ethiopian rule. Prior to the 1993 referendum, the Eritrean embassy in Ethiopia enumerated the Eritreans living throughout Ethiopia and placed the number at 160,000 (Kibreab 1999). At the time of the border war, Ethiopia estimated that there were approximately half a million Eritreans in Ethiopia. Others note that the population prior to the deportations was probably closer to 130,000 (Kibreab 1999).

In 1991, Eritrea immediately began governing as a sovereign entity distinct from Ethiopia, but at this time, the question of the citizenship and nationality of Eritreans residing in Ethiopia was not clarified. There was never a process in place to determine the citizenship of people of Eritrean descent in Ethiopia or for Eritreans in Ethiopia to formally declare or renounce their Ethiopian or Eritrean citizenship (Campbell 2013; Human Rights Watch 2003). The citizenship status of Eritreans in Ethiopia was a legally gray area, but in practice, Eritreans living in Ethiopia believed they could *legally* retain their Ethiopian citizenship even if they *felt* Eritrean. Ethiopia, which at that time had undergone a radical political transition of its own, did not disavow Eritreans of either the notion that they were Eritrean or the idea that they could hang on to their Ethiopian citizenship.

In 1993, Eritreans around the world voted in a referendum for independence. In Ethiopia, the referendum on Eritrean independence did not lend any clarity to citizenship questions. Instead, citizenship continued to be a gray area. Seventy-eight polling stations were set up in Ethiopia, and 57,706 Eritreans in Ethiopia voted in the referendum (Kibreab 1999). At this time, Ethiopia did not require Eritreans to renounce their citizenship. Eritreans who voted in the referendum continued to live, work, and function as if they were Ethiopian citizens (Campbell 2013; Human Rights Watch 2003).

In May 1998, tensions over disputed sections of Ethiopia and Eritrea's shared border erupted into an all-out war. Through the border war, it appeared that Ethiopia was intent on delineating both territorial and identity boundaries with Eritrea, leaving a large number of people feeling trapped "in between nations" (Riggan 2011). For the first time, Ethiopia rejected the membership of Eritreans in the national polity. The rationale for the expulsion was that by virtue of voting in the referendum and engaging in a number of other nationalistic activities, Eritreans had chosen Eritrean nationality and therefore were foreigners in Ethiopia (Legesse 1998; Klein 1998; Human Rights Watch 2003; Amnesty International 1999).

The deportations were a watershed moment in determinations of not only citizenship and nationality but also belonging. In an interview with Radio Ethiopia on July 9, 1998, Prime Minister Meles Zenawi declared, "As long as any foreign national is in Ethiopia, whether Eritrean or Japanese . . . [he/she] lives in Ethiopia by the *goodwill* of the Ethiopian government" (Kibreab 1999). This quotation is significant because the prime minister indicates, publicly and for the first time, that Eritreans in Ethiopia are *not* Ethiopian and casts them as *guests* who can be disinvited. The deportations themselves then signified that Ethiopia intended to treat individuals of Eritrean descent not only as aliens but also as citizens of a hostile enemy nation and effectively as unwelcome guests. This was both a declaration of enmity and an assertion that, for the first time, Eritreans *did not belong* to Ethiopia. When deported, their documents were stamped, "Deported, never to return" (Campbell 2013, 95).

In August 1999, the Ethiopian government ordered all Eritreans above the age of eighteen who had voted in the referendum for independence to register and obtain an alien residence permit. They were given a residence card stating that they were Eritrean, even if they were born in Ethiopia (Campbell 2013, 46). This illustrates the Ethiopian government's retroactive claim that Eritreans who had voted in the referendum were of Eritrean nationality, not Ethiopian, by virtue of voting in the referendum, despite the fact that there had never been a process in place for them to renounce Ethiopian nationality. From this point on, people who had voted in the referendum were regarded as having Eritrean nationality.

The mandate that all Eritreans register as alien residents was implemented in an arbitrary manner. Some Eritreans were targeted; others managed to keep their identity obscured. For their own safety, some Eritreans hid their Eritrean identity from authorities, sometimes at great risk. Several of Jennifer's interlocutors told stories of having to change jobs, avoid friends, and move to a different part of the city, sometimes several times, to avoid someone finding out that they were Eritrean and reporting them to the authorities. Many eventually fled to other countries to avoid persecution.

By 2003, Ethiopia had gradually begun to warm up to Eritrean people but not to the Eritrean government. The number of Eritrean refugees fleeing to Ethiopia gradually began to increase, leading Ethiopia to establish the Shimelba camp to house Eritrean refugees in 2004. However, questions of the nationality of people of Eritrean descent remained unclarified until the Ethiopian Nationality Law Proclamation of 2003, which restates that "a person shall be an Ethiopian national by descent where both or either of his parents is an Ethiopian" (Proclamation No. 378/2003). The proclamation also states that "any Ethiopian who voluntarily acquires another nationality shall be deemed to have voluntarily renounced his Ethiopian nationality" (Proclamation No. 378/2003). This means that people of Eritrean descent in Ethiopia who either voted in the referendum, were registered as alien residents, or were deported have been retroactively classified as Eritrean, not Ethiopian.

Eritreans have alternately been citizens of Ethiopia, enemy aliens, and refugees/guests. They have moved in and out of stages of being welcomed and expelled, but more importantly, the modality of belonging shifted to one in which hospitality came to frame the regional political relationship between refugees and the hosting state. Hospitality entails a recognition and management of difference. As such, it is a new modality through which Eritreans are seen to belong *in* Ethiopia but not *to* Ethiopia. Hospitality thus reinforces their precarity in a country that has previously oscillated between the forcible incorporation of Eritrea (and Eritreans) into

Ethiopia and the violent rejection of Eritreans as enemies. Ironically, although the discourse of hospitality posits an extension of welcome and protection to refugees, it also serves to depoliticize them. They are cast as guests who should be grateful for protection rather than as people who might demand rights of and from the state or who had been victims of that same state (Fassin 2012).

The Micropolitics of Hospitality

"Where can they go?" mused a representative from the aid organization attached to the Ethiopian Orthodox Church. We asked him about Eritrean refugees and onward migration, and he balanced the lack of mobility of Eritreans who remained in Ethiopia against the hospitality offered them there: "Better to be here comparatively. Our people are good for guests. At least we don't loot them. At least we sympathize. So, they prefer Ethiopia."

The narrative of hospitality draws from cultural practices that span the border between Eritrea and Ethiopia and form part of people's self-identification. As many Ethiopian aid workers and government officials asserted, Ethiopians are good for guests. Indeed, refugees often said as much, but this guest-host relationship, as we have noted throughout this chapter, is riddled with paradox. Hospitality involves a warm welcome and protection, but it also involves security, dependency, and, often, a neglect of basic needs. It contains inherent contradictions due to its temporality that renders guests as temporary while shaping the parameters of expected behavior. It also masks the broader context in which the mobility of refugees is constrained due to the risks posed by structural and direct violence.

Here, we explore these contradictions first by looking at guest-host relations as they play out between camp refugees, local community members, and Ethiopian aid and administrative staff. We then further explore this dynamic with two main examples—students who are "gifted" with scholarships to attend university and refugees who are the recipients of permission to live "out of camp." In both cases, the etiquette of generosity and *qelíálem* obscured the fact that refugees had real but unmet needs and interlaced the (anti)politics of being a refugee with the positionality of Eritrean guest-hood in Ethiopia.

Cartographies of Care and Segregated Communities

Hitsats refugee camp in northern Ethiopia was known for its heat and malaria. Settled in a dust bowl and divided from the town by a thin trickle of river, the camp sat under the glare of the sun, and everyone moved as slowly as possible during the hottest stretches of the afternoon. We began each period of fieldwork in Hitsats by checking in at the ARRA office to get permission to enter the camp. The ARRA office was located across a bumpy dirt road from the camp. ARRA shared a compound with a large structure for processing new arrivals and a massive World Food

Program shed where rations were distributed. Beyond the offices where we checked in, laundry was often hung out to dry in front of dormitories housing ARRA employees, including Ethiopian school teachers that were working in the camp. The residences and offices of various INGOs were situated farther up the hillside away from the camp and somehow obscured from view.

On our third or fourth visit to the camp, we were hosted by an INGO that had recently begun working in Hitsats and did not yet have a building of its own there. Our INGO contact took us to the International Rescue Committee compound in search of a bathroom. Although the compound itself was rather desolate (indeed it was full of piles of not-yet-used playground equipment), we were immediately struck by the view from high up on the hill and the cool breeze that relieved some of the oppressive afternoon heat. We sat on a shaded porch and gazed toward the sprawling dust bowl of the camp below us. A brand-new UNHCR residence perched above us, shimmering on the edge of the escarpment. It was literally both on top of the camp and tucked away from view, existing in what seemed to be a completely different ecosystem.

The social cartography of the camp becomes apparent if we consider one category of actor who, in theory, should be able to move across these separated spaces—teachers. In the Hitsats camp, half of the elementary school teachers were ARRA employees who were paid a salary to teach, and the other half were refugee incentive workers. When we asked if teachers socialized together, we were always told that they did, but when we asked *where*, our interlocutors, both refugees and ARRA workers, hesitated, saying that salaried teachers tended to only go into the camps for special events, like baptisms. Whenever we went to the canteen in the ARRA compound next to the dormitories, we noted a strong sense of sociability between Ethiopian teachers and other ARRA workers, but no refugees were present. Eating together and food sharing are a particularly important way of building community (Tesfay 2016). But the cartographies and geographies that separate refugees from humanitarian workers, including Ethiopian and Eritrean teachers, also make it difficult to engage in practices that establish relationships of reciprocity.

This separation between refugee and Ethiopian teachers was not unique to Hitsats, nor was it purely spatial. When Jennifer once asked an Ethiopian teacher to help her find a refugee's house in Mai Aini camp, he accompanied her but was clearly uncomfortable. He had never really been in the camp itself before, despite the fact that it was right across the street from the school where he had been working for over two years. He hesitated before entering a bar to get directions, an encounter that he rushed through awkwardly in broken Tigrigna. In the refugee's house, he sat uncomfortably on the edge of a low concrete bed.

The lack of intimacy built into the cartography of care arguably also frames the micropolitics of hospitality vis-à-vis camp-town relationships. Whenever we arrived in the camp, we received news of refugee-host relations. The fact that camp administrators and refugee staff repeatedly brought this up, even when we had not asked, shows the importance placed on this relationship. Like a weather report, this briefing seemed to shift according to a variety of somewhat predictable factors, namely the presence or absence of resources. A great deal is already known about how the lack of resources can strain relations between camp refugees and their host communities (Kibreab 1996), and indeed, we were often told that a scarcity of firewood or water was straining otherwise good relations between host and guest. But often, the presence of resources—and the humanitarian/bureaucratic requirement that refugees share resources—could also be a barrier to crafting enduring sociality between refugees and local communities. Even though relations between Eritrean refugees and local communities were typically quite cordial, there was little that would suggest the presence of the kinds of dense networks of reciprocity and sharing that Tesfay argues are essential for building community.

Both Mai Tsebri, which borders Adi Harush and Mai Aini camps, and the town of Hitsats, which was connected to Hitsats camp by a long gravel road, had grown from sleepy villages to bustling towns since the camps were constructed. The camps were a captive audience of potential consumers, at least some of whom had money to spend. Town residents could provide services to refugees and sell things in the camps. In Mai Tsebri, streets full of suitcases, backpacks, and winter coats seemed completely out of place for northern Ethiopia but were an indicator of lucrative markets developing in these towns around refugees' onward journeys. Residents of Hitsats had started a thriving transportation business that started as motorcycle taxis and then turned into three-wheeled *bajaj*, which carried refugees to the town about a kilometer away and at times to far-flung parts of the camp as well.

The flow of economic resources, however, was mostly one directional. Refugees were not permitted to engage in the transport business in Hitsats. As we walked down the market street of the Mai Aini camp, we noticed a girl selling vegetables next to a refugee-run shop. Our refugee host that day noted that people from the camp could not sell in the town, but town residents could sell things in the camp. The one exception to this was the weekly Saturday market in Mai Tsebri, where refugees could sell rations to the local community. We met a handful of other refugees who were even more economically integrated and, indeed, buying and selling livestock. But for the most part, it seemed clear that given restrictions, the presence of refugees was a boon to the town's economic development, but not the other way around.

The presence of refugees also brought in other kinds of resources. The mandate of several local integration initiatives, namely the CRRF and the Regional Development and Protection Program (RDPP), was that 70 percent of donor-funded services should go to refugees and 30 percent to the host community. Strict quotas determined that this percentage of host community members must participate in any service, from job training to university test preparation to schooling. Yet restrictions placed on refugee work and mobility meant that the outcome for these shared programs was very different. For example, as we explore in more detail in chapter 4, refugees who graduated at the top of their class from Ethiopian universities were relegated to working for incentive pay, while their Ethiopian colleagues advanced in their professional careers.

The proviso for distributing resources between locals and refugees also required joint educational opportunities at the secondary school level. Schools that were established in the camps (such as in Mai Aini and Hitsats) operated relatively smoothly, particularly as they incorporated local students and made previously unavailable educational opportunities accessible to surrounding villages. In Mai Tsebri, however, a different dynamic took shape. Refugee students from Adi Harush camp were required to attend the existing school in the nearby village of Mai Tsebri. Tensions emanated from the need to treat students differently because of their status as refugees, and the role that some refugee students and families assumed in asserting their needs. For example, refugees were not required to wear (nor did they have access to) uniforms, which are symbolically potent in shaping the notion of proper student behavior and discipline. While we detail these tensions in chapter 3, here we would like to point out that these events could be interpreted as refugees failing to perform their role as guest properly. By asserting that they needed something other than what the host community was providing, they were not acting as grateful guests.

As we noted earlier, sharing resources, particularly food, is an important index of relationality in Tigrigna communities. It delineates and creates social hierarchies but also binds communities together and forges networks of relationships. Within this system of gifting, sharing, and reciprocity, there are inequalities and social hierarchies, but there is a symbiotic relationship between giver and receiver that binds them together. They need each other, and while they may have different resources, they enable each other's dignity.

In contrast, we would like to suggest here that, in the case of refugee-town/host relationships, there is a different kind of symbiosis in which giving and receiving are mediated through a humanitarian, bureaucratic intermediary and can therefore never fully create this relationality. There are rules, regulations, and laws that prevent town residents and camp refugees from engaging with each other in a truly reciprocal relationship. Thus, these networks of reciprocity are incomplete, meaning that refugees and hosts do not function as one community but as two distinct ones. Also, because refugees were limited in their ability to earn income, they had far less to share at a personal level. Their containment and legal restrictions on work limited their capacity to truly integrate with local communities by forming and cultivating reciprocal gift exchanges. Instead, refugees who called attention to their needs were seen as a burden, as bad guests without *qelíálem* who asked for too much.

"We Are Thankful, but . . ."

The performativity of the role of grateful guest, of refugee *qelíálem*, existed in tension with refugee attempts to get their needs met. When we conducted focus groups with university students and others, they invariably began with a near-ritualized observance of gratitude toward Ethiopia as a host for providing them with the opportunity to live safely and to attend college in the country. They began with praise for Ethiopia and the opportunities they had there that were not available in their home country—opportunities to study, advance their education, and learn about specific topics like civics and democracy. Even when refugees were struggling to survive and enduring abhorrent conditions, their narratives were shaped by the expected gratitude that a guest extends to their host. As one male refugee who was struggling to get by in Addis Ababa under the out-of-camp program shared: "For two years I lived in a room which was a toilet for many years. The landlords just closed the opening and provided that space for lower rent. I have no choice than living there because it is the one that I can afford paying. I thank the people of Ethiopia very much for their hospitality. They are welcoming."

Praise was often followed by a *but* and carefully couched critiques of what refugees lacked. For example, refugee university students were thankful for the opportunity to study in Ethiopian universities, *but* the stipend they received to buy books was not enough. They were appreciative of ARRA and UNHCR *but* they relied on their self-created refugee student organization for support and advocacy and really wanted that organization to be officially recognized to better facilitate its work. They were grateful for the opportunity to live out of camp *but* desperately needed protection from exploitation by landlords, business partners, and sometimes even the police. As one refugee noted bluntly, "We are thankful for the effort, but the money isn't enough." Another said, "The Ethiopian government has been generous enough to let us stay here, and we sleep safely with a roof over our heads, but that is not enough. . . . However hard we try to settle here, Ethiopia has a hundred million people to give jobs to and then they can help others."

These critiques were typically tempered and framed by a ritualized enactment of praise that is part of the performance of the guest-host relationship. Just as Ethiopia portrayed itself as a good host, refugees seemed to play the good guest. The etiquette of *qeliálem*, as we noted above, was supposed to inhibit Eritreans from asking for what they needed. When they did call attention to needs, they failed at playing the good guest by exposing Ethiopia's weakness as a host and feared being regarded as ungrateful.

The limiting nature of the guest role is reflected in the careful discourse of refugees themselves, but it is also reinforced by the expectations about refugee behavior held by aid workers. In part, this reflects what many scholars have noted is a broader undercurrent in humanitarianism that constitutes refugees as mute victims in need of assistance rather than fully human actors (Malkki 1996; Ticktin 2011). Yet the discourse of hospitality reinforces this expected subjectivity and the way it is embedded in hierarchical relationships. For example, at times the NGO provider community expressed resentment toward refugees who asked for too much. In interviews with aid officials in Addis, there was an attitude that refugees would ask for things endlessly, along with a sentiment that refugees sometimes felt like they had a right to things (such as resettlement) that were actually privileges they should be grateful just to have the opportunity to access. This sentiment also played out in the resentment that some of the aid workers held toward a few refugees who were elected to the Refugee Camp Council (RCC) in one of the camps. These RCC representatives began to demand payment for their time and efforts in administering the camp. This labor involved responding to long lines of people seeking their signatures for things like pass permits, gathering refugees to participate in aid programs, and carrying out other aid agency agendas. To do so willingly involved fulfilling one's role as a good, worthy guest. To demand payment, voice complaints, or refuse to participate in requested services violated this role.

Welcome and Security

Many Eritreans reported feeling surprised on their arrival in Ethiopia that Ethiopians did not hate them. And yet, the border war—particularly the deportations—loomed large in people's imaginations. Refugees noted that the vast majority of Ethiopians were welcoming and demonstrated tremendous hospitality, with one Eritrean university student stating, "One of the basic inviting parts in this area is social hospitality to the Eritreans. I expected before coming to Tigray, the issue we know from the news in Eritrea—I wasn't expecting like this. This was very good for me. There is, I mean, collaboration between all the faculty and students in trying to help us."

When he mentioned the news in Eritrea, the student was referring to the frequent propaganda of Ethiopian enmity that Eritreans are exposed to in their home country. They are led to believe that Ethiopians personally hate Eritreans and subsequently, many people arriving in Ethiopia expected to be met with hostility. Although Eritreans came to feel personally welcomed by Ethiopians, this sense of welcome was tempered by two things: an awareness that security was deeply intertwined with hospitality and a sense of bureaucratic invisibility.

Earlier in this chapter, we showed that ARRA and the roots of Ethiopia's refugee-hosting bureaucracy are directly attached to the security apparatus. While this security apparatus generally remained latent in refugee lives, it always made its presence felt through various prohibitions, such as the ban on forming groups, organizing the community, holding political protests, or making demands. One way to look at this is that the security apparatus could be deployed to ensure that Eritreans would remain good, uncomplaining, grateful guests. As we have shown above, the logics of generosity on the part of the host and *qelíálem* on the part of the guest forged a cultural framework through which guest behavior was disciplined by the expectation that they defer to hosts, not complain or call attention to their needs, and be thankful. But in the face of severe needs, this cultural frame often fell apart. Refugees did complain, call attention to their needs, and organize themselves.

When the cultural logics of *qelíálem* broke down, refugees stopped acting like good guests, instead politicizing their needs and flagging the securitization of their status. The most extreme examples of this breakdown show up in Addis Ababa. Refugees explained that Eritreans generally got along very well with Ethiopians, but they also struggled and felt stigmatized. Landlords discriminated against them. Refugees were unable to work legally and were therefore exploited by employers. Additionally, they could only run a business with an Ethiopian partner, who might also exploit them. These limitations placed tremendous strain on refugees in urban settings. For the most part, refugees knew that they were supposed to not be angry, but sometimes the veneer of *qelíálem* and gratitude cracked. Many urban refugees shared stories of friends who were becoming exasperated with their lives. At times, this frustration manifested itself in such behavior as getting drunk, singing patriotic Eritrean songs, loudly complaining, and eventually getting in fights with Ethiopians.

A more moderate example concerns refugee attempts to organize, particularly around the camp setting. "We are not allowed to form groups. We are not allowed to organize," was a common refrain that we heard, particularly among university students. Still, refugees in camps and universities formed an organization, provided support to each other, used their organization to advocate for themselves, raised funds, and planned activities for host and refugee communities. ARRA would not recognize their group officially or release funds to them directly, citing security concerns and Ethiopian law, which prohibited foreigners from forming political parties. In one particular instance, we conducted a focus group with Axum University students who had become aware of some rifts within the camps related to ethnic and regional origin in Eritrea. They decided to start a public education campaign about the importance of national unity. ARRA immediately put a stop to it and confiscated the flyers, saying they were too political. Because of these and other instances, refugees felt constrained. Where organizing efforts did work and could thrive, they were an incredible boon to refugees, making them feel that they belonged. But there was a widespread sense that this kind of activity was not allowed, particularly in the camps. Thus, part of the role of the guest is to be not only uncomplaining but also apolitical.

Eritreans were always aware of security formulations around their shifting role as Eritreans in Ethiopia and the fusion of this with economic limitations and the bureaucracy of hospitality. One refugee university graduate we spoke with echoed a common complaint about the limitations on their ability to achieve social, economic, and spatial mobility: "We saw the opportunities in Ethiopia, and they are not encouraging. We are not only second-class citizens, we are Eritreans. The Eritrea-Ethiopia relation affects us very much. So, it is not easy to get a job in Ethiopia. Security is the main issue. In Ethiopia, it is not encouraging."

Refugees often talked about their future in combination with both the political and economic situation in Ethiopia. Although most did feel that Ethiopians were welcoming to them and expressed gratitude for being cared for, they also felt that pervasive surveillance and bureaucratic distance impeded their ability to advocate for themselves.

They described this bureaucratic "hospitality" as problematic. Refugee students assigned to Axum University arrived in fall 2016 to find that the university was not prepared for them. They were sent away. Through organizing and collective advocacy, refugees approached the university president and renegotiated their situation. The president later apologized for his lack of welcome and proved to be tremendously supportive of this particular group of refugees. But to get to that point, the students had to step out of their role of deferential *qelíálem* and ask for their needs to be met—to assert their status as students rather than guests. University students suggested that the mechanism of protection under ARRA was part of what impeded their ability to be treated as they had expected. As one student noted, "The basic problem still remains, we are under ARRA protection—the government of Ethiopia—but there is no authority that can speak with us [directly]. That is the main problem that remains. . . . I mean, as Eritreans we need to have our own organization to speak with the leadership. We need the guarantee of ARRA to speak with us and to create everything in this relationship."

Earlier in this chapter, we discussed the cartographies of the camp that promote physical distance between Ethiopian staff and refugees, even when they are counterparts doing the same job. We noted the economic limitations that promote distance between refugees and host community members. Bureaucratized hospitality also creates distance. Refugee university students wanted to be respected to advocate for themselves and did achieve some success—for example, in the case of students assigned to Axum University. But where ARRA was concerned, they wanted a closer link, one that recognized their status and stature. They wanted to shorten the distance and be regarded as equals who had rights, not guests who had to defer to hosts.

Conclusion: The Slow Temporality of Hospitality

Hospitality, as we have shown, is rife with contradiction. While many scholars have observed this, particularly in the growing literature on hospitality toward migrants in Europe, these contradictions are amplified in the Global South, in countries that are envisioned as end points by policy makers but way stations by refugees. When we shift our perspective on hospitality to refugee hosting in Ethiopia, we are forced to center important questions about time, precarity, and danger in a different way, highlighting the tension between care and containment, security and protection, and the gap between the teleology of local integration and the temporariness of hospitality in a place where long-term stability and safety are deeply in question.

The presence of a bureaucratized hospitality that illuminates the performance of being a good host and neglects the needs of the guests only furthers mistrust in the host. In the previous chapter, we noted that the temporalities of development are longer term than the temporalities of humanitarian emergency aid. The telos of developmentalism is supposed to lead to something permanent and enduring. In contrast, hospitality is impermanent and temporary. Guests can wear out their welcome—particularly guests who are needy, fail to show the proper deference, and become too demanding. Slicing across temporalities of humanitarianism and developmentalism are the temporalities of bureaucracy, which are notoriously sluggish. Slow bureaucracy keeps the future permanently at a distance. One cannot plan to go to school when the building of the school is delayed. One cannot plan to get a job when the passage of the law that allows one to work is delayed. The temporalities of hospitality are thus temporary but also painfully slow and insufficient.

Arjun Appadurai asks, "How can hospitality toward the stranger be made a legitimate basis for the narrative of citizenship?" (2019). We would answer that it cannot. While hospitality displays political and cultural generosity, by definition, it cannot serve as a blueprint for belonging. Guests go home. They cannot strain the host's resources forever. As we have emphasized here in the context of Eritreans in Ethiopia, the ongoing performances of *qelíálem* also strain the guest. Thus, over time, guests develop real needs that hosts may or may not be able to accommodate. As Shryock (2012) observes, it is in the slippage between scales that bad hospitality happens, like when people can only be hospitable in ways that the nation-state allows. In Ethiopia, this slippage happens when the slow temporality, material scarcity, and spatial hierarchy built into bureaucratic hosting prevent people from engaging in networks of reciprocity. And when bad hospitality happens, the stranger may no longer be a guest but is also no longer a stranger (Pitt-Rivers 2012). This slippage is a potentially dangerous one in the fraught regional and historical politics of belonging.

The resultant effect is a bureaucratized hospitality coupled with a political performativity in which guests are disciplined by both a cultural etiquette of deference and the security apparatus. The paradoxes of hospitality are particularly acute for Eritreans in Ethiopia, who face such profound ambiguities of belonging. They have belonged in Ethiopia in the past, and they fought—and to some extent still fight—against forcible inclusion in the Ethiopian polity. They have also been violently and suddenly ejected from Ethiopia and fear that that could happen again. It is thus not surprising that Eritreans would be wary of Ethiopian hosting and instead prefer to be negotiated with as equals.

Notes

1. The possibilities of ethnography are rooted in the complexities of hospitality, which mediate, facilitate, or block the efforts of anthropologists. Julian Pitt-Rivers explores the complicated relationship between ethnography and hospitality via his experiences conducting

research in Andalusia, where the community suspected him of being a spy and reinforced a hosting relationship with him: "I was never allowed to escape from my status of being a guest, where I had no rights, into that of community member where I might assert myself, make demands and criticism, and interfere in the social and political system" (Pitt-Rivers 2012, 512).

2. Matei Candea and Giovanni da Col (2012) question what kind of work may have been done in anthropology if Mauss (1990) had focused instead on hospitality, arguing that while both gifting and hospitality involve tensions between friendship and enmity, improvisation and calculation, hospitality goes further in raising important questions about economy and time and negotiating the relationship between sovereignty, identity, politics, inequality, and belonging.

3 School Time

Teleological Violence and the Pain of Progress

Education: A Powerful Weapon

A banner over the school director's office read: "The future is in school today" (see fig. 3.1). A painted metal sign standing in the school compound stated: "Education is the only powerful weapon to change the world!" (see fig. 3.2).

Taken together, these two statements link the school with the present and future, tying both to a progressive vision of changing the world. The belief that education aligns the present with the future and brings about a positive change is, perhaps, as old as formal schooling itself. So strong is this faith that, at present, development organizations, educational policy makers, and school systems around the world continue to promote education as a tool to get ahead, despite increasing evidence that for many, it may not fulfill its promises (Jeffrey 2010; Jeffrey et al. 2004, 2005; Mains 2011; Honwana and De Boeck 2012; Stambach and Hall 2016).

The school enrollment rates tell the story of those failed promises for refugees. A hand-drawn attendance chart on the wall of the school director's office showed a clear progression in the enrollment numbers for local and refugee children since 2010. While the overall enrollment had been increasing, there was a steady decline in refugee enrollment. In the 2014–2015 academic year, the number of refugee students dropped from 300 the year before to a mere 167. Since then, it had continued to decline. Yet the camp was full; new arrivals were packed in warehouse-like structures at the edge of camp, where they waited for up to a month to be allocated housing. The Mai Aini secondary school is not alone in its low enrollments. The newly built secondary school in the Hitsats camp, along with the elementary schools in both camps, was also thinly enrolled.

Why, we wondered, if schooling had such positive connotations, were there not more refugees in school? If education is such a powerful weapon to change the world and if the future is, in fact, in school today, why were refugees not in school?

The temporality of education presupposes a forward march toward progress. Education produces a linear, unidirectional track between present actions and future accomplishments in which one step builds on the previous and leads toward the next. This linear ordering inherently disciplines its subjects, situating them in a position where they are led to believe that their actions in the present will shape their future (Foucault 1978). However, refugees are often situated on the sidelines of

Fig. 3.1. Sign in secondary school in refugee camp. Photo by Amanda Poole.

Fig. 3.2. Sign in secondary school compound in refugee camp. Photo by Amanda Poole.

that linear pathway, and those who attempt to get ahead face cruel forms of social, economic, and spatial immobility.

Teleological time becomes violent when people believe that hard work, discipline, having a plan, and attaching that plan to broader developmental goals will lead to personal and collective progress and prosperity but also know, without a doubt, that they will face very specific impediments that will block their progress and aspirations. In other words, teleological violence exists when the logics of progress confront the realities of structural barriers.[1] Additionally, teleological violence masks the work done by these barriers.

A key component of teleological violence is what Pierre Bourdieu and Jean-Claude Passeron refer to as *symbolic violence* (1990). Symbolic violence is the violence done to nondominant groups struggling to succeed in education systems designed for dominant groups.[2] Symbolic violence results in the stigmatization of nondominant groups by masking the structural barriers to success (the real reasons for the nondominant group's inability to succeed) and instead blaming these groups for their "failure."

Teleological violence might be thought of as an acute form of symbolic violence resulting from the temporal contradictions produced when disadvantaged populations engage in activities that they believe will enable them to achieve a particular end—in this case, progress through schooling—and that end is then understood to be impossible. Experiences of formal schooling, in general, and success at schooling, in particular, produce an orientation toward the future and present in students that is rooted in individual ambition and a sense of duty to help society develop. But the refugee condition entails structural constraints that prevent refugees from actualizing those ambitions. Teleological violence ensues when refugees feel beholden to temporalities that promise the rewards of a bright future but also know, with certainty, that that future is out of reach.[3]

Although the crisis of teleology has the potential to harm refugees in very specific ways, they are not the only ones who experience teleologies violently. Indeed, the precarity of youth is a manifestation of the rupture of teleological time (Mains 2011). Marginalized youth in many circumstances have a problematic relationship with time and the future. For example, Craig Jeffrey, Patricia Jeffery, and Roger Jeffery note a rise in alcoholism and criminal activity among educated, unemployed lower-caste men in India (2005). Drug use and a turn to irregular/illegal economic activities are apparent in other studies of marginalized youth as well (Mains 2011; DiNunzio 2019). Marginalized youth may be made available for various forms of labor that are violent or place them at risk of experiencing violence (Hoffman 2011). Indeed, the failure of youth, both educated and uneducated, to "grow up," find work, and forge a future for themselves is so prevalent that a number of studies have questioned whether youth are "vanguard or vandals" and "makers or breakers" (Abbink 2005; Honwana and De Boeck 2005). With the exception of Daniel Mains's research, these studies do not use teleological time as an analytical frame specifically, but they do point to similar phenomena and conditions that can be thought of as akin to teleological violence.

The refugees we talked to were able to sharply articulate these paradoxes and the violence inherent in them. One refugee who had graduated from college in Ethiopia reflected on the pain of unmet aspirations created by education: "If you teach someone that going out in the sun is harmful, and then you send them out without shelter . . . [it is] better to never know the sun is bad." The awareness that the sun is bad, like the awareness that education is good, is posited as knowledge that makes us better, but it only does so if we can change our behavior. If we are structurally prevented from changing our behavior by being systematically denied shelter (in the case of sun exposure) and jobs or opportunities (in the case of education), the knowledge gained becomes worse than worthless. When refugees do everything they are supposed to do to succeed and adapt to the strict teleological discipline of education only to find themselves stuck once more, unable to work legally, advance professionally, and assume the responsibilities of adulthood, it burns them. As another refugee described teleological violence, "Four years ago, I graduated. I have an asset. But if you have a big asset and you cannot use it, it is like a virus. It will drive you crazy."

What kind of powerful weapon is schooling? Our answer is that it is a teleological one that turns on those it purportedly enlightens and uses those supposedly enlightening processes to do so. Education, we found, was often described by those we interviewed as a sort of double-edged sword—having all the potential to change the world in positive ways but often causing harm to refugees themselves.

In the following section, we explore the various intersecting components that make up teleological violence, particularly as it manifests among educated refugees. We unpack the way education and schooling function as the machinery that produces modernist, progress-oriented notions of teleological time—or, in other words, how schools function as factories of teleological time. We then look at the ways that the teleological expectations placed on and enacted by educated people are bisected by the temporalities of humanitarian bureaucracy to produce a paradoxical subject: the educated refugee. The educated refugee experiences the contradictions of teleological violence in a particularly acute form where their future is concerned—a future, we should note, that is aborted due to structural barriers to progress, such as prohibitions on legal work and further education. We then illustrate the moral freighting of teleological time and how that places it in a relationship between migration and camp time. And finally, we explore how refugees attempt to produce alternatives to the contradictions of teleological violence.

Schools as Factories of Teleological Time

> In order to get satisfaction from work, you have to finish it on time. This is because the reason you work is to do something useful that will be ready when it is needed. (Mehari et al. 2002a, 112)

> When you work hard there is another benefit, there is an increased production of goods and services. (Mehari et al. 2002b, 100)

In formal schooling, particularly in the developing world, the teleology of education inherently binds individual behavior to temporalities of progress and to the notion of national development (Fuller 1991; Katz 2004). Taken from units on industriousness in the Ethiopian Civic and Ethical Education (CEE) curriculum for grades ten and eleven, the quotations above are examples of this. These quotations are taken from units that explicitly link individual work habits and work ethics to economic production and national development. They are preceded by units that focus on individual habits and behaviors, which cover topics such as savings. The following unit on macroeconomics puts individual hard work and industriousness into a broader frame so that students visualize how their self-discipline aligns with the trajectory of the nation. For example, the curriculum explains the benefits of having a parsed-out daily schedule by linking it with the value of accomplishing larger goals. A lesson titled "Knowledge and the Habit of Reading" presents a case study of a student schedule and asks students to discuss the importance of having a daily schedule, even when not in school. It then provides an example of an influential journalist, noting that reading "offers an opportunity to get more knowledge and make a difference" and that "people with knowledge command respect in society. You can be one of them" (Mehari et. al. 2002a, 162).

The Ethiopian civics curriculum is an example of a phenomenon common elsewhere; it illustrates how the teleological time of education manifests in the developmentalist state where ideals, practices, and institutions of schooling have been imported to explicitly link students and their communities to a modernist trajectory (Katz 2004). Time and space are thus co-constituted and bound to the notion of progress. In this context, schooling doubly binds people to place and community on one hand and to dominant structures and notions of modernity and progress on the other (Hall 1997; Stambach 2000). Schools are prime institutions through which the linear and teleological temporality of modernity, however contradictory it may be, is socially reproduced and internalized. Modern schools are among the many industrial-era institutions designed to parse time by the hour, day, week, and year, aligning smaller units of time with increasingly larger ones and producing a subject that understands the benefits and consequences of adhering to or deviating from this temporal discipline (Foucault 1978). The rise of modern schooling in Europe, for example, came to be organized according to a linear, chronological temporality, such that homogeneous groups of children could progress in learning together through small temporal units, each tethered to stages of development (Biesta 2013). However, the temporal discipline promoted through schooling in particular, and education more broadly, is distinct because it attaches smaller units of incrementally organized time to distant goals and broader notions of progress. In *Discipline and Punish*, Michel Foucault highlights schools as particularly adept at producing and normalizing subjects' attachments to incremental time, aligning time with categorized knowledge, and giving that knowledge power through the surveillance techniques of the examination (1978). Schooling accomplishes this through spatial and temporal ordering.

This model of scheduled time that orders smaller increments (periods) with ever larger ones (days, weeks, terms, years), assigning each a task (knowledge to be mastered) that is evaluated and for which rewards will be granted, is still, arguably, the way schools are structured. Thus, schools teach students to keep time, use time, and master time; progress is assessed based on how well one adheres to and performs within these temporal structures (McClaren 1986).

Schools in the refugee camps were no exception. Students were expected to be punctual and to devote a great deal of time to their studies, despite the fact that their time often had to be spent on other things, such as waiting for humanitarian bureaucracy or conducting necessary everyday chores. Schooling operated according to daily, weekly, semester-long, and yearlong schedules that were interlocked and nested within each other, enabling the systematic movement toward a goal or outcome, often embodied by end-term examinations and report cards. The entire multiyear experience of schooling then builds toward the culminating national examination.

The teleological nature of education also ascribes a morality that entails a sense of individual responsibility for progress. Mains notes that education produces expectations in the educated individual: "The educated individual expects to be transformed so that his future will be better than the present" (Mains 2007, 665). An actor who is temporally disciplined and uses their time well is supposed to be successful, and conversely, one who lacks temporal discipline has failed to use their time well (Mains 2007, 2011).

If we understand that teleological time, as it shows up in processes of schooling, is organized incrementally, then it is easy to understand how schools are like factories designed to assert the normalcy and benevolence of these teleological trajectories, even when they systematically leave behind and weed out certain people. The sociology and anthropology of education literatures have carefully and ethnographically diagrammed the ways that schools reproduce inequalities while producing ideologies of meritocracy and achievement (Bourdieu and Passeron 1990; Bowles and Gintis 1976; Willis 1977), in no small part through the inculcation of teleological temporalities, the disciplining of students to adhere to these temporalities, and the attachment of morality to their success or failure at doing so (Foucault 1978). Anna Bennett and Penny Jane Burke (2018) illuminate how the meritocratic logic of education presents a linear and rigid understanding of developmental time frames that tends to assume that problems encountered by students are due to individual deficit and can best be fixed by developing the right personal habits (i.e., setting goals, creating action plans, using calendars, and chunking tasks). All of these strategies prioritize institutional, homogeneous time frames and problematize students unable to conform to them. Furthermore, they find that students themselves internalize this sense of personal deficit, failing to recognize structural and temporal barriers to their success.

Returning to the CEE curriculum that we began this section with, we might read that curriculum as a teleological chronotope (Bakhtin 1981; Keunen 2011). Mikhail Bakhtin's notion of the chronotope illuminates genres or narratives in which time and space shape and animate each other (1981). In a teleological chronotope, the narrative involves a sequence of events oriented toward progress; a protagonist follows certain steps to arrive at (or fail to arrive at) a previously understood goal or outcome (Keunen 2011). The teleological chronotope bundles together incrementally ordered time, the morality of student discipline and "hard work," and notions of progress both for the individual student *and* for national development. A teleological chronotope, we argue, functions to flatten space into a preset path of predictable steps, while time is funneled into a unilinear progression toward a known end with consequences for deviating from the precise steps on the path.

We might think of CEE as the blueprint for what an Ethiopian citizen should be. The teleological chronotope apparent in Ethiopia's CEE posits students as the protagonist who, if temporally disciplined and engaged in a prescribed set of behaviors, will bring about a better future for themselves and the nation. The curriculum thus binds daily time, the future, and Ethiopian national development together in a narrative of progress encapsulated in the epitaph from the previous section: *The future is in school today.*

These curricula contain messages that frame and illustrate the teleological orientation of schooling by focusing on responsibility, industriousness, self-reliance, saving, community participation, and the pursuit of wisdom. Throughout the curriculum, students are given the message that their duty is to study hard to have a better future for themselves and to bring progress to the nation. The idea conveyed is that hard work, timeliness, and discipline will enable individuals and the country to march toward a more prosperous future. Indeed, that future is held up to be inevitable if only each actor plays their part to the best of their ability.

But where do refugees, who are not Ethiopian citizens but temporary guests, fit into this national, teleological chronotope? The modern temporalities produced by schooling exist in an uncomfortable relationship with alternate ways of imagining the future, particularly in the context of hospitality, which renders connection to place more tenuous and temporary for guests. Hospitality, as we noted in chapter 2, is welcoming but exclusionary; it denies refugees full membership in a polity. Thus, hospitality produces structural barriers to progress, even as performances of being a good host disguise those barriers. Meanwhile, teleological chronotopes position educated refugees on a developmental trajectory. For Ethiopian students, the teleological orientation of schooling links notions of national space with future development. It also tethers refugees to these same notions of development and progress; however, refugees have no legal attachment to the nation. For refugees, as we explore later in this chapter, imaginaries of development and modernity are appealing, but they are imagined as somewhere "out there" in the world, not in the refugee camp, and often not in Ethiopia. Refugee students may be attached to teleological notions of time, but they are also keenly aware of how out of reach progress is and how their status as refugees makes it so. The next section details the processes through which refugees are impeded from full participation in teleological time.

Telos in the Time of the Camp: Hospitality, Humanitarian Bureaucracy, and the Cultural Production of the Educated Refugee

As we toured the Mai Aini secondary school, the director kept repeating, "You wouldn't expect a school like this to be for refugees." The school was well equipped, clean, and relatively new, having been constructed to serve refugees and local students shortly after the camp opened in 2008. The teachers were motivated, and the library was relatively well stocked. It was indeed a beautiful school, but why was the director surprised? Through his praise of the school and his expression of surprise that a school "like this" was built for refugees, the director positioned himself as a generous but skeptical benefactor who was subtly questioning whether or not refugees merited such a gift. The overt message was that refugees were lucky to go to such a school. The implied message was that as refugees, they somehow deserved less.

A closer look at the school director's statement—"You would not expect a school like this to be for refugees"—reveals the productive work of teleological violence; the teleological orientation of schooling and the constant assertion that schooling is a gift for refugees, rather than a necessity or human right, work together to culturally produce a particular kind of educated subject: an educated refugee.[4] Refugee schooling is simultaneously posited in different ways: a human right; a reward for the disciplined, hardworking, and meritorious; and a gift for the underprivileged. The school director's statement encapsulates all of these meanings, asserting the bold generosity of the host while reifying the otherness of the refugee-guest. While the conceptualization of education as a reward for the meritorious suggests that anyone who works hard enough will accomplish good things, the conceptualization of education as a gift for the needy fundamentally posits refugees as somehow less deserving than others. The contradiction between these two framings of education results in a painful and dangerous condition. The subject position of the educated refugee is marked by this frustrating paradox: the teleologies of education claim to propel refugees forward—to enable to them to progress if only they do the right things—while the structures of being a refugee hold them back, relegating them to the status of temporary guest.

Another illustration of this contradiction between education as a reward for hard work and education as a gift can be found in conflicts in a school that served residents of the town of Mai Tsebri and refugees from the Adi Harush camp. We had heard there were tensions in the Mai Tsebri school, the only school in our study that was located in a village. The school's teachers and administration were

scrambling to accommodate both a fluid population of refugees and a rapidly growing population of Ethiopian students arriving each year in the booming town. The
challenges were in many ways obvious, involving a severe shortage of resources and
impressive ingenuity on behalf of the teachers and administration who repurposed
materials for ad hoc classrooms, raised funds for a new building, and found work-
arounds for book shortages. Yet the school director also described social tensions
between refugees and locals that centered on the perceived desire for refugees to be
treated differently. The thornier concerns revolved around the production of social
difference.

A central tenet of the literature on cultural production holds that processes of
schooling not only *reproduce* existing social differences and inequalities; they also
produce tastes, habits, and identities that may resist, contest, or alter social categories or status groups (Levinson et al. 1996). In many circumstances, student difference is reinforced, reified, and reproduced without their doing a single thing or
simply because they have tried to advocate for themselves in positive and proactive
ways. Here we explore the subject position of *educated refugee*, which is produced
through the logics of progress, on one hand, and hospitality and bureaucratic humanitarian care, on the other.

The cultural production of the educated refugee is not only inculcated with
and implicated in very particular notions of progress and telos but also embodies
the contradiction inherent in being an educated refugee that is the focus of this
chapter. As noted earlier, the paradox of educated refugees is that they, by virtue of
being educated persons, are heavily socialized to understand their potential, possibility, and responsibility, but as refugees, they are also made keenly aware of very
clear structural limitations to progress. Here we focus on how humanitarian care
of refugee students demarcated them as refugees and produced the conditions for
their differentiation. Refugees' own understandings of and advocacy for themselves
as protected subjects also contribute to their framing as refugees.

Tensions that arose every year in the Mai Tsebri school around school uniforms
are an apt illustration of how refugees are culturally produced through slow humanitarian bureaucracies. In Ethiopia, as in other parts of the developing world, wearing
a uniform is important. It serves as a marker that one is a student—a distinct and
often privileged identity. It further communicates that discipline is fundamental
to being a student. The consistency with which a student wears their uniform and
the condition in which the uniform is kept are often thought to reflect on the quality and character of the student. However, refugees, as well as many lower-income
students, often cannot afford a uniform. Jennifer's research in Eritrea and Ethiopia
found that teachers in both places, despite saying that they understood the financial constraints that some students faced, still judged students who failed to wear
a uniform and blamed problems with school discipline on this (2016, 2019, 2022).
Even when students had a legitimate reason to not wear a uniform, they could be
disciplined, punished, scrutinized, and judged for not being appropriately attired.

In the case of refugees, the Administration for Refugee and Returnee Affairs (ARRA) was supposed to provide their uniforms. However, ARRA was always late with the funds. In the Mai Tsebri secondary school, this created problems: refugee students felt discriminated against when the government failed to provide uniforms for them; Ethiopian students, many of whom came from poor, rural communities, felt that refugees were being given an unfair exception to the dress code; and teachers were unhappy to have a sizable number of students out of uniform. The annual late arrival of refugee uniforms served as an important means to demarcate who the refugees were, but it also inadvertently set them up for moral judgment. On the one hand, they were not regarded as "real" students because they were out of uniform. On the other hand, they were perceived as entitled, because exceptions were made for them that were not made for students from the host community, including those who struggled to afford uniforms. The late arrival of uniforms also illuminated the ways refugee students were victims of slow humanitarian bureaucracies; they were dependent on an institution (ARRA) that failed to provide for them in a timely manner. This reinforced lines of social difference in their school experience.

There were many other examples of the failure of humanitarian bureaucracy to provide for refugees in a timely manner in ways that disadvantaged them and challenged their dignity. On our first visit to the camps, we asked about refugees' university experiences, and one student told us about a friend who was preparing to give a presentation that was required for graduation. He was expected to wear a suit for this talk. His understanding was that ARRA was supposed to provide him with additional funding for things like this, but despite some assurances that this would happen, ARRA never gave him the money. He ultimately had to borrow a suit from someone else. We heard reference to this story several times and found it significant that this story about a suit meant so much to refugee students. The fact that he told this story—and that this story circulated more broadly—shows the importance of feeling cared for and the painful stigma of feeling singled out. They wanted to be able to present themselves and showcase their accomplishments just as any other student, but doing so required getting assistance, and assistance moved at the glacial pace of bureaucracy, often arriving too late to be useful.

The late provision of necessities was a common complaint in refugee interactions with ARRA across educational settings. University students also complained that their monthly stipend was often late, a huge problem given that these funds were necessary to photocopy readings so that they could keep up with classes. This stipend also enabled refugees to purchase food and even showers in cases where the campus plumbing was nonfunctioning. This delay impacted refugees in other ways as well. Refugee applicants to university were only allowed to take the national exam after Ethiopian students, and their results were released late, meaning that they enrolled in university later and had limited selection of what to study. Most concerning to them, they had to start the school year up to three months late, meaning they had to ask for extra help from the instructor or other students. It was often difficult for them to catch up.

The slow, disconnected, bureaucratic temporality of hospitality conflicts with the way teleological, educational time requires that its subjects take responsibility for their success or failure. This leaves refugees facing such challenges as having to make up for two months of university education or figure out how to eat on no stipend. To face these challenges, they have to ask for help either from professors or fellow students. They also have to ask that special accommodations be made for them. This characterizes them as both needy and demanding, belying the prescribed "good guest" behavior that we discussed in the last chapter. All of this results in indignities that are uncomfortable and make it difficult for refugees to succeed.

These indignities extend to other perceived forms of discrimination that reproduce social difference for refugees in tertiary education. Many of the college students we spoke to had a distinct sense that they were only allowed to study at the convenience of the administration. Because they took the matriculation exam late, they were assigned to universities where there were slots left over in universities and programs that were less desirable. As the school director we quoted earlier implied, there was a sense that refugees somehow deserved—or at least should expect—whatever they were given and should be thankful for whatever that was. In a focus group discussion with refugees who were waiting for their matriculation results we heard that they would like to study subjects such as computer science and engineering but they were not assigned to those programs. They also said they would prefer not to study in Tigray and had requested universities in other parts of the country but were typically placed in Tigray because of "the need of the officials," rather than their own desires and academic interests. The lateness of the refugee matriculation exam was a key reason why refugees were relegated to the "leftover" university assignments, but this was not just a temporal problem. Refugees had a strong sense that this occurred because of a belief that refugees did not merit the same treatment as Ethiopian students.

Refugees felt they were second-class citizens, devalued and differentiated from Ethiopian students and unable to compete on an even playing field. For example, several refugees noted that no matter how hard they worked, they would not be given the same rewards or opportunities as Ethiopian students. One young graduate shared a common complaint that we heard often from university students: "Your achievement is your achievement regardless of your school. There are awards given to top students in each college. These awards are not given to Eritreans, even if they are the top student scoring the highest marks. If an Eritrean scores top marks, it will be given to the next student." While students frequently described this practice as demoralizing, others noted that the various forms of recognition denied to refugee students also harmed them in material ways. We often heard that professional leadership opportunities, such as serving as a prefect or teaching assistant, were preferentially allocated to Ethiopians regardless of refugee student accomplishments. These kinds of prizes and opportunities are essential for all students in a tight job market but are particularly essential for refugees, who compete in this tight market without the benefit of the legal right to work, further narrowing the opportunities available to them.

Many of the complaints about being stigmatized, not looked after, and not cared for stem from the nature of bureaucracy, which moves slowly, adheres to its own temporality, and therefore cannot be responsive to the individual needs of refugees. Bureaucratic temporalities serve and respond to the needs of the program, not the people it is supposed to serve. They not only move very slowly but are often unpredictable and impossible for refugees to control. Meanwhile, the requirement that refugees engage with and master the teleological time of schooling is extremely challenging given these sluggish bureaucratic temporalities. Bureaucratic time thwarts self-discipline, and it thwarts structured and planful time. It is anti-teleological because it works against refugees striving toward progress and accomplishing their desired ends.

The harm caused by bureaucratic time is compounded by the fact that refugees are under a system of bureaucratized hospitality that reinforces both the status of the host and the dependent, temporary status of the refugee. As we described in chapter 2, hospitality in refugee management concentrates power through a profoundly unequal "gift" exchange and distances the host from the quality or appropriateness of the gift. The gifts provided by humanitarian bureaucracies—UNHCR resettlement processes, WFP food distributions, and the array of services ARRA provides—seldom meet refugees' needs fully and often work against their goals, plans, and teleological aspirations. Teleological violence is apparent in the disjuncture between the teleological time of school and the slow bureaucratic time of hospitality, but some of the extremes of teleological violence are experienced when refugees encounter a bleak and empty future.

Teleological Violence and the Aborted Future

"An asset you can't use is an expense," a university graduate and resident of Adi Harush camp told us. We were conducting a focus group with university graduates who were back in the camps in a bar owned by Berihu, our friend and interlocutor. A group of about ten university graduates sat under the shade of an awning drinking cold Cokes off low tables. The awning, the comfortable plastic chairs, the tables with their shiny plastic tablecloths, and the refrigerator were all purchased with the loan Berihu had taken out to buy his bar. Everyone nodded in agreement with the first speaker and chimed in. Another former student added, "When we stay here for a long time, our minds are damaged." Members of the focus group then made frequent, almost poetic statements about the damage, not simply of living in the camp, which was hard enough, but of being relegated back to the camp. The value of their education, the fruit of their hard work, had been destroyed, and they were being forced into low-paying incentive jobs with no future after having been to university.

The lack of opportunity after graduation was experienced as a particularly acute form of temporal suffering; it was fueled by a sense of failed promises, of having been cheated out of something they were taught to believe they merited by virtue of their hard work. Theirs was an unsuccessful success (Varenne and McDermott 1998). In higher education, students are not only taught the curriculum but trained for a profession. Yet the end point for refugees is being stuck in the camp, unable to work legally except as incentive workers. A refugee commented that they expected a different outcome in their life: "We are at the same level as the ignorant people. What will be our output at last? Even though they gave us this chance for education, what is our output?" This suggests that education without "output," or purpose, is meaningless. Another refugee expanded on this thought, noting that he had hoped that education would at least make him self-sufficient yet had failed to produce even this: "We are visionless. What are we going to do? We don't know. We are visionless. We learn here and go to camp. What will I be later? Nothing. I will be the same as those who are not educated. If you always give food, it is not good. You need to teach a man to fish, so we need a change. We don't have a chance to do anything."

Educated refugees felt that they had learned to fish but were then not allowed to fish and instead were relegated to living in the camps, getting handouts to eat. If camps are, as Elizabeth Cullen Dunn says, "an engine" that "keep[s] people frozen at the cusp of futures just out of reach" (2017), then refugee schools are a particularly acute manifestation of that engine. Teleological time in refugee camps, as with other settings in which the developmental ethos is predominant, was put forward as the norm that everyone should strive toward. And yet teleological time promoted through schooling in the camps did not provide a return on its investment or hold true to its powerful promises.

Teleological violence and its relationship with the sense of an aborted future are illustrated in the stories of Berihu and Gerie, who attended university together; both experienced teleological violence in different ways. Berihu's story, which we detail more in the next chapter, illustrates the traumas of empty, endless time and of teleological violence. During one of our conversations with him, he shared a picture of friends—seven polished young men—in his graduating class. As graduation neared, refugee students had meetings about their future every three months, asking each other, "Where will we go from here?" After graduation, all of them but Gerie were back in the camps. Berihu listed their fields of study as an index of their identity and accomplishment, yet the sense of hope and pride faded when he described how they were stuck in the camps, unable to get a proper job or continue their education: "Until now, I was happy to get this opportunity to have a bachelor's degree. If I got the opportunity or chance to keep on my progress, I will have success. But if I sit here for three years and forget what I learned . . . Nobody is happy after graduation because they returned back to the camp and they simply live as the others. We have to use our knowledge to give something back to society. This one graduated one year ago but now is simply living the same as the illiterate refugees. He gets rations each month."

His suffering is not just due to his low-incentive wages (about forty dollars per month) but is distinctly linked to his inability to progress despite his educational successes. In the next chapter, we discuss Berihu's temporal suffering in more detail as well as his efforts to alleviate it through acts of caretaking. Here we emphasize the role of education in producing temporal suffering. Education, both his own and that of the young people he was charged with teaching, was a particular source of pain because it served as a constant, insistent reminder of what he was not permitted to accomplish.

Gerie's story in some ways could not be more different from his friend Berihu's, yet the elements of precarity and uncertainty and the effects of teleological violence are similar. Gerie was the educated refugee success story. He spoke flawless English and was bursting with charm and positive energy. He went to a university in Ethiopia under the refugee college scholarship program and started an organization to motivate refugee youth to attend school and avoid secondary migration. He married an Eritrean woman he met in the camps, had two children, moved to Addis Ababa, and was one of the rare few who managed to secure himself a relatively good, if informal, private-sector job.

It was challenging for us to get on Gerie's schedule and meeting him required multiple schedule changes and a long taxi ride to the outskirts of Addis Ababa, where he rented a unit in one of the newly built condominium blocks. Gerie and his wife had just celebrated the second birthday of their son and the birth of a second child a few weeks before. Their apartment was decorated with colored posters and trays of candy and popcorn. While his wife remained secluded in an adjoining room with her newborn baby, Gerie simultaneously entertained his vivacious two-year-old and engaged us with sparkling conversation and keen insights into the plight of educated refugees in Ethiopia.

It would seem that Gerie had succeeded. He described his persistence: "I am very bold. I see my vision and the people behind me." But Gerie also had the profound sense of running in place. As with many people who cling to the edges of the middle class in Addis Ababa, his low wages and the city's sprawling demographics and geography meant that he lived far on the outskirts of town, with an onerous commute to a job where he worked long hours. Time, once again, was a problem: "I am getting tired all day in the school. I am teaching, and when I come home, I've got little time to spend at home."

His time and energy were spread thin as he simultaneously worked on multiple strategies to *get ahead*. Some of that time and energy went to organizing university students—work that had come to mean so much to him—but he had thus far failed to have the university student organization officially recognized by ARRA, which both limited its effectiveness and exposed structural barriers to refugee participation in civic life. He had also been trying to pursue a graduate degree but was finding innumerable formal and informal barriers. Additionally, in an effort to gain control over his life and to get ahead, when we last saw him, he was trying to raise capital to start a business by drawing on church connections abroad. These efforts required a constant exertion of social and cultural capital and the leveraging of hard-won connections gained through bureaucratic office visits that ate up all his spare time. Time and again, he smacked up against legal barriers that limited the efficacy of the cultural capital he had carefully cultivated in his schooling.

Both Berihu and Gerie were deeply inculcated by teleological time, but despite doing all the "right" things and achieving a great deal of success in education, they struggled to get ahead. This pained them in no small part because they knew that the constraints that the refugee label placed on them caused their failure. They were socialized, through many years of education, to have goals and to parse out their time incrementally on a daily basis in service to those goals. However, Berihu and most refugee university graduates were floundering, living partially in a trauma-ridden past, always aware of the option of leaping to the distant, unknown future of migration. Time back in the camp was not merely emptied of telos; it involved a kind of progressive degeneration. Degrees became stale, knowledge and skills atrophied, bright work opportunities faded. Without professional experience, certifications expired.

Everything about schooling created temporal expectations—having control over time and moving through time in a progressive way. But this teleological time was troubled. Gerie and Berihu felt it was their responsibility to encourage young people in the camps to go to school, but they themselves were routinely confronting the reality that education did not get them anywhere. Berihu was all too aware that he served as a negative role model to youth in the camps and represented the myth of teleological time. This myth was exposed when the illusion of being able to arrive at a bright future through self-discipline and actions involving incremental progress toward a reachable goal confronted the reality of educated refugees languishing in the camps or struggling in the cities. Graduates felt as if they had been tricked, and it became increasingly harder to wait hopefully.

While there was a sense that promises were not fulfilled, often the deeper regret came from an internalized blame for wasting years in pursuit of an empty future. Berihu mused with regret, "We have gone to school. We have followed the classes for twenty years. So, we blame ourselves: Why did I go to school? Why didn't I try to solve the problem for myself?" In all of our conversations with refugee graduates, they talked about the future as if it had abandoned them and about education as if it had been some sort of cruel trick. Teleological time forged a "cruel optimism," to borrow Lauren Berlant's concept, which explains how attachments to an object of desire, an imagined "good life," are not only impossible but can be injurious (Berlant 2011). As Shahram Khosravi notes in his writing on unemployed youth in Tehran, "To pursue a goal which is by definition unattainable is to condemn oneself to a state of perpetual unhappiness" (2017, 72). Teleological time produced and reinforced exclusions, exposing and bolstering the illusion that education provides a viable path forward. Educated refugees were frozen out of the future (Dunn 2017).

Teleological violence did not just result in deep unhappiness; it also led to risky decision-making regarding migration. One of the arguments refugees commonly made for not attending school was the understanding that education would not get them *anywhere*—that it is just one of the more onerous ways to kill time in the camp. Nearly every time we asked why people were not in school, we heard similar responses. As one refugee university student who was waiting out the summer break in the camp noted, "There are many young people here, but their plans are not to study. Their plans are to go abroad, secondary movement." He explained that it was hard for him to deal with the emptiness of camp time; he was just waiting and sleeping. He explained that youth who are not in school "are playing football. There is the JRS [youth center] where they spend their time playing billiards. But ninety percent of them are in bars." This was a temporal problem. His description of activities that fill time suggests that refugees were focused on the temporariness of Ethiopia as a stop in a longer journey. As one young woman reflected about the youth in camp who refused to attend school: "Those who are of age are busy taking care of themselves. They think they are leaving tomorrow. The process may come early, we may leave, and so why worry about education here? For those who are underage, they are dreaming and wishing to be abroad."

Educated refugees were acutely aware of the way education more often than not led to stasis rather than progress, and they therefore felt the pull of migration. That pull was arguably stronger in some ways because of the pressures of "failing" at making progress through education. The risks of migration were well known, particularly for those who lacked the financial and social capital to fund the journey. Although many of these frustrated graduates do wait in the camp for years, the possibility that, in desperation, they might decide to migrate is a specter that haunts all of them. Berihu told us a story about one of his mentors, a refugee who had encouraged him and many others to go to university and not to migrate. "Because of this person, I did not migrate and instead I went to university," Berihu said. "But then I heard that he himself left the country. This kind of thing makes you confused. . . . I saw so many of my friends lose hope. Why so many travel through the Sahara Desert—because they lose hope. I stayed here five years. A refugee is a person who is not stable. Everyone is changing his decision day by day." Those who attend university and return to the camp are not generally predisposed to leave. And yet the pain of coping with time without telos after having been in university often drives them, if not to migrate, to at least consider it as an option.

Futures in Conversation: Schooling, Migration, and the Camp

It was hot by the time the school closing ceremony got off to a start, an hour or so later than it was supposed to. By then, the space in the shade under the awnings made of blue tarps was crowded. Students, parents, and teachers squeezed onto benches that had been dragged out of the classrooms. Music blared over a sound system. Refreshments (tea and *embasha*, a homemade bread) circulated through the crowd. There was a festive air.

The end-of-year ceremony in Mai Aini camp's senior secondary school was a teleological event. It marked the end point in the school year and created a sense of progress. It was supposed to motivate students by making them feel like schooling was important, their efforts valued. Lasting an entire morning in early July, the ceremony included speeches by the school director and head of the Parent Teacher Association (PTA), comments from the audience, performances by students, and an awards ceremony. Interestingly, most of the speeches and comments addressed the lack of a bright future in Ethiopia and in Mai Aini. They cautioned students to avoid wasting away in the camp by drinking and acting badly and also warned about the dangers of irregular migration. Throughout the ceremony, schooling was cast as a valiant alternative, a sort of antidote to "deviant" behaviors.

Nothing illustrated this better than a short play that was written and acted out by the students. In the play, a young man cuts class and plays hooky to go to the bars and drink with money he cons from his sister in the United States by telling her the money is for school and assuring her that he has top grades. Despite warnings from his mother, his teachers, and an old man in the bar, the young man continues along his wayward path until his sister calls with news of a scholarship. With great glee, he goes to the embassy to receive his scholarship, but much to his surprise, he is given a test that he fails spectacularly, causing him to lose the scholarship.

The play is a morality tale—work hard at your education and do not succumb to the vices of empty time, because education will help you one day, and it might even help you leave the country. It celebrates the virtues of education, hard work, and disciplining one's time to attend school. It demonizes the evils of falling into the timelessness of the bar. In doing so, the play, and the ceremony overall, set up education as a moral project in which those who work hard and settle into school-based discipline will have access to better things and will progress to a brighter future.

The play puts the time-space of schooling in a conversation with the time-spaces of both the camp and migration.[5] Two of those time-spaces—schooling and migration—are teleological, while camp time is not. But the time-spaces of schooling and migration convey very different kinds of teleology.[6] The former can be equated with modernist notions of progress prescribing a linear movement forward through a series of stages to a known and predictable endpoint. The latter is open ended—the desired outcome is clear but the way to get there is not. This open-ended teleology exists in the space of the distant, rather than the near, future.

Putting migration, schooling, and the time-space of the camp in conversation with each other was certainly not limited to the play or the school closing ceremony. In almost every discussion we had about education, the relationship between education, the empty time of the camp, and migration was evoked. As we explore in the next chapter, the space of the camp is always seen as a temporary one linked to the vices of succumbing to interminable empty time or marked by helplessness in the face of bureaucratic processes. Temporal suffering is produced by this temporariness and cruelties of bureaucratized "care." Migration, as we explore in chapter 5, is attached to an unknown space and an unknown time; it links an indeterminate space *beyond* Ethiopia and the camp with a distant imagined future. The school offers up a different imagined future, one which is drawn near to the present through the disciplines and everyday structure of schooling. The future offered up through schooling is presented as an attainable goal.

Ideas about progress are infused in discussions of both secondary migration and camp time. For refugees, secondary migration held the possibility of acute trauma and death but also progress, while remaining in the camp was known to lead to suffering (and potentially slow death) with little hope for progress. Meanwhile, progress promoted through schooling promised to offer a leg up and over these impasses but did not. Each time we returned to the camps, we learned about students who had succumbed to one or the other pathway, leaving people behind them a little less certain—or forcing them to shore up their own resolve about the path they were on. This, perhaps, is where teleological violence poses the greatest risk of physical violence to refugees. When educated refugees abandon the hopes for the future their education has promised them, they are posed with a choice, much as the character in the school play is depicted as having a choice: abandon hope for progress and succumb to the dangers of empty camp time or hold on to hopes for progress and face the severe risks of migration as the only remaining possible pathway. Some refugees, however, were seeking out alternative ways to make time by engaging in the politics of reclaiming teleological time on their own terms.

Time-Making and the Politics of Reclaiming Teleological Time

Teleological violence does not simply entail being highly educated so that one can face the precarity of incentive work in the camps. It is also working so hard to graduate and facing the shame of borrowing a suit for the final presentation or achieving top grades and finding there is no trophy for you after all, simply because you are a refugee. It is being told that you are lucky to have these opportunities but not having anyone concerned that the implementation of opportunities winds up placing you at a disadvantage because you arrived to school months late and did not receive a sufficient stipend to purchase materials to study. Teleological violence reveals that the best-laid plans for refugee care become plans for refugee containment, reinforcing lines of social difference and generating political and economic vulnerability. And yet refugees did constantly push back against their relegation to the empty time of the camp and against teleological violence.

The temporality of educational teleology required and expected that students were good at planning, goal setting, and managing time. Indeed, these are integral to what it means to be a "good student." However, the experience of being a refugee—specifically refugees' lack of control over time—works against the utilization of these skills.[7] One of the reasons teleologies are harmful is because there are so many temporal barriers to refugees' achieving their goals. We have seen several examples of these barriers throughout this chapter. Refugees are not without agency, but they have to go beyond being planful and organized to enact temporal agency. They have to be more than managers of time; they have to be makers of time. They turn to activism in an attempt to lay claim to their right to progress and to make teleological time work for—rather than against—them.

In conclusion, let's return to that attendance chart we problematized earlier in this chapter. Every chance we got, we continued to ask why enrollments among refugees were so low. Why had they fallen so suddenly in that particular year? If schooling was such a great opportunity, why had enrollments not risen again? Repeatedly people responded to our question with two answers: onward movement and hopelessness. Both are true, but finally, after over a year of asking, we got an answer that specifies teleological violence and complicates our understanding of the relationship between schooling, the camp, hopelessness, onward movement, and refugees' lack of belonging in Ethiopia.

The year that saw the steepest drop in enrollments, 2014, was the year of the Lampedusa boat wreck. Lampedusa was certainly not the first, last, or even most deadly of the many boat crashes in the Mediterranean, but it captured the international imagination. Less covered was the fact that the majority of migrants on that boat were Eritreans, many of them from the Mai Aini camp. Refugees in the Mai Aini camp were outraged and openly protested conditions in the camp such as low rations and a lack of resettlement opportunities. They believed these conditions had directly led to the mass migration that resulted in deaths at sea. The Ethiopian government clamped down brutally on the protests, which in turn led to another wave of mass migration and a general increase in disillusion about Ethiopian goodwill. School enrollments plummeted. We argue that this is reflective of a lack of trust in both the Ethiopian government and the outcome of schooling. The two are connected; there is no purpose for education if the Ethiopian government doesn't guarantee rights for refugees, such as the right to work.

This brings to the fore the complexities of refugee political action. The subject position of being a refugee in Ethiopia was brutally reinforced, undercutting the subject position of being a student on a path toward the future. "They had hope before," explained one long-term resident about the sudden and enduring drop in enrollment. "After that, the government and the UNHCR told them, 'You will live your life in this camp.'"

In conclusion, we want to explore a form of temporal agency, or time-making, that emerges from political action and responds directly to teleological violence by reclaiming one's space in a teleological narrative. The protests following Lampedusa were an attempt to claim status as rights-bearing subjects—subjects who had the right to a future. It is significant that one of the things that protesters were asking for was more transparency around resettlement opportunities. The firm clampdown on the protests indicated that refugees did not have the right to lay claim to a future. Interestingly, the response after the protests was to abandon the institution often most closely associated with producing the future: schools.

Since the Lampedusa protests, refugees have been cautious about political organizing but have not failed to organize themselves, as doing so gives them a sense of dignity and purpose that we might argue forged an alternate teleology. They might not be able to get jobs or advance their education beyond the postsecondary level (and thereby will be blocked from continuing on an imagined trajectory toward material success). However, they can use their clout as students and graduates, their confidence, their sense of themselves as leaders, their communication skills, and, at times, their contacts to forge an alternate teleology, demand dignity, and serve as role models. Educated refugees claim a leadership role on the basis of being educated. None of this is a replacement for the stability or livelihoods denied them, but it is a way of claiming agency amid severe structural barriers. We suggest that such organizing efforts are an attempt to reclaim the right to progress, to forge a pathway to a meaningful future, and to carve out a special role for educated refugees.

One of these organizing efforts resulted in the formation of the Eritrean Refugee University Student Association (ERUSA) in 2015. One of the founders of ERUSA described the motivation that drove him to form the organization with other students at Adigrat University: "As educated people in our community, we began talking about our future. It was very heavy. People were dying in the sea, even students who had been with us. What do we do? Do we just keep working for other organizations? At least let's give some advice to the unaccompanied youth. Let's share our love. They are away from family, far from older brothers. Let's be their older brothers."

He described this work as meeting the needs of both the unaccompanied youth and the refugee college students: "We can be of some service and ask some privileges from other organizations and governments. We are suffering from lack of opportunities. So, let's ask the UN, NGOs, the Government of Ethiopia. If a friend of ours graduates and is just here in the camp, not allowed to work, he goes to the Mediterranean Sea—sinking there. Let's help our community and be helped by others."

The organization quickly expanded to include Eritrean refugee students at other campuses in the Tigray region and those who attend the University of Addis Ababa in the capital city. Most of the nearly one hundred members loosely organized via a social media app that allowed students to pose questions and share experiences and advice. For some of these students, their membership was more about support than political organizing. However, more formal leadership structures took shape at campuses with a larger population of refugee students, and these groups were more expressly political and more active in attempting to attract resources and recognition from the humanitarian aid industry.

In the summer of 2016, members of ERUSA partnered with the Norwegian Refugee Council to conduct workshops with youth in the camps, a project they extended in 2017 with funding from UNHCR. They arranged a sports festival for youth in two camps and in surrounding villages to create opportunities for positive interaction and community building. They also conducted three workshops in Mai Aini to address what they felt were the most pressing topics facing youth in the camps: the danger of addiction, the usefulness of education, and the risks of secondary migration. During the school year, they organized after-school tutoring for elementary children using resources they were able to secure from a church abroad. More recent efforts have involved a public health campaign to educate refugees in the camps about COVID-19. Access to external resources has been sporadic, however. ERUSA's application for the small summer grant from UNHCR was unsuccessful in 2018, and despite repeated office visits to ARRA officials in Tigray and Addis Ababa, the group did not gain recognition as a formal organization from the Ethiopian government. Indeed, ERUSA's activities in the camps have been heavily surveilled. As such, the organization has tended to shift in membership and orientation as varied cohorts of students enter and leave the university. And, as a result of the difficulties communicating across great distances with few resources to meet in person and sporadically available internet, more than one manifestation of ERUSA emerged.

The work of ERUSA blended ethical, social, and political commitments, thereby crafting an alternate narrative of the role of educated refugees in the region. They framed their work with Ethiopian communities as a kind of grassroots diplomacy rather than a form of local integration. When the organization formed at Adigrat University, one of their first initiatives involved designing a campus greening project with the goal of contributing to the local community—a goal that was similarly embedded in the sports events. These objectives involved a long-term vision for their own role in the region. As one leader explained, "We can preserve our resources, the educated scholars, if God willing a change happens in our country. We can preserve it right here." The work with community building, social organizing, and networking links directly to an imagined future of political transformation. If humanitarian borderwork depoliticizes the effort to stem secondary migration as a kind of "compassionate" act of saving the individual lives of young refugees, ERUSA explores the politics of staying close to home, the collective impacts of migration, and the stakes of building positive relations with local border communities that have oscillated between enemies, friends, and brothers during a tumultuous history.

Eritrean student groups on various university campuses also organized to push back against the structural barriers imposed by a slow-acting bureaucracy. On Axum University's campus, they formed a group and elected leaders who approached the university administration to ask to be admitted to class, despite the fact that they had arrived late and the school did not want to enroll them. They also asked for support given that they had missed two months of class, did not speak the language that many classes were taught in, and often ran out of money before they could photocopy their course materials. This same group was working to create a direct line of communication with ARRA to ensure that ARRA was also trying to better support them and ensure their success.

Although these organizing efforts may have had limited success in terms of stemming onward movement and securing future opportunities for refugees, they were important in other ways. They were acts of temporal agency—time-making—that asserted that refugees were subjects who had the right to a future. Although this refusal to abandon teleological aspirations was one of the things that made teleologies painful, it also restored dignity, a sense of purpose, and a sense of agency over forward-moving progress. Even if refugee university students could not go on to graduate school, move to another country, or get a job, they could use their special status as educated people to help their community and that of their Ethiopian neighbors. They could advocate for their right to a future.

Notes

1. The notion of something you work hard to accomplish harming you is similar to Lauren Berlant's (2011) concept of "cruel optimism." Like cruel optimism, teleological violence incentivizes and disciplines people to act in particular ways, making them hopeful and expectant of outcomes that remain out of reach due to substantial structural barriers. The facet of teleological violence we discuss in this chapter resonates with this notion of the thing you strive for causing harm. However, the concept of teleological violence emphasizes the temporal dimensions of striving and also serves to explain why one might respond to this violence either by not striving or by striving in a different way—for example, by migrating.

2. Bourdieu and Passeron (1990) posit that education systems are designed to benefit the politically and economically dominant groups in society for whom formal schooling mirrors their habitus. Students from dominant groups, therefore, come to school equipped with the cultural capital to be successful at schooling. When there is a disconnect between pedagogical style and student habitus, symbolic violence results. For refugees, there is a complex relationship between habitus/cultural capital and symbolic violence. While many refugees may already have the habitus/cultural capital of an educated person, they are stigmatized and often suffer material deprivations as refugees. For example, they may know how to act and dress like a student, study and take notes, and talk to teachers and professors, in some cases more adeptly than members of the host community, but they may not have money to buy appropriate clothing, books, or even food. It is important to note that Bourdieu and Passeron's emphasis on habitus and what might be thought of as complex, nuanced, "cultural" impediments to

success do not preclude or erase structural barriers but do specify their function. We emphasize structural barriers to success more than cultural barriers such as habitus but still find their basic premise that schooling produces false promises a useful starting point.

3. See Dunn (2017) for a detailed discussion of the ways the refugee camp produces a sense of futurity that leaves the future perpetually out of reach.

4. Here we draw on the rich literature on the cultural production of the educated person (Levinson et al. 1996; MacLeod 2008; Levinson 2001). Drawing together social theory from Bourdieu and Passeron (1990) and Foucault (1978) and other work on cultural production and social reproduction (Willis 1977; Bowles and Gintis 1976), this body of work explores the confluence of cultural, historical, and economic factors to show how education, rather than empowerment and the provision of opportunities, has complex effects that often reproduce inequalities while also producing new ways of relating to the world.

5. Our thinking here is informed by Hilary Parsons Dick's analysis of migrant speech practices, which describes the imagined relationship between different time-places (2010). Migrant narratives place the United States and Mexico in a contrapuntal relationship between "there" (the United States) and "here" (Mexico), which serves as an index for the imagined moral and economic trade-offs of migration (Dick 2018). Similarly, refugees bundle together an array of times and spaces, including daily time in the camp, the time of schooling, and the future-making inherent in thinking about migration.

6. As we noted in the introduction, there are distinct but closely related notions of teleology, with one notion of *teleology* being synonymous with *progress* and associated with modernity. A more open-ended teleology is associated with the notion of an end (see Bryant and Knight [2019] and Ramsay and Askland [2020] for further discussion). Rebecca Bryant and Daniel Knight argue that teleology as associated with progress has gotten something of a bad rap and, in their discussion of the anthropology of the future, make open-ended teleology central. In contrast, we suggest that to understand the future from the vantage point of refugees and other marginalized people, we need to put teleological notions of progress in conversation with open-ended teleologies.

7. This is similar to what Arjun Appadurai (2004) would call lacking "the capacity to aspire," although we note that educated refugees knew how to aspire, they knew how to plan, and they knew how to succeed educationally. What they faced was less a lack of the "navigational capacity" that Appadurai describes and more an attempt to aspire in the face of repeated—and unpredictable—barriers.

4 Camp Time

Suffering and Care in a Time without Telos

Libraries and Gardens

Berihu

"A graduate is living for three years, useless. After graduation, I returned to where I was—just sleeping and sitting," Berihu told us. He wore a sharp dress shirt and invited us to drink chilled soda in the shade of woven reed mats in front of a restaurant he had recently opened. After graduating at the top of his class through the university scholarship program two years earlier, he found himself back at the camp, subsisting on rations and incentive pay (about forty dollars a month) for his work as a volunteer teacher at the camp primary school. He lived at the far edge of the camp, where the dirt roads and houses were surrounded by a landscape of reddish earth, grasses, and grazing cattle. Berihu reflected on his struggle to remain hopeful while stuck at the camp facing an uncertain future. He described a period when he had stopped acting like a teacher. He would show up for class late, unbathed, in casual clothes. Teaching for incentive pay, he explained, "is killing time. It is all about how to kill time," and that is "demoralizing." After all, he says, "You need to eat to live, not live to eat."

He eventually righted himself, thanks in no small part to caring for others and the land. In addition to his teaching position, he started working with other refugee college students to design education programs that would encourage youth to stay in school and avoid secondary migration. "If you support somebody, you feel proud," he said, mentioning repeatedly, "It makes your mind rest."

Berihu was also trying his hand at farming. He took us around the back to see his new garden. He had spent tremendous effort digging rocks out of the soil behind his house, and over the course of a week, he had excavated a pit filled with rocks, some as large as boulders. He was cheerful and undeterred by the momentous task and proud of the progress he had made. But he also said he was farming the land without permission and faced the risk of the camp administration pushing him out at any time. Similarly, when he expanded his home to build the restaurant, Administration for Refugee and Returnee Affairs (ARRA) representatives told him he could not continue, but he risked building it anyway. Although it was still just red earth and rock, Berihu told us the garden "is what makes his place special." As we admired his work, a local Ethiopian man from a nearby village approached to ask for money for his sick child. Berihu pulled Ethiopian bills from his pocket without hesitation. Local people often asked him for help here, he explained, assuming because of his appearance that he was in a position to assist them.

But despite—or perhaps because of—his efforts to care for the land, the children in the refugee camp, and even his Ethiopian neighbors in the host community, Berihu was keenly aware of his precarious future. He told us that most refugees were reluctant to invest time and money into long-term projects because of instability and not knowing the future: "What refugees are feeling is we don't know where we are. Will we go forwards or backwards? They are worrying about that, and since they are worrying, they don't want to do anything. If I get out after one year, I will not see the profit from my business."

Andebrhan

Andebrhan had been a science teacher before leaving Eritrea. His English was excellent, and he had hoped to pass the matriculation exam and attend a university in Ethiopia. He had a mother and younger sibling in Addis. They had avoided deportation during the border conflict because his mother was caring for his critically ill father. But Andebrhan had been deported as a child to Eritrea, where, like so many others, he was forced into military training and endless government service. When he returned to Ethiopia as a refugee, he stayed with his mother for a short time before returning to the camp in an attempt to continue his education and prepare for the matriculation exam. Andebrhan suffered from memories of the deportation and separation from his family, and his relationship with them was strained. Unfortunately, Andebrhan failed the matriculation exam and was told that he was not allowed to take it again, dashing his hopes.

Recognizing his skills, the local branch of an international nongovernmental organization (INGO) asked him to run a new camp library—a resource room with Ethiopian textbooks and some shelves of fiction written in English and Amharic. Andebrhan lived in a small room adjoining the library. He made us tea over a charcoal burner and told us about his daily work there, which began as early as 6:00 a.m. on days when the water was not working, because he would open the library for people to gather and kill time while they waited for the nearby tap to turn on. Andebrhan kept a meticulous log of books that were loaned out and a box of ration cards that were held until the books were returned. He had constructed an additional shelf for scrap materials and decorated the space with inspirational phrases in flowing English letters: "Trust yourself. You survived a lot, and you will survive whatever is coming." Mostly, though, only a handful of people trickled in to borrow books throughout the day, and he faced long stretches of empty time. He seemed hopeful and determined, even though he was struggling with a recurrent bout of malaria and chronic pain in his leg from a botched injection he had received when he was serving in Eritrea, a time that he referred to repeatedly as "in my previous life."

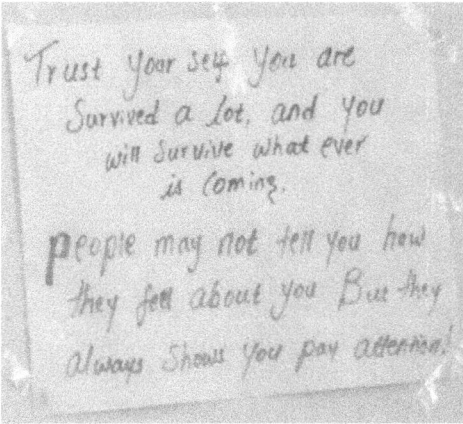

Fig. 4.1. Sign in refugee camp library. Photo by Amanda Poole.

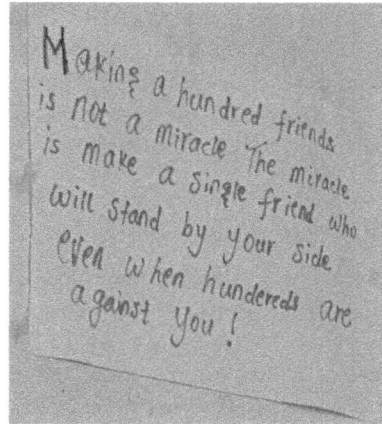

Fig. 4.2. Sign in refugee camp library. Photo by Amanda Poole.

Fig. 4.3. Refugee camp library. Photo by Amanda Poole.

The present was also a challenge for Andebrhan. Working and living alone for two years at the library was difficult. He said he was lonely and could not stop himself from drinking. The low pay and lack of educational opportunities also got to him. Not knowing the incentive scale, the INGO that employed him had paid him well until other organizations learned about his salary; the INGO was then forced to reduce it by nearly half, which was demoralizing and made him feel like he was going backward. Andebrhan ended up getting fired from his position after he got drunk during work hours and talked poorly of the INGO's partners—UNHCR and ARRA. He complained publicly that ARRA workers were paid so much more than refugees, and word got to the camp administrator, which looked bad for the INGO. Andebrhan said it was the stress that drove him to do it and that it was his own fault he lost what he called "a special job."

Temporal Suffering and Caretaking

Both Berihu's and Andebrhan's experiences illuminate the intertwined relationship between what we call temporal caretaking and a kind of temporal suffering associated with living in the camp. What is special about Berihu's garden and Andebrhan's library is that they are places imbued with care. Caretaking clearly lent meaning to otherwise devastating circumstances; as Berihu noted, helping others "makes your mind rest." But caretaking is also a constant reminder of the emptiness of time and of the interminable present that is the humanitarian condition. The small library that Andebrhan cared so much for became something that caused him harm, amplifying his isolation and sense of stagnation. The garden became a source of food and pride for Berihu, but at the same time, it served as a constant reminder of how he did not belong, had no control over the place where he was living, and his hard work could at any moment be rendered purposeless, draw attention to his illegal efforts, and cost him his business. Care for place is palliative but also amplifies the precarity and potential temporariness of any endeavor in the refugee camp.

In refugee studies, attachment to place is often investigated as an index of belonging. Place-making is seen as an agentive way that refugees connect to communities of asylum and resettlement (Brun 2001; Eckenwiler 2016; Hammond 2004; Vasey 2011). Therapeutic landscapes can become a source of healing in the context of resettled refugee youth (Sampson and Gifford 2010; Townsend and Pascal 2012) and other migrant communities negotiating the meaning of home and health (Dyck and Dossa 2007). There is a kind of future orientation in thinking about place as a crucible for healing past wounds, building something new, and moving forward and onward. Certainly, caring for these places served as a kind of balm for Andebrhan and Berihu, who spent their time in ways that avoided the grinding boredom of the camp—a boredom that eroded well-being, a sense of purpose, and hope. However, we argue that these acts of caretaking are more temporal than spatial and far more about the present than the future.

Refugees engage in processes of caretaking (for their community and for themselves) that might appear or be designed to produce a sense of belonging and permanence. However, when these forms of caretaking are examined through a temporal rather than a spatial lens, they are revealed to be inherently temporary. Rather than building enduring ties to place, they are focused on caring for the present. Temporal caretaking, we argue, is one way that refugees take agency over time—by giving meaning to the present in the context of permanent temporariness. Ultimately, however, these efforts at agency generate the very harm they are designed to alleviate.

The experience of indefinite temporariness is directly linked to forms of temporal suffering. Time often can be experienced as painful. Bruce O'Neill has argued that boredom is a "traumatized structure of feeling" (O'Neill 2014) endured by people living in conditions of deep material and social precarity. Similarly, the stress and despair accompanying empty time in the camps can be understood as a form of temporal suffering. Waiting is possibly one of the most troubling forms of temporal suffering for refugees, as it evokes ideas of progress and presupposes the notion that life will get better while enforcing a temporal and spatial containment in the endless present of the camp. Temporal suffering is an experience that is intimately intertwined with caretaking.[1]

Refugees themselves clearly and consistently describe the chronic stress generated by life in the camp as traumatizing. This is partly what drives people to risk their lives in irregular migration but also what triggers malaise, depression, despair, and addiction. A growing body of research on the mental health of refugees shows that trauma results not just from preflight experiences; symptoms of trauma are also linked to postmigration stressors and worsen with the length of time that refugees spend in detention (Getnet et al. 2019; Miller and Rasmussen 2017). For Eritrean refugees in Ethiopia, a recent study suggests that symptoms of depression and post-traumatic stress disorder are closely related to the length of time spent in the camps. Berhanie Getnet, Girmay Medhin, and Ataley Alem (2019) speculate that this is caused by the persistence of stressors such as limited resources and meager support, the likelihood of being exposed to traumatic events in the camp, and a loss of hope, all of which erode coping strategies. Recovery and mental health are not simply an individual matter; they depend on environmental and social factors, and negative conditions can lead to worry, anxiety, and a sense of personal inadequacy. Similarly, Nancy Farwell found that the ability of Eritrean youth in the aftermath of the liberation struggle to heal and recover from trauma was directly linked to their access to economic necessities and social support (2001).

Temporal harm is traumatic because it links very real material precarity to the drudgery of the chronic present and the sense of time passing by. It is an experience of trauma that can be thought of not as the outcome of a dramatic singular event in the past but as a process that unfolds in particular contexts—"trauma-as-ongoing-lived-experience" (Lester 2013). In the anthropological literature, trauma is caused by events or situations that push people to the edge of their existence, stretching or tearing "the bonds that tether a person to the everyday world" (Lester 2013). A focus on trauma can help illuminate "the social and cultural processes through which some experiences are recognized as 'traumatic' and others are not, what this reveals about local understandings of moral responsibility, and the pathways by which recovery is imagined" (Lester 2013).[2] Temporal harm helps to illuminate how refugees are not defined by past trauma so much as they experience an unfolding trauma caused by humanitarian care/containment in the present.

People seek to find their footing, make their way back, and "retether" the world through practices that are culturally meaningful. There is agency here, not just victimhood. Indeed, in the context of "waiting" and painful boredom, people create culture, ideas germinate, and caretaking occurs (Janeja and Bandak 2018; Jeffrey 2010; Khosravi 2017). In the context of temporal suffering, refugees imagine pathways of recovery and retether the world through acts of caretaking for themselves and others. We argue here that these acts of caretaking are central to how refugees wait hopefully and take agency over time. In this chapter, we explore how time in the camps is traumatizing but then look at the agency and ambiguity of caretaking practices, focusing on small businesses, incentive work, child tutoring programs, and a grassroots mental health project. These practices do not supplant the unfolding trauma of temporal suffering, but they make the interminable present more livable.

As we develop these concepts, we refer to the stories of Andebrhan, Berihu, and other refugees, ultimately arguing that both the programming oriented at giving refugees something to do and their own efforts to improve their communities are palliative forms of time-making by which they resist and attempt to heal from temporal harm. Ultimately, however, even as temporal caretaking is essential for refugees' well-being, it still operates as a facet of prolonged suffering.

Waiting

Berhane understood the political operation of waiting. One year after we met him, he was elected to the position of refugee camp coordinator in one of the camps in the Tigray region. He described this as a demanding position that placed him in the lower rungs of a long bureaucratic chain that other refugees had to pass through to access such resources as replacement ration cards and the pass permits allowing them to travel out of the camp. When he described his role, it was with a dry humor; he was a leader, yes—a leader in unpaid work. One of the afternoons we spent with him, this work entailed a visit to his office, a small room in a long structure built from corrugated metal. It contained two desks, thin wood benches, and dog-eared notebooks that recorded the activities of the office in precise writing in the Geez alphabet. Though he had only planned to stop in and leave quickly, when people noticed the door open, the line began—a long line. People arrived bearing papers with the ubiquitous series of stamps from one layer of authority to the next.

Berhane admitted that he hated his job and the incessant line of people seeking his signature. "It is very disturbing," he said. "So many people cry." He shared the story of a woman who had recently come to him in tears, asking for help after her rations were stolen in the night. He signed the request for replacement rations, but he knew that ARRA would do nothing to help her. Although he often felt upset, he explained that he had no power to help them—no power, he said, to even help himself. Pass permits were also restricted to those who "participate," and they were doled out by neighborhood. It was often impossible, he said, for a married couple to get passes to travel together in this system. Although he signed these requests, they ultimately went to ARRA for approval, requiring another period of waiting for the permission to be approved or denied.

Bureaucracies of care relegate refugees to a painful position of waiting for things beyond their control. This is not unique to humanitarian aid. Making people wait is an exertion of power, an assertion that some people's time is less valuable than others' (Khosravi 2017). And keeping people waiting without losing hope has "been part of the mechanism of domination" (Khosravi 2017, 79), a technique of statecraft that produces dependent subjects, or what Javier Auyero refers to as "patients of the state" (Auyero 2012). Lines of migrants waiting, Shahram Khosravi argues, are a paradigm of our times, reminding people of their place in a racial hierarchy (2021).[3] As such, waiting as a technology of power characterizes the management of refugees, even when it conscripts the refugees themselves into these bureaucratic positions, providing a semblance of local governance that operates to create more waiting. When migrants are kept waiting, their time is being wasted; in a sense, it is stolen in the way that "wastelands" were appropriated under older forms of colonialism (Khosravi 2019).

The bureaucracy of humanitarian care also consumes time and is one of the primary ways the "endless present" is constructed (Dunn 2017). These bureaucratic processes are designed around the assumption that refugees have a lot of time. However, waiting devours refugees' ability to be in control of their own time. Getting the rations needed for survival can involve spending days each month waiting in line, with no provision for students who are frequently forced to miss class. Refugee students explain that the lengthy resettlement process through UNHCR involves "long lines" and "no consideration" for school schedules. "I am living alone," one tenth-grade student remarked. "I have something to process with the UNHCR. No one will do this for me. I try to work, feed myself. And I spend five working days as a student." Similar accounts emerge from those refugees in the out-of-camp program, most of whom describe the difficulties dealing with UNHCR, including long lines and a lack of respect. As one man noted, "Going one day, to be turned back and told to come the next day, and when you return, they turn you away again. They expect that refugees don't have a life. But we are trying to build a life here."

Refugees are ostensibly protected subjects but often lack the legal rights to movement and work that citizens have. In exchange, they are provided with aid, shelter, and care that are often inadequate, leaving them in overcrowded conditions, hungry, sick, and, in some cases, susceptible to violence (Agier 2011; Betts and Collier 2017). Humanitarianism thus holds refugees, who typically lack legal status and the right to work in their host country, in a condition of stasis—unprotected from precarity and constrained by the very machinery of humanitarianism that seeks to care for them. Elizabeth Cullen Dunn (2017) argues that the temporal harm experienced by displaced people in camps emerges from refugees being reduced to a technical problem to be addressed through bureaucratic control—an aspect of the depersonalizing and depoliticizing logic of humanitarianism. In the humanitarian logic of depoliticized care, the lack of respect for refugees' time corresponds to a lack of appreciation for their complex and contextualized lives and futures (Brun 2016). Humanitarian aid keeps refugees alive, barely (Redfield 2005). Cuts in rations combined with inflation mean that refugees struggle to survive on their aid allotment and must constantly seek out means to supplement their income.

We can think of waiting as a mechanism through which structural forms of violence create uncertainty and precarity for refugees.[4] They are stuck waiting for things they need to survive, not knowing when or if they will appear. As such, their dependent position is reinforced, as is their feeling of being temporary (guests rather than citizens). At the same time, it is important to keep in mind that structural violence is backed up by the brute threat of force by the state. As we described in the last chapter, when refugees organized to protest their conditions, they were quickly and violently subdued by Ethiopian military. Yet these more direct threats of violence are hidden by bureaucratized governance, which also renders the effects of this violence on refugees' lives and well-being far less visible, as they are ostensibly "cared for" by actors and institutions in the constellation of the humanitarian aid industry.

Being Stuck While Time Moves On

There is a heavy silence around the topic of time in the refugee camps. During one of our early visits to the camps, we took refuge from a thunderstorm in the home of a woman named Trhas. We came to know her well over the course of three years, but that afternoon, we quickly learned that time was not a subject of small talk. We asked how long Trhas had been in the camp, and her reply was brusque: ten years, almost as long as the camp had existed. A heavy silence followed this statement, during which no one seemed to want to meet each other's eyes. Trhas's adopted niece hugged her legs against the cold and rocked back and forth in a thin sweatshirt. Trhas's small children, born and growing up in the camp, snuggled close to her as the rain pounded the tin roof. Refugees do not come to camps to have children and settle down. But as they feel the pressure of time, many do have families. Growing children become an index of passing time.

While waiting for the rain to end, Jennifer, whose husband is Eritrean, pulled out her phone and shared pictures with Trhas. "*Shukor*," Trhas muttered as she scrolled through pictures of children in America only a few years older than her own. "*Ma'ar*." "Sugar" and "honey," she said admiringly. Although sharing pictures was often a way to get to know each other, in this particular moment, seeing Trhas and her children, who were stuck in a refugee camp, gazing at the pictures of Jennifer's half-Eritrean children, who were growing up in America, threw the constraints of the humanitarian condition into sharp relief. Some refugees called our attention to these constraints. While sharing lunch with another refugee, we noticed a small tricycle at the door to his house. Unthinkingly, Jennifer made what she thought was a rote comment on the boy's new toy, saying, "What a lucky boy."

"He is not lucky," our host said sharply, "to grow up in a refugee camp."

These anecdotes illuminate the problems with the present and its relationship with care in refugee life and particularly the camps. The condition of feeling stuck is not a simple or straightforward one. As Catherine Brun (2016) observes, there is always some movement in people's lives. In the camp, children are born and grow. Resettlement opportunities trapped "in process" for years suddenly and fantastically appear. Some decide to leave illegally. Yet the never-ending present, a constant sense of precarity, and an enduring temporariness constitute defining features of what we call *camp time.*

Camp time, as we pointed out earlier, is produced by a particular teleological temporality oriented around the notion of progress and time marching incrementally forward. Within this configuration of space and time, space can be thought of as both enabling and preventing forward movement, indicative of the presence of progress or its absence. The camp is described as a space of constraint where refugees are held back. The hallmark of the camp is "empty time," which is often described as a product of humanitarian care and control but is simultaneously experienced by refugees as a space-time that cuts them off from the future and from teleological notions of progress (Allan 2013; Dunn 2017). As Dunn notes, "Camps . . . are engines that produce longing, inactivity and anxiety"; they are spaces of "nothingness" that are "not just the result of violence, but also the result of care" (2017, 111). Empty time, during which refugees are kept busy with activities oriented toward their survival, converges with bureaucratic activities to serve as a constant reminder of refugees' inability to have any control over the future.

For many refugees, empty time is painful because they are unable to assume social and familial responsibilities that would allow them to progress to adulthood. Young refugees grapple with the "intolerable pressure of having nothing to do" (Allan 2013) in spaces of long-term humanitarian confinement from which there is no clear pathway *out.* Empty time thus exists as a specter to be feared. Camp time can erode and absorb efforts to avoid it, particularly the longer people remain in the camp. As such, tending to the library or garden, running small businesses, and even the act of raising children come to be described as temporary ways that people care for themselves and survive in the face of the empty space-time of the camp.

The Trauma of the Empty Present

One of the primary symbols of empty time in the refugee camps in northern Ethiopia are youth who drop out of school and become idle, often drinking. On walks through the camp or while sitting at cafés, our interlocutors would almost always reference these young drinkers as being emblematic of being stuck. Aster, a young woman who left the camps shortly after arriving in the country, noted, "There are so many people who just sit around all the time drinking in the camp. Sometimes they fight." Aster explained how the excess of time in the camp was distressing and dangerous and was something she was glad to leave behind when she joined extended family in Addis Ababa. Similarly, a long-term resident of Hitsats camp described new arrivals: "They are just enjoying in the bars. We were all like that at first." However, he also described his fear of falling back into such behavior and said that people sometimes returned to the pattern of drinking all day if they heard bad news, if a business failed, or if the endless waiting just finally got to them. In Mai Aini, a long-term camp resident observed that all but a few of the young people were in bars instead of schools or even camp programs like sports or vocational training and attributed it to the temporality of the camp: "Being in the camp, idle, without any work, is the result of this harsh situation. We are spending our time waiting for changes. We are not able to create changes by ourselves. Everyone is waiting for changes." In Hitsats camp, another man explained that the idleness and the loneliness were both oppressive. He shared a room with eight strangers from different parts of Eritrea. "They are drunkards," he said. "Rather than studying or trying to develop themselves, they drink." Another young woman, newly arrived to Hitsats camp, shared that the stress related to this empty time was keenly experienced by her roommates, who, unlike herself, did not have the option of living with family members in Addis or the preparation needed to attend college in Ethiopia. "They are emotional wrecks," she shared.

The concern with slipping into empty time relates to the inability of individuals to remain hopeful in the face of precarity. Precarity may be caused by social abandonment, exclusion from work, or an inability to connect the present to a desired future (Allison 2016; Khosravi 2017). As such, precarity exists on material, social, and existential levels and entails the unequal distribution of vulnerability and hope. Precarity produces a gap between "a sense of the actual and a sense of the possible" (Treiber 2014, 132). For those displaced by conflict and living under protracted humanitarian care, precarity is not just uncertainty about the future; it amounts to what Dunn describes as an "existential instability": "It is a risk that whatever fragile structures of meaning, whatever frail networks of sociality and sense that are built up, might be exploded in an instant" (Dunn 2017, 196). If we understand the fragility of sociality and indeed everything that refugees attempt to build in the camp, we can see why caretaking is only ever a temporary strategy.

Refugees often actively work to get unstuck but then experience the anxiety of falling back into a temporal stasis (Brun 2016). They experience this as a form of temporal suffering because they do not control their lives, mistrust entities that govern them, and fear for their survival (El-Shaarawi 2015). They are left to wait for the resources they need to survive without knowing if and when those resources will materialize. Our interviewees frequently voiced anxieties about further cuts to rations they depended on for survival and fears that relations between Ethiopia and Eritrea would shift, making them vulnerable to political violence.

Andebrhan, who we introduced at the beginning of this chapter, embodied the dangers of empty time as well as alcoholism. His efforts, like those of many of the young people in the camps, demonstrated how people attempt to care for the present by finding meaningful work, opening a business, or starting a family. These activities give people's daily lives a veneer of normalcy in the face of the endless empty present, but none of it is permanent, and none of it actually creates an attachment to place in the way refugees imagine wanting to be attached to a place. The trauma of protracted time and displacement often overtakes efforts to give the present meaning.

The Fullness of Empty Time

Empty time, however, does not mean that refugees have nothing to do. Instead, time is experienced as oppressively consuming. In the camps in northern Ethiopia, the excess of empty time and the painful boredom of the camp were also linked to activities that usurped time without filling it meaningfully. Survival in the camp was tremendously time-consuming and often entailed waiting in long lines to collect water or rations or to acquire firewood. Brikti, a young woman who was enrolled in Hitsats camp as a ninth-grade student, explained, "For me, living with my parents, I don't have a problem. But from my observation in the camp, people who live alone have to care for themselves." She explained why it was difficult for people who don't have families to attend school and complete chores. "Fetching water [before] going to school, [we need] to do all household activity first. When they come it is midday." At other times, she explained, if the water supply is disrupted, students miss school altogether.

Brikti also pointed out the gendered nature of these tasks, explaining that it was more difficult for men, who were not used to cooking, a task that is often done by women. Young men who we interviewed frequently noted that mundane chores were a burden that ate away at their time and prevented them from attending classes regularly. In a focus group of refugee college graduates, all of them men, one joked that he had no time to do anything since he was cooking and doing work like a woman. As he made his point, he gestured toward the woman who had silently made us three rounds of coffee, served with sugar in small espresso cups, from a stool in the corner of the café. The gendered nature of domestic labor is meaningful in a cultural and historical context. The traditional subordinate role of women in Eritrean society was challenged during the independence struggle, when 30 percent of the guerrilla fighters were women. While the Eritrean People's Liberation Front (EPLF), the leading guerrilla movement, promoted the status of women, it did not challenge the low status of their labor (Bernal 2000). Cooking and washing were assigned as punishments for male and female soldiers alike, and Eritrean women fighters struggled with a return to civilian life after the end of the conflict, when they were expected to resume these domestic tasks. While the endless lines for inadequate resources made daily tasks of survival more protracted and less pre-dictable for everyone in the camps, it was a further burden because the camps were heavily populated by young people—mostly men—who had come without their families. These tasks were untethered from the work of creating sociality and fam-ily life and instead reinforced the endless time of living without progress in the present and with an uncertain future.

In the Georgian internally displaced person (IDP) camps researched by Dunn (2017), long-term IDPs came to attribute stress and trauma not to war but to the "daily, non-eventful conditions of life constructed by humanitarian aid" that they experienced as both constricting and degrading. She argues that camps are "a zone of temporal indistinction between permanence and transience that leaves displaced people in a state of waiting and stasis" (Dunn 2017, 111). This "chronic present," she asserts, is not static and unchanging; "rather, it is characterized by a slow, grind-ing decline" (2017, 128). In Ethiopia, this facet of camp time was strongly present in stories of youth who felt the possibilities for their lives were slowly dying. One man, who had worked as an engineer and innovator in Eritrea before fleeing to Ethiopia, mused, "My golden years are passing here."

This sense of decline is also illustrated by Semere's story. When we met with Semere for tea at one of the camps, he had been living there for the past four years without options for employment, despite having graduated near the top of his class from a university in Ethiopia. He described spending his time "with routine, with daily actions." He explained, "We have no future plan, because we are a refugee." He associated empty time with a crisis of hope that could lead to migration and the risk of death: "We have hopes. But you know if you stay a long time in the camp, that hope may evacuate. We cannot give up. Life may change. The only hope we have is if we get a chance out of the camp, legally through the resettlement process or even illegally by crossing borders to other countries like Sudan. But as refugees inside the camp, you can do nothing. Our hope is finishing."

What makes refugees temporally suffer in the camp is not just boredom or hav-ing nothing (or nothing meaningful) to do, it is the sense of time passing them by. Teleological notions of progress bring time in the space of the camp into relief. In the face of desires, expectations, and hopes for progress, time in the camp thickens, weighing down the efforts of refugees to move forward or even to stay afloat. As such, the temporality inherent in Habtom's statement "We are like animals," discussed in the introduction, is illuminated by what Dunn calls "the suspended temporality of absolute zero" (Habtom and Ruys 2017, 113) experienced as a dehumanizing state of enforced passivity in which the humanitarian condition only forestalls death. How-ever, refugees take agency—they make time—even in the endless present.

Caretaking in the Endless Present

The activities that fill empty time illuminate a process we call temporal caretaking but also the problems with it. Caretaking efforts were always constrained in ways that made them temporary. They were constrained by the bureaucracies of care and the stilted economics of the camp, itself produced through humanitarian and Ethiopian regulations. Caretaking efforts were also constrained by humanitarian logics that seldom noticed what refugees themselves were doing to make their community better.

What does it mean to care for the present? Berihu, once again, provides us with an example. In the face of being stuck, Berihu turned things around by cultivating ways to spend his time meaningfully—starting a business, planting a crop, and working with children. He asserted: "If you saw where I was eight months ago. . . . Now, I feel proud. I have lifted one leg. If you come back again, I will be on two legs." His hope, though, was always standing on precarious ground. He was constrained by the limitations he faced as a refugee living in a place of "permanent temporariness" (Bailey et al. 2002). Berihu had an interesting way of articulating the tensions between caretaking and the future: "Two hands are pulling each other. One says, 'Go with your business. Make a profit. Marry.' The other says, 'Take care of your people. Help someone below you. Don't think about money. It makes your mind rest. If you pass someone lying on the ground, you cannot leave them. You help them up.'"

We suggest that caretaking is deeply intertwined with the paradoxes of caring for a temporary place, the temporariness of which may be permanent. A recent shift to focusing on care in anthropology seeks to highlight the agency and creativity of marginalized people beyond a focus on suffering (Black 2018), as care can shift attention to shared responsibility and intersubjectivity (Raghuram et al. 2009) with the constitution of ethics in the context of everyday struggles and experiences (Mattingly 2014). Applying an ethics of care lens to humanitarianism in the context of protracted displacement, Brun (2016) argues that an ethics of care can potentially be transformative by working against the depersonalizing biopolitics of emergency care that forecloses the future by focusing on physical needs in the present. Brun advocates instead for an ethics of care, which entails a temporal shift: "When we care about an 'Other,' we acknowledge their future, their welfare and their ethical significance is bound up with our own future" (2016, 405). But Brun's focus is on care *of* refugees by aid workers. Far less work has focused on care practices *by* refugees for each other (for a notable exception, see Carruth 2021). When we consider caretaking as an agentive practice enacted by refugee communities, we see that the future is not easily opened up. Indeed, we would argue that the limit of caretaking among refugees is that it does not have the capacity to create future possibilities. It is a practice oriented toward the present.

Care is always paradoxical. For example, the broad literature on neoliberal capitalism and care work (health care, teaching, eldercare, etc.) demonstrates how care is exploited while workers in such fields are disciplined and their labor simultaneously monetized and structured in ways that impede them from giving care without tremendous self-sacrifice (Abramovitz and Zelnick 2010; Pyle 2006).

Another paradox of care, as Steven P. Black argues, is that the giving and refusal of care always go together and that "moral and ethical care is never devoid of issues of power and vulnerability" (2018, 80). This is an important point, but how do these power dynamics play out when refugees themselves (the "cared for" population) are the ones providing the care?

Many of these paradoxes are present in some form but appear differently when we consider the community care refugees provide. The problem here is less about the exploitation of care and more about the invisibility of care. It is also less about the refusal of care and more about the limits to the care refugees can provide to each other. As we have shown throughout this chapter, the efforts of what Berihu calls the first of two hands would inevitably and almost always be futile. Indeed, Berihu tried this strategy, but his business failed. Restlessly ambitious, he was still trying—with another business, a wife, and a growing family. But here we would like to call attention to the other hand: "Take care of your people. Help someone below you. Don't think about money. It makes your mind rest." We would like to particularly call attention to Berihu's assertion that helping others is *restful*. What better way is there to describe the palliative nature of caretaking? At the same time, Berihu and so many others were always at risk of falling back into the despair generated by being stuck at the camp.

Many of these caretaking efforts are linked to INGO programs aimed at helping refugees integrate or at least stemming onward movement. Common wisdom in refugee camps is that vocational training, incentive work, recreational programs, and small business development will curb onward movement because they give refugees something meaningful to do and generate an attachment to a future in Ethiopia. However, we have argued throughout this chapter that caretaking is a fundamentally temporal strategy to make life in the endless present of the camp bearable.

As Michel Agier (2002) observes, people in camps often conduct lives *as if* they are in a town or city. But the camp is a temporary space, and people do not inhabit it as they please (Hyndman and Giles 2016). Earlier, we explored how time in the camp "thickens" and becomes downright sludge-like in response to two factors: teleological notions of progress and humanitarian/bureaucratic constraint in the space of the camp. In response, refugees attempt to fill the endless present with acts of caretaking for themselves and the places they inhabit, but these acts are not linked to progress and the notion that they are moving in meaningful ways toward some desired future. As we explore in the next section, caretaking includes such practices as starting a business with the awareness that there is no way it can be successful or planting a garden that the camp authorities may uproot. Caretaking also includes diligently caring for a library and keeping it open for long hours even though few visit, and participating in INGO vocational education programs knowing that the skills one learns have no use in camp life. Additionally, it includes starting groups that will improve life in the camp for a time but that receive no support from camp administration. While these processes of caretaking might create an illusion that refugees are integrating, adapting to their circumstances, and fitting in with local communities, caretaking is always talked about as an impermanent, imperfect, and unfinished process, often because humanitarian organizations, laws, and policies fail to provide the resources and support needed to make these activities sustainable. Caretaking is a temporal strategy of enforced presentism always limited by the sense of confinement created by bureaucratized care, both within and outside of the camp.

Jobs without Pay: Incentive Work as Caretaking

Incentive work is one way that refugees engage in time-making in the chronic present, revealing the ambiguity of time-making as both palliative and harmful. UNHCR and NGO partners engage refugees as "incentive workers" for service provision to displaced communities globally, both within and outside of camps. *Incentive* refers to the compensation that refugees receive and is used to distinguish their work from wage labor. Incentive work is often characterized as volunteering; it is "grounded in the idea that refugees should actively participate in efforts to support their own communities, which is seen to promote empowerment rather than dependencies" (UNHCR 2014, 1). Systems like incentive pay are often described by UNHCR and implementing partners as a means for refugees to participate in humanitarianism rather than merely being the beneficiaries of aid. Incentive positions with humanitarian organizations are also envisioned as part of a solution to secondary migration in that they not only provide opportunities for refugees in the camps but also mobilize refugees to work on projects designed to stem secondary migration (e.g., youth programming, counseling, and education). Ethiopia developed guidelines for incentive work in 2010 that standardized incentive pay levels across agencies and instituted a scale that allowed for some recognition of differential qualification. At the same time, these guidelines reinforced the goal of incentive pay as a means to promote volunteerism and community participation rather than as a form of salaried employment.

While Ethiopia had announced a plan to provide work permits to refugees, the formal labor market was (and largely remains) inaccessible, leaving those in the Tigray region dependent on an informal labor market that entailed few, low-paid, seasonal manual-labor jobs. The humanitarian aid ecosystem, on the other hand, generated numerous positions for skilled workers such as translators, teachers, and refugees working in various health care roles, including, as we later describe, psychosocial support and counseling. Due to the national policy on incentive work, the incentive pay was standardized across organizations, which included not only UNHCR but also Ethiopian institutions such as the Ministry of Education, Ethiopian NGOs such as the Development and Inter-Church Aid Commission (DICAC), and international nongovernmental organizations (INGOs) such as the Danish Refugee Council, Norwegian Refugee Council (NRC), International Rescue Committee (IRC), and Jesuit Refugee Services (JRS).

For some refugees, incentive work was viewed as a way to counter camp time; it offered a means to contribute to the community, develop professional skills, and connect to professionals from other parts of the world. Iyob is a case in point. He had lived in the camp for ten years and became an incentive worker for an INGO that provided psychosocial support and counseling for refugees. He was trained to work as a counselor, and he often spoke about the desire to help people in his community, making his work with the organization fulfilling. He also valued the relationships he formed with INGO workers. During the state of emergency that led up to the change in leadership in Ethiopia in early 2018, pass permits to travel out of the camp were suspended for refugees. When Iyob was recognized as Eritrean in a nearby town, he was taken to prison. The head of the INGO waited with him the entire time, making sure he was treated well and ultimately released.

Iyob's ability to draw from his position to build professional relationships and work meaningfully on mental health care in the camps is counterposed to the experience of many of the other refugees we spoke to, like Berihu, who tended to describe incentive pay as primarily a means to "kill time." It was also counterposed to the experience of Andebrhan, whose incentive work reinforced a sense of being othered and devalued and ultimately failed to fend off the despair and alcoholism generated by temporal harm in the camp.

Many similar critiques of incentive work originate with refugees like Berihu who graduated from college in Ethiopia only to find themselves barred from salaried employment. Humanitarian aid keeps refugees alive, barely. Cuts in rations combined with inflation mean that refugees struggle to survive on their aid allotment and must constantly seek out ways to supplement their income. However, incentive pay is far from sufficient. When this is described as something that refugees should value doing as volunteers, it comes to feel like the coerced and interminable national service work that Eritrean refugees experienced in Eritrea. One college graduate now working for incentive pay remarked, "We left our own homeland, where we were forced to work government jobs. Even an engineer there is forced to teach in a remote post. If the same thing is happening here, what is the difference? You have to have a future." Incentive work was perceived to be part of the mechanics of aid that immobilized refugees in a chronic present. Indeed, many of the young men who had graduated and served as incentive workers felt that they were less visible to aid organizations and were less of a priority for resettlement. Gerie observed, "The government and UNHCR, they think that we will be OK. They don't care about us. They don't care about our lives. Some of us are leaders. Freely we are administering the camp. It is a benefit to the UNHCR and to the government to keep us here."

It is no surprise, then, that there is a high turnover rate for refugees serving as teachers and other incentive workers in the camps. As the director of the primary school in one of the camps explained to us, each year they lose about half of their incentive teachers. Refugee teachers are in a particularly challenging role.

Nearly every incentive teacher we spoke with mentioned the low pay as a problem, including Berihu, who, when we asked him why he had stopped dressing for class and showing up on time, explained, "What can you buy for nine hundred birr? Clothes?" However, the other most common complaint that teachers had was the lack of motivation among the refugee students; low pay for teachers and lack of motivation among students were explicitly connected. Although education was seen as key to deterring secondary migration, every camp primary and secondary school struggled with absenteeism, high dropout rates, and low enrollment. Volunteer teachers commonly expressed the feeling that they could be important role models for students, but they set a negative example instead; they urged their students to adopt an educational path toward a hopeful future, yet personally demonstrated the lack of a tether between the future and the camp. "Everybody has a responsibility to nurture children, as a society," explained Berihu. "But they see the reality of what we are still."

There are some alternatives to teaching for incentive pay. If incentive work is a way for refugees to kill time, working with children through grassroots initiatives can be a mechanism of time-making that taps into and reaffirms the will to spend time meaningfully and wait hopefully. Eventually Berihu left teaching, but he found other ways to care for the community. Outside the administrative structure of the education system, he worked with other university graduates to coordinate tutoring sessions for refugee students in the camp. One initiative lasted five months and involved tutoring students in grades six through eight. The program, called Save Eritrean Seeds, was formed around a vision of caring for youth and hoping that the future may be better. This is one example of what we think of as invisible caretaking, discussed later. Getting permission to run the Save Eritrean Seeds program required extensive efforts at navigating the humanitarian and governmental bureaucracy. It ran without support and with little acknowledgment, and yet to Berihu, it was preferable to working for incentive pay as a teacher.

Incentive work embodies the paradox of the refugee condition. Because they are receiving aid and protection, refugees may not work. They may do incentive work, which is conceptualized as a sort of volunteer work, for a small amount of pocket money. Yet aid is never enough to live on, forcing refugees to work at artificially depressed wages. Thus, humanitarian logics directly produce an economy of constraint. Many refugees still undertake incentive work—some for survival, others because it keeps them meaningfully busy—but it can never be equated with development or progress and only ever serves as a reminder of their relegation to the interminable present.

Businesses without Customers: Entrepreneurialism as Temporal Caretaking

Berihu's business ultimately failed, as so many did. The loan proved too difficult to pay off. One year after taking out the loan, he and his business partner were forced to close the café. The restaurant was located at the edge of the camp, and the small generator had died. He explained, "There has been no change in my life for the past ten years. When I think about this, I feel like crying. The generator crashed, and you can't do a business in the dark. It's been more than two months without light. I am fighting. I am fighting not to fail." A few months later, Berihu opened a new café, this one more strategically located toward the center of camp. Like the last restaurant, it may not work out, but it does *do work* in other ways.

For Berihu, the business provided an alternate way of spending his time. Rather than wallowing in the endless present of camp time, he was running a café, an activity that he linked to caring for family. In fact, he got married to a woman from his hometown and fostered a number of younger family members. In many ways, the café was restorative. It provided a fulcrum for sociality through meaningful labor, countering camp time and the oppressive nature of bureaucratic "care." However, in the context of the precarity that refugees face, temporal harm and caretaking mutually constitute each other. Caretaking is therapeutic, but these activities are so often doomed to failure, which can ultimately come to amplify the stress of empty time. They accomplish palliative work but are prevented from being transformative by the possibility that all of this could change at any moment.

The precarity of caretaking, its intersection with temporal trauma, and its encounter with the paradox of permanent temporariness were apparent in the numerous stories we heard of businesses opened and closed and of those that limped along without much expectation that they would turn a profit. Hitsats camp, for instance, was replete with small shops attached to refugees' houses. Idris's shop was typical of these. He had recently sold it to a friend when he decided to go to university under the refugee college scholarship program, but he still lived adjacent to the small store when he returned to camp during school holidays. The shop had few items—juice, soda, soap, and cookies. There was also shade. Idris smiled warmly and pulled out a blanket to place on a concrete slab where he invited us to sit. He explained that he had started the shop after he arrived in the camp nearly three years earlier, leaving a wife and daughter in Eritrea.

"This shop was mine at first," he said. "From the beginning, I was more clever." In an effort to keep busy when he first arrived, he started the shop, took on a local leadership role, and volunteered as an incentive social worker for an NGO. Later, when he returned to camp for the long summer break from university, Idris struggled with boredom. When he reflected on the past in contrast to the present, he felt like his mind had gone dormant because of having too much time to worry. He also expressed that the shop had been more viable in the beginning, but too many shops had opened in recent years, leaving one for every three or four houses. For the most part, people shopped in the adjacent town of Hitsats, which had been booming since the camp was established. The refugees who owned small shops in the camp bought things in bulk from the town to resell, but overall, the camp economy was stagnant, and legal restrictions prevented refugees from working or opening up businesses outside of the camp.[5] As another man joked when we passed by his small shop, where he was lounging with friends on a mat in the shade of an awning, "This is not a shop. This is a place to sleep."

Joking aside, people congregated in these spaces, chatting, listening to radios, or playing the *kirar*, a stringed instrument. When the owners left, the shops were often sold or passed to friends or family. These shops were important as a form of temporal care that, like Berihu's restaurant, meaningfully filled the present. Furthermore, these businesses were spaces of sociality that served as gathering points and markers of one's role in the community. But there was no illusion that these endeavors would lead to progress. Refugees were keenly aware that, given the lack of customers who could afford to make purchases and the inability of shop owners to competitively price goods, camp businesses were structurally doomed to fail. They were thus nonteleological.

Vocational training and certificate programs also functioned as a form of temporal caretaking rather than as a way to help refugees feel settled or attached to a future. Numerous international NGOs coordinated vocational training and certificate programs in the camps that were often accompanied by assistance in establishing small businesses there. For example, the NRC operated a vocational training program in Hitsats camp that, according to a camp-based representative, trained around six hundred people a year, providing classes in food prep, furniture making, garment work, metal work, and information technology support. Yet there was little potential to sustainably add more of these businesses in the camp. Each time we visited Hitsats, we drove by the NRC market building designed for these refugee graduates—a large compound on the NGO side of the road across from the refugee residences. The individual stalls were almost always closed when we passed. Once, we managed to secure the promise of a tour, but the NGO worker never showed up. Although it seemed to be largely unused, the compound was an example of place-making in camp time. The NRC market compound, along with numerous other start-up businesses that were only occasionally occupied, bore the prominent logos of humanitarian aid organizations. Indeed, nearly every tree and latrine were marked this way, crediting the organization that contributed to its presence in the camp. Some signs were only in English, lacking a translation in the Geez alphabet that would be legible to Tigrigna or Amharic speakers. While these places offered some opportunity for refugees to spend time engaged in activities and avoid the boredom of camp, they also emphasized the role of international agencies as the place makers and the role of refugees as temporary residents in a space designed and controlled by others. This branding reproduced teleologies because these programs were supposed to move refugees in a progress-oriented direction. However, for refugees, the shuttered shops and branded trees were indicative of the time-space of the camp where they were stuck waiting in permanent temporariness.

Even when businesses succeeded, they reflected the profoundly temporal nature of these activities. Mai Aini camp, which was located farther from local towns and had a more settled population that included many family households, offered more lively market opportunities for refugee entrepreneurs. Trhas' husband, Tsegay, was a successful businessman who earned a livelihood through his expertise in mechanics, cultivating a clientele of local Ethiopians. He slowly bought and rented out prime real estate in the camp along the main road in an informal housing economy that emerged over time with the expansion of the camp. He was always busy when we encountered him and worked long hours at his shop. Trhas was busy as well; she cared for their kids, fostered another teenager from their home village, and attended Bible classes at one of the churches in the camp. On one afternoon, we arrived to find the household turned upside down. They had received word that they would be resettled and should be prepared to leave at any moment. There was a palpable air of excitement in the house. Just two weeks had passed since they were notified. We return to their story in more detail in chapter 5 but mention it here to illustrate that all strategies in the camp, even if they do succeed in generating wealth, are made temporary by the assumption that at some point, the refugees will no longer be there; in other words, the permanent temporariness can be ruptured at any time.

Invisible Caretaking

Time-making as a therapeutic act also appears in the grassroots efforts of volunteers to address the needs of refugees suffering from severe mental illness. We learned about these organizations from Iyob, who we described earlier as a person who had worked with an international NGO on mental health care. Iyob had taken on numerous volunteer roles in the camp—both formally as an incentive worker and elected leader to the refugee camp council, and in various grassroots groups, most notably as one of the founders of a refugee-led organization that provides care to people with severe mental health problems.

Iyob extended his role as a psychosocial counselor beyond the incentive pay position. He worked to form a residential home for refugees in the camp who were suffering from severe mental health problems. Identifying a serious gap in care, Iyob explained, "They were sleeping in the street, beating people, hurting themselves." Beyond some psychosocial counseling programs, there were few other mental health services available in the camp. In contrast to humanitarian organizations, which tend to stress the need for mental health services to address traumas endured in the past, Iyob described a growing crisis in the camps because of distress and hardship endured there in the present. "The number of mentally ill is increasing," he explained when he gave us a tour of the compound—a cement block structure with a small ancient television playing in one of the residential rooms. "This comes from the harsh life here. That is why you will see more people when you come back."

Iyob worked to solicit support, mostly from other refugees and also from the Orthodox church in the camp, to locate a compound where people could safely reside, be fed, and be cared for. The facility, known as Hawat ("brotherhood" in Tigrigna), housed seventeen people when we visited in 2018; they were cared for by refugee volunteers and funded by money collected by people in the camp. The facility was associated with the Orthodox church but served both Muslim and Christian refugees using a combination of psychological counseling, holy water and prayer, recreation, and general support from community volunteers. Although this facility was necessarily temporary in the context of the camp, and the volunteers would come and go, it provided a crucible for caretaking that redefined refugees as givers of care rather than mere recipients. At the same time, it pushed back against the bureaucracy of "care" that relegates refugees to a painful position of waiting for things beyond their control—a situation that exacerbates people's stress in the camps and creates the conditions for temporal trauma.

Hawat provided a nexus for community members to care for a vulnerable population that was not being served by the humanitarian apparatus, but it also emphasized the gaps in care experienced by the refugee community and the precarity of life and well-being in the face of these gaps. "They just collected the people to live together without any support from the government or an NGO," Iyob explained as he narrated the history of the facility. "Nobody supports them," he insisted. He said that an international NGO provided one-day training on counseling for the volunteers working at Hawat, and the volunteers solicited the occasional assistance of an Ethiopian psychologist from a university in the regional capital, Mekelle. Still, they were reaching out to other organizations, hoping to secure water provision and assistance with clothing and equipment. But so far, these resources had not been channeled to grassroots efforts like Hawat. The number of refugees with severe mental health problems was growing, Iyob asserted, as was the length of time people lived in the compound, and the facility's beds were already full.

Hawat is but the clearest example of several unrecognized efforts by refugees to take care of the camp. Alongside incentive work with no pay, small businesses with no customers, vocational training programs that led to no jobs, and NGO recreational programs—all of which filled the present but did not address the future—refugees found ways to make the present meaningful by doing things to care for the camp. They did so by taking in unaccompanied minors, tutoring younger children, and addressing community needs even in the absence of governmental or nongovernmental programming to assist them. These efforts were admirable, and refugees did feel good when participating in them, but without greater support, they were always only partial solutions. And like Trhas and Tsegay's family, refugees at any moment might move on. Indeed, they hoped that they would, meaning that these efforts were never intended to be long-term strategies, but only temporary, palliative measures.

Caretaking as Place-Making or Time-Making?

Early in the book, we introduced the concept of time-making to temporalize place-making. In the context of refugee studies, place-making entails the processes through which refugees navigate belonging and establish homes, despite possibly feeling powerful connections to the homes they were displaced from (Denov and Akesson 2013; Eckenwiler 2016; Jean 2015; Rios and Watkins 2015). Place-making is closely related to the concept of place attachment, a process whereby people come to identify with particular places of resettlement (Boğaç 2009; Rishbeth and Powell 2013). Place attachment references psychological processes of group and individual identity formation as they are linked to meaningful social spaces (Giuliani 2017). Similarly, Laura C. Hammond uses the concept of emplacement to describe the ways resettled refugees transform an unfamiliar landscape into a home both materially and symbolically, replete with social relationships (2004). This research has helped denaturalize the links between people and place and consequently depathologize refugees as people defined by their displacement from a native homeland. It has also explored how refugees exert agency in forging new connections to places and people in the context of mobility (Brun 2001). Place-making is also considered central to healing via the creation of therapeutic landscapes (Bell et al. 2018; Doughty 2018; Gesler 1992; Sampson and Gifford 2010). However, in situations of deep and protracted precarity, such as refugees living in long-term emergency containment, temporality takes on critical importance. In these situations, the concept of *therapeutic landscapes* must foreground the temporal, rather than spatial, projects through which people care for themselves and others.

Consequently, we need a better theoretical lens to understand the temporality of place-making. This is critical because, without an assessment of time, spatial analyses risk obscuring the enduring precarity and forms of violence that confront refugees. Georgina Ramsay argues, "Displacement is also an existential condition that is realized through shifts in the temporalization of everyday life: that is, when the predictability of the present and the assumptions about the future are jeopardized and made precarious" (2019, 203). While displaced people are assumed to be able to rejoin society by constructing new lives and homes when they are resettled or encounter opportunities for local integration, they still face "regimes of temporal incommensurability" (Ramsay 2019, 203). Focusing on spatiality alone risks missing the agentive ways in which refugees care for themselves and each other, particularly in temporary places, in conditions of radical precarity, and in the face of profound structural barriers.

Place still matters. Indeed, without an analytical lens focused on place, the theoretical turn toward investigating temporalities of precarity can lead to research that describes what life is like when people are confronted with profound material and social insecurity but not how things came to be that way in particular times and places. However, place is always imbricated with time. When we center temporality in our analysis, we can better understand how activities like building a business, going to school, growing food, starting a tutoring program, or establishing a religious community are not necessarily indicative of place attachment and the desire to stay in Ethiopia. They are temporal acts through which, in the condition of endless waiting, refugees care for themselves and others and hold open the possibility of other futures.[6] These are the methods by which refugees "reclaim waiting as a livable space" (Kallio et al. 2021, 4007).

This possibility of other futures—and the efforts to hold them open—is a critical aspect of temporal agency. Care for the present, as we described here, is similar to Kirsi Kallio, Isabel Meier, and Jouni Häkli's concept of *radical hope*, which they define as the "ability to maintain a meaningful existence when a person's life is at the brink of losing all meaning" (2021, 4008). Radical hope involves orienting oneself toward the present to detach from despondent futures and opens the possibility that people may take up the challenge of "making it through the day-to-day life that has become unlivable and by doing so deny[ing] the right of other actors to define the direction of their active presence" (Kallio et al. 2021, 4008). Radical hope illuminates how temporal agency may be hidden in activities that seem passive and mundane, like disengaging or withdrawing from organized activities and turning away from teleological linear temporalities. Yet the ambiguities of caring for the present in a temporary place make these projects unstable. Furthermore, as we explored earlier, while withdrawal, disengagement, and abandoning hopes for progress may be agentive acts of time-making, they are always intertwined with temporal suffering.

This focus on time-making can illuminate why top-down place-making initiatives do not necessarily succeed in attempts to curtail secondary migration. Outside of the ethnographic literature, place-making generally entails a design framework rather than a grassroots process. In the spheres of public and global health and urban planning, place-making is the purview of the policy and design experts, who configure places to cultivate certain kinds of desired social, economic, and (increasingly) ecological relations. For example, Lisa A. Eckenwiler (2016) lauds refugee management initiatives as shining examples of place-making in urban design and global health, because infrastructure is designed with humanitarian goals, such as reception centers that not only ensure shelter but also foster stability and integration. Projects designed to encourage refugees to stay in Ethiopia operate according to a similar ethos—crafting opportunities for livelihood and sociality that would foster integration and root people in place. But people are caring for temporary places. In doing so, they are engaging in profoundly temporal acts of caretaking that offer some respite from the kind of temporal incarceration of camp time. When we understand waiting as temporal suffering, we can better appreciate how people are also engaged in restorative projects of time-making.

Notes

1. We assert that temporal suffering is experienced as traumatic while recognizing that trauma is a loaded term in research with refugees. Didier Fassin (2012) cautions that humanitarian reason tends to reduce violence to trauma and translate complex social processes into a clinical language of suffering. Refugees come to be defined by their past trauma in ways that further categorize them as victims, stripped of history and agency. In the process, the

structural causes of violence are obscured. Similarly, in work with war-displaced youth in postconflict Eritrea of the late 1990s, Farwell (2001) cautions that translating war experiences into biomedical categories through which we measure trauma often entails diagnosing individual distress, which can obscure the collective and temporal nature of trauma as it is experienced across families through generations. The concept of temporal suffering opens the possibility for emic depictions of trauma and healing that make space for these varying experiences.

2. Anthropological studies of trauma also help to complicate the notion that people are simply victims of trauma. As Rebecca Lester (2013) explains, trauma is a kind of experience that involves a rupture from everyday modes of human relationship and connection and a nonlinear process of recovery.

3. Khosravi (2021) draws from Frantz Fanon in his discussion of the racialization of time, arguing that colonial racism is built on the idea of the belatedness of non-Europeans: white time is thought of as civilized, modern, and neutral, while the racialized Other always arrives too late.

4. Khosravi (2021) describes waiting as a colonial technology that renders some people's time as less valuable than others', reminds people of their place in a racial hierarchy, and renders people's time as wasted in a way that means it can be stolen. These violent processes play out in migrant experiences with deportation, detention, and the long, uncertain processes surrounding resettlement and local integration.

5. Indeed, urban refugees that we interviewed talked about innumerable failed businesses due to their vulnerability at the hands of legal restrictions and the challenges that accompany caring for sick and displaced family.

6. Karen Fog Olwig (2021) describes how asylum seekers refuse to live in a time of suspension waiting for the teleological end point of resettlement by keeping various end points open—for example, by entertaining ideas about varied future trajectories.

5 Moving Time

Time-Making toward the Distant Future

"Do you know Tony Stark?" Tesfay asked us.

We stared blankly at him, not expecting him to open the conversation with a reference to the Marvel Comics' Iron Man alias. We were sipping cappuccinos and hot tea at a café near Addis Ababa University on a cold, rainy summer day with Tesfay and Haile, two of the rare refugee students to attend the country's most prestigious university. We met up with them whenever we were in Addis, but this time, when we were setting up our meeting on the phone, Tesfay was particularly excited and noted that he had a lot to tell us.

Seeing the blank looks on our faces, Tesfay continued, "Iron Man? How about Elon Musk?"

Snapping out of our stupor, we nodded and said, "Yes. Yes, of course we know Iron Man, Elon Musk, and Tony Stark."

Tesfay then talked rapidly, with passion, and told us about his plans for a drone controlled by brain waves and a circular motorcycle of bulletproof plastic. He had been developing the material in the university science lab by melting down used plastic. "I've already developed a plastic that can stop a bullet," he said. Tesfay explained that he had always been an inventor. He developed one of his earliest inventions in secondary school in Eritrea: shoes that allowed him to walk out over the Red Sea, at least a few steps, by freezing the surface of the water beneath them. Tesfay's ideas quickly flowed from him, sometimes aided by sketches on a café napkin.

As he enthusiastically fielded Jennifer's questions about his inventions, his friend Haile tried to explain the start-up they were developing to Amanda. It was formed by linking inventors in a kind of horizontal social network; it was similar, he explained, to blockchain-based cryptocurrencies. Haile was as excited about linking people together in a decentralized network by way of a social media app as Tesfay was about his inventions.

The conversations that we were separately drawn into converged around the mining of Bitcoin. Tesfay and Haile were both animated by this topic; they spoke rapidly, completing each other's sentences. They planned to use Bitcoin mining as a mechanism to not only generate funds for their start-up but to bypass the banking and regulatory institutions whose operations concentrate wealth and exclude people without citizenship, such as refugees. We had a lot of questions, as our twentieth-century brains accustomed to linear planning attempted to grasp the pragmatic and logistic leaps that their plan seemed to take. We managed to squeeze these questions in only to be met with a long explanation from each of them, accompanied by more diagrams on the napkin.

After a couple of hours of talking, the conversation wound down. Tesfay and Haile had an appointment with another student who was interested in investing in their Bitcoin project, and we had a meeting at the university. But before we wrapped up, Tesfay looked down sheepishly and said, "I have something else to tell you." He confessed that he was considering dropping out of school. He evoked Elon Musk again and said that school was too small for him; it was not allowing him to think the way he wanted to.

We felt ourselves begin to panic a bit and said something to him along the lines of, "Don't do anything too rash." We stammered out that we wished he had brought this up earlier and asked what we could do to help him think this through. We glanced at Haile, who shrugged and said, "I told him these things." Tesfay agreed to show us the lab where he was working in the university later that day; we hoped we might be able to convince him that the university had something left to offer him.

Why would Tesfay, a refugee who had a highly coveted spot at the most prestigious university in Ethiopia, complain that education had nothing to offer him and threaten to drop out? Tesfay's temporal orientation reflects a reworking of teleological time. It claims an end point, but one that is on a distant horizon, located outside the frame of the near future. If the near future entails planning and staged growth toward a goal, the distant future, in contrast, is better arrived at through dreams, faith, magic, and hope.[1] We refer to this particular form of time-making oriented toward the distant future as future-making.[2] Unlike the discipline and planfulness embedded in school time, which is often disempowering, future-making is creative, open-ended, and hopeful. Future-making is an imaginative, phenomenological process that makes the distant future tangible in the present. We consider it a type of care akin to the forms of caretaking we discussed in the last chapter but focused on future-leaning care rather than care for the present.[3]

Refugees often weigh these different notions of teleology (one that is open-ended and oriented toward a distant future and the other that populates the near future with activities, plans, and goals to provide a linear pathway toward progress) against each other. Habtom, whose story we have discussed throughout this book, was capable of seeing his future simultaneously unfold across these different temporal trajectories and in multiple spaces. He understood the risks inherent in each choice and was capable of shifting between multiple temporalities, each of which placed differential emphasis on the present, near future, and distant future. Tesfay and Haile, in a very different way, existed in multiple temporalities and were keenly aware of the points of overlap as well as the incompatibility and the trade-offs between them. Habtom feared getting stuck in the empty present of the camp but could simultaneously envision a teleological near future for himself attending university in Ethiopia and a distant future for himself "out there" in Europe with his siblings, even though he was keenly aware of the risks involved in migration. Similarly, Haile and Tesfay were extremely successful in terms of getting a formal education, but, like Habtom, they also saw the limitations of this teleological pathway. Even though Haile and Tesfay were fortunate to live and study in Addis Ababa and did not have to bear the kinds of pressures brought on by the empty time in the camp discussed in chapter 4, the "chronic present" (Dunn 2017) still pressed in on them. While they had the ability to move with relative freedom through space, they shared with refugees in the camps the difficulties with being able to move in time—or, more specifically, to make time move. And, because they were students, they keenly felt the failures of teleological time and its inability to produce a viable future.

In chapter 4, we explored how refugees make time by caring for the present. In this chapter, we look at future-making as another form of time-making. To better understand future-making, we turn to explanations of "prophetic time" (Guyer 2007; Robbins 2004). Prophetic time manifests in numerous ways. It is teleological in the sense that it orients toward an end point (some would argue the ultimate end point). However, teleologies that are prophetic, apocalyptic, or millennial forge a very different relationship with both the present and the near future than modernist, progress-focused notions of teleology. Although Jane Guyer does not explicitly note the teleological nature of these shifting temporal paradigms, she proposes this notion as a temporality that "evacuates" the near future and attaches the present to a distant future.[4] Furthermore, she suggests that these kinds of futuristic temporalities are showing up in seemingly disconnected fields. In our work with refugees both in camps and in Addis Ababa, we observed the numerous ways in which refugees prophetically ordered their future and present. We demonstrate here that the temporality of formal legal migration processes and their illegal "other"—irregular migration—were both structured prophetically. We also explore an array of other activities that are temporally prophetic—joining religious cults, trading in Bitcoin, and bringing "fantastical" inventions into being, as Tesfay was trying to do.

Future-Making, Choice, and the Distant Future

Many of us, refugee students included, function under the hegemony of conventional notions of teleological time that emphasize the necessity, if not the inevitability, of progress, making the lack of progress seem like an aberration and a personal failing, something we detailed in chapter 3.[5] Given the powerful ways in which the temporal hegemony of progress-oriented teleologies structured the lives of refugee students, this leaping over the near future might seem surprising, particularly for talented and accomplished students like Habtom, Haile, and Tesfay, but, as we describe in this chapter, under the circumstances that refugees face, it often became the only logical form of temporal agency and, more precisely, the only viable way to "make" the future.

Much of the work on refugee futures suggests that the problem is that the future is uncertain, unknown, and unknowable (Dryden-Peterson 2017). While this is indubitably true, much of the literature on refugee futures stops with making the case that refugees need and deserve a much more predictable, knowable future, using this as the rationale for refugees to have better access to education as well as expanded opportunities for local integration. We agree (and more importantly, most refugees would agree) that enhanced local integration and access to education are essential. Educational opportunities should be advocated for, but we also note an absence of theory that helps us understand what refugees do in the face of this painful uncertainty.

Future-making is a process of holding open the potentiality of the future by making choices. As we have detailed throughout this book, refugees are faced with weighing many risks: like the risk of waiting and experiencing the kinds of temporal suffering we discussed in the last chapter versus the risk of irregular migration; or the risk of investing in an education that seems likely to lead nowhere, which we discussed in chapter 3, versus the risk of abandoning dreams of education, which may lead to a different nowhere. We often focus on how refugees are victimized by the trauma and violence associated with these risks, but here we would like to emphasize the choices they make about the present and the future and the actions they take based on those choices. Even though they know they may not control the outcome, having a choice between risky outcomes is essential, as it provides an agentive pathway through uncertainty. It can give rise to extraordinary creativity and care. But the extreme risks on all fronts—psychological and physical—expose the effects of the intertwining of teleological violence with temporal agency.

Future-making also entails aligning the temporality of the present with a distant, hopeful future and considering how the distant, hopeful future gives shape and meaning to the present. In other words, future-making requires taking specific and direct actions in the present to move toward the distant future on the basis of faith that a particular future will *be* even in the absence of knowing *when* it will be. Tesfay's futuristic inventions and the way he diligently worked to make his inventions even in the absence of materials and technology are a prime example of this disciplining of the present and attaching it, materially, to the distant future. As we explore in this chapter, rituals performed in the service of unlikely and unpredictable resettlement processes and decisions to leave Ethiopia through irregular migration are also acts of future-making—they discipline the present through an orientation toward the distant future—as are planning for risky irregular migration and, conversely, rejecting migration.

Guyer's framing of prophetic time allows us to parse out futurity in a way not often developed in the literature on refugees and temporality.[6] Little work has looked at the phenomenology of how refugee agency forges a relationship between present and future.[7] We show that prophetic future-making both imagines this relationship and brings it into being; it leads to decision-making that has consequences that are imaginative *and* material. By bringing Guyer's work into conversation with work on cosmologies, magic, and hope, all of which provide frameworks for understanding how we take agency over the distant future by acting in the present, we can begin to understand how those who have very limited futures apprehend the distant future and use it to frame decisions. We can then begin to understand certain actions that refugees take as specific acts of future-making.

Guyer emphasizes the "fantasy futurism and enforced presentism" (2007, 410) that accompanies the evacuation of the near future. This framework entails a "downplaying or rejection of *durational human reasoning*" (Guyer 2007, 414, emphasis added). Durational human reasoning is a central component of modernist forms of teleological time in which time is thought to move (and improve) through controlled and measured steps from present to near future to distant future. Durational time moves forward incrementally toward its end, often assuming the certainty that we will arrive at that end point. Prophetic time, in contrast, is unpredictable, focuses on distant end points, and entails "no stages to reach for, no synergies of forces picking up on one another over time: no organization and no midterm reasoning" (Guyer 2007, 416). Thus, we consider our exploration of how refugees engage with the distant future as an effort to understand how they claim temporal agency and agency over the future without resorting to the kinds of modernist teleologies that have failed them.

Guyer calls on us to explore ethnographically "what becomes of 'near' when 'near' fades from collective consciousness" (2007, 410). This, in effect, is what we seek to do in this chapter. She provides us with several key analytics through which to explore ethnographically what happens when the near future recedes and the present is "indexed" to an "infinite horizon in the future" (Guyer 2007, 413). She questions what internal logics emerge when we find ourselves living in a "pause" or a "parentheses," when time becomes "episodic." These three analytics: living inside a pause, parentheses, or hiatus; the indexing of the present to a distant future; and the nature of episodic time are useful to understand how refugees make the future. As we discuss each category, we weave together a discussion of several other concepts: cosmologies, hope, and magic. These ideas help us demonstrate that the indexing of the present to the distant future is not a new thing; people have long had ways of enacting temporal agency amid uncertain circumstances in which they lack power.

Living in Parentheses

The notion of the pause, parentheses, or hiatus from durational time is key to understanding temporality among refugees. When constituted as a hiatus, the near future, according to Guyer, is "evacuated, in a way that is . . . disorienting and yet internally logical" (Guyer 2007, 414). Others liken this experience to "living in [the] parentheses" of prophetic time in which one reads signs and ritually orders everyday life while waiting for new temporal rhythm to begin (Robbins 2004, 159) or living in an unfinished pause or a break in temporal rhythms (Agamben 2005).

What does time look and feel like in this unfinished pause? It can look and feel like Haile and Tesfay putting their futuristic fantasies into action in the everyday sphere. It can look like the various forms of caretaking we described in chapter 4, such as joining a vocational education program knowing there are no jobs or opening a shop knowing there is no market for one's goods. It often entails long periods of waiting. And in these parentheses, people experience a meticulous ordering of the present in the service of a distant future, either by planning for irregular migration or by engaging in the time-disciplining bureaucratic processes of resettlement or family reunification. The unfinished pause can also lead to risk-taking when waiting for the pause to end becomes unbearable, and one feels compelled to make time move again, even if that movement entails risk. It can also engender tremendous creativity and wild leaps of ingenuity based on a faith that a future that does not exist will one day come to pass.

The pause is interesting, because while prophetic time is teleological, the pause is not. The telos—or desired end—of what lies outside the pause can either make the pause bearable or put pressure on life in the pause. The former enables agentive waiting and caretaking. The latter has the potential to create an urgency and lead to risk-taking, particularly migration. Different kinds of teleologies exert pressures in different ways. For example, a need to progress in the near future may make the pause unbearable and create pressure to end it, but a focus on the distant future may order time in nonteleological ways and populate the present with meaningful activities.[8]

Time in parentheses is a pause, but it is a pause in which a particular outcome is imagined and the present is ordered by the daily, often ritualized, preparation for that outcome. The way in which prophetic time attaches the present to the future is distinct from durational, linear, punctuated time marching in stages toward its teleological end. Prophetic time is nonlinear, taking large but logical temporal leaps. Guyer notes that temporalities that abandon the near future set up the "distant future as the moment of truth" and the present as populated with choice, ingenuity, experiment, risk, and discipline; this "new indexing" of the "present to an infinite horizon in the future places people in emotional and sociological *terra nova*" (2007, 413). This raises the question of how the present becomes indexed to the distant future, which is not a new question in the anthropology of refugees, forced displacement, and precarity (Ramsay 2019; Dunn 2017; Khosravi 2017; Jansen 2008).

Indexing the Present to a Distant Future

Whether the experience of life in parentheses is bearable or unbearable depends on the level of faith in and hope for what lies outside the pause as well as the capacity of that faith and hope to order life in the pause. Anthropology has several tools to help us understand how life in the pause might index the present to a distant future. The concept of cosmology provides one such tool. Cosmologies might be thought of as religious or spiritual beliefs, but the concept has been used to understand how daily lives come to be structured and endowed with meaning through their connection with beliefs about how that which is beyond is ordered. According to Georgina Ramsay, "Cosmologies are those seemingly self-evident laws and logics of human experience and the universe that make some ways of being seem natural" (2019, 29). Cosmology can be an "important heuristic tool for linking representations of reality with perceptions of morality and prescribed actions" (Belloni 2019, 3). In her highly influential study of historical memory and political identity among Hutu refugees from Burundi in Tanzania, Liisa Malkki notes how refugees create cosmologies centered around a mythical future of return (Malkki 1995a). Malkki describes cosmological praxis as a "form of acting upon the fundamental *order* of the world" as people rework systems of categories and the relationships between them: temporal, material, spiritual, and social (1995a). In a similar vein, Elizabeth Cullen Dunn notes that refugees often ascribe the future with a mythical quality and long for their return to a place that likely no longer exists (Dunn 2017). These cosmologies of return frame decisions about how the present is lived and exert a kind of discipline over daily life.

Refugee cosmologies are not always oriented toward the myth of return. Indeed, they are specific to historical, political, and cultural contexts. For example, Ramsay (2019) notes how cosmologies among Congolese refugees in both Uganda and Australia are oriented around regeneration, feeding, fertility, and biological motherhood. This cosmology traverses space but is placed in crisis due to radical ruptures to familiar rhythms of daily life.

The cosmologies that organize Eritrean migration are oriented around the narrative of leaving to return. Many Eritreans view leaving as a patriotic duty that reflects the culture of sacrifice produced by the Eritrean state (Bernal 2014) and the unequal burdens placed on its territorially bound vs. diasporic citizens (Riggan 2013; Woldemikael 2018). Eritreans long to leave so that they can return and forge a different, diasporic relationship with their country (Riggan 2013). By leaving Eritrea, an Eritrean is transformed from a territorially bound citizen who is unable to leave the country and expected to provide forced labor for the state to a diasporic citizen who is free to come and go but expected to contribute financial resources to the state. The latter is the more valued and less oppressive contribution (Riggan 2016). Eritreans thus long for return, as do refugees in other contexts (Malkki 1995a; Dunn 2017; Allan 2013), but they long to return *after* having left, settled elsewhere, and transformed into diasporic citizens. Leaving in order to transform the nature of their national duties requires Eritreans to be successful in their migration. Milena Belloni's argument that Eritrean migrant decisions are framed by a hierarchical "cosmology of destinations" helps us understand how migration trajectories, choices, and pathways are bound to the broader cosmology of return (2019).

Another way of indexing the distant future to the present is through hope. Hope might also be thought of as cosmological in the way that it hinges the present to the distant future. Hope points to an imaginative *horizon* (Crapanzano 2003). As Rebecca Bryant and Daniel Knight note, it "draws the not-yet into the present and motivates activity in the here-and-now" (2019, 157). Grasping the nature of hope is key to understanding how refugees make the future while existing in parentheses. Hope is a means of laying claim to the future and structuring the present according to that future (Jansen 2016).[9] It is intricately connected to the "capacity to aspire" (Appadurai 2004) and is a component of "tricking" the future (Ringel 2016).[10]

Hope is a central feature in a number of studies of refugees. We observed that hope was extremely important to our interlocutors. Recall Berihu's comment in the introduction, just before he told us about the traumas he had endured in the war, that he did not want to talk about his troubles, he wanted to talk about his hopes. Throughout the course of our fieldwork, in the face of extreme challenges, Berihu and others repeatedly returned to hope, clung to hope, asked us to help give them hope, and noted the dangers of losing hope. Hope in this sense—and in the sense that many refugees experienced (and mobilized)—resonates with Kirsi Kallio, Isabel Meier, and Jouni Häkli's notion of "radical hope," which we introduced in the last chapter. They argue that radical hope requires not only an "active orientation toward the present" (which resonates with our concept of caretaking for the present discussed in the last chapter) but also a "dissociation from the facts of anticipated futurity that constantly threaten to thwart people's agency" (Kallio et al. 2021, 4008). We found that the facts that "threaten to thwart people's agency" are often located in the near future. This means that the distant future is an important site for the maintenance of radical hope.

There are numerous examples of the ways refugees index the present to a distant future. Catherine Brun's concept of "agency in waiting" allows us to understand how those facing protracted displacement link the everyday time of the present to an abstract future elsewhere through hopeful waiting, enabling them to cope with indefinite uncertainty (2015). Cindy Horst (2006) similarly illuminates how *buufis*, or dreams of resettlement, may help Somali refugees in Kenya survive despair and endless waiting, yet she cautions that these dreams can be painfully maddening when they fail. Diana Allan's work reveals how talk about migration and dreams generates hope and a sense of futurity for Palestinian refugees long confined to the Shatila refugee camp. Allan argues that "emigration is tantalizing because it introduces the possibility of *discontinuity*—both spatial and *temporal*—between who (and where) one is and what one might become" (2013, 167, emphasis added). Emigration talk "creates space for fantasy, speculation and the promise of a meaningful life; as such, it represents an arena in which aspirations are cultivated and acted upon" (Allan 2013, 33). It serves as "a kind of anti-empirical approach to making sense of uncertainty" (Allan 2013, 156). Eritrean refugees in Ethiopia also turned to emigration as a way to structure their distant future. However, future-making was not limited to thinking about emigration; it enabled the imagination of other, sometimes surprising, futures as well.

Cosmological time and the temporalities of hope give the distant future mean-ing and make time in the parentheses—a time without telos—bearable.[11] Cosmolo-gies and hope order time in the present in meaningful ways. Because of this, pro-phetic temporalities can lead to inspiration, creativity, and generativity. But they are also always intertwined with forms of temporal suffering, constraint, and an awareness of stalled futures.

Agency and Episodic Time

To say that refugees do not have control over their time would be a vast understate-ment. Not only are refugees subject to the regimes and power structures of being made to wait, but they are also subject to substantial date regimes (Strathern 2000). In other words, they are disciplined by a series of high-stakes dates, such as ap-pointments with UNHCR, monthly rations allocation, and others (Guyer 2007). These high-stakes dates are disjointed, episodic events that are detached from other everyday occurrences and distinct in the way they punctuate the present with vague promises and threats of negative consequences should a refugee not show up for an appointment at the allocated time. This is particularly the case for refugees engaged in legal migration processes. Time in parentheses is a temporality in which the actor—the refugee in this case—does not have the power to produce a particu-lar outcome in the distant future or even to determine when time would begin to move again. However, our interlocutors did believe themselves to have influence over the distant future and, perhaps more importantly, believed they could situ-ate themselves for a distant future outcome and prepare themselves for when time might start moving again. This imagined relationship between present responsibil-ity and future outcome attaches the present to the distant future in a very particular way. The stance toward the distant future reflects what Guyer says is emblematic of prophetic time as the time of "an enduring attitude of expectant waiting" in the gap between the past, when time was moving "normally," and the distant future, when time is expected to start moving again. The "temporal sensibility" that has emerged inside the pause is "episodic" (Guyer 2007, 409).

How do we understand temporal agency inside the pause, when subjects lack the ability to plan or predict when the pause will end, on one hand, or to make time move, on the other? To understand temporal agency in the unpredictable and uncontrollable nature of living episodically inside a pause, we turn to stud-ies of magic. These theories may provide us with some analytic frameworks that help specify what life looks like inside the parentheses and enable us to better understand the agency refugees take by making their own future.[12] Magic helps us understand the nondurational, nonteleological unpredictability of living in the episodic time of the pause, and theories of magic help us grasp the relation-ship between structural violence and temporal agency. Magic responds to unpre-dictable circumstances by situating routine and ritual everyday action within a broader cosmology. It does this by enabling actors to act on, or "trick" (Ringel 2016), an unpredictable future and simultaneously recognize that they are imbricated in a broader complex of power, a system in which they are not entirely powerless but are definitively subject to a power greater than them. Theories of magic give us tools to understand the phenomenology of indexing the present to the distant future.[13]

Magic can simultaneously provide an interpretive framework through which people make sense of power, especially when its function is mysterious and obscured, and form an agentive means of claiming power, in a limited way, in the midst of an overall condition of powerlessness (Geschiere 1997; Whitehead and Finnström 2013).[14] The ways in which refugees make sense of and respond to the powerful, unfair, and nontransparent nature of resettlement programs resonate with how magic is used to make sense of other contexts that are opaque, mysterious, and violent. Seen through this lens, the magic of legal migration processes involves the creation and deployment of social categories, including powerful methods of dehumanization that temporally displace and incarcerate populations of people, leaving them suspended and expectant. Refugee attempts at future-making take these magical elements of power and invert them so that the future, a thing denied to refugees, becomes a tool to remake the world. We will now explore how people make meaning of and attempt to chart a path through an obscure, unpredictable, and high-stakes (life or death) process of refugee resettlement.

Life inside a Process: The Temporalities of Legal Migration

Jennifer and her colleague from Addis Ababa University, Dr. Alebachew Kemisso Haybano sat at a café in front of a tall building in the Mebrat Haile condominium complex on the outskirts of Addis Ababa, an area known for its large number of Eritrean urban refugees. We were talking with a group of women, many of whom had come to Addis Ababa to join their husbands or other family members who had already migrated, as part of a study of urban refugees. A few had gotten permission to leave the camps through the formal out-of-camp program, but most had left without official clearance and were effectively living as undocumented urban refugees. All were living without the benefit of assistance from UNHCR or the Administration for Refugee and Returnee Affairs (ARRA) or the right to work legally while they waited. The phrase *I have a process* and the question *Do you have a process?* punctuated this conversation.

These women were somber as they described the strain of waiting, which clearly wore on them. Some had processes in progress, while others were waiting for their processes to start. The stories about processes varied widely but were often filled with accounts of loss and disconnection, such as not being able to get in touch with husbands or fiancés abroad. It was also common to hear stories of women who had come to Addis hoping to be reunited with husbands or fiancés only to learn that they had been abandoned for another woman. One woman had accompanied her extended family's children to Addis. The children were reunited with their parents abroad, and she was left alone in Addis. Although they made a clear distinction between those whose processes had started and those whose processes had yet to start, all of them described suffering from interminable waiting in similar ways.

In simplest terms, a *process* refers to a specific bureaucratic proceeding involving a trajectory toward migration either through refugee resettlement or family reunification. But what is the temporality of a process? Temporally, these processes, whether or not one has one, order time prophetically such that the everyday present is disciplined by waiting for an outcome whose existence was believed in but not known for certain. Having a process was a painful but coveted condition in which a refugee had theoretically moved from aimless waiting to waiting for something, but having a process did not create certainty; rather, it deepened the mystery that existed around legal migration.

Resettlement through UNHCR is a rare opportunity. In Ethiopia (and globally), fewer than 1 percent of registered refugees are accepted for resettlement (Paszkiewicz 2017). Still, this rare opportunity ordered the everyday lives of many refugees. Most expected prior to their arrival in Ethiopia that the resettlement process would be more transparent and much faster. They were often surprised to find that they had extremely limited access to UNHCR and were only able to meet with a resettlement representative once every few months. Even if they did manage to meet with UNHCR, they were seldom given adequate information about legal migration processes.

Resettlement processes were opaque and so complex that even UNHCR resettlement officers struggled to explain them clearly. These processes hinged on an outcome in the distant future that was hoped for but unpredictable and uncertain. To refugees, it felt as if a power beyond their reach was structuring outcomes in material ways. Refugees found it impossible to acquire information about these processes. The time spent waiting for resettlement was time in parentheses. Refugee behavior in response was disciplined and ritualized.

The frame of magic, or more precisely witchcraft, helps us understand how refugees made sense of resettlement processes, because in both cases, an opaque and far-reaching power was believed to structure outcomes in material ways (Geschiere 1997). Magic is a useful lens through which to view resettlement processes in no small part because refugees found it impossible to acquire information about these processes and had to resort to what might be thought of as ritualized behavior as well various forms of divination to develop a theory of how this power operated. Indeed, there were so many moving, interlocking parts involved in resettlement that even those who had power in the process never fully controlled it or grasped its mysteries.

Vetting refugees for resettlement is a lengthy process that often takes several years, particularly for resettlement to the United States, which remains the country that resettles the largest number of refugees from Ethiopia. A resettlement officer at UNHCR explained to us that keeping the right number of refugees in the pipeline so as to ensure that all resettlement slots are filled requires a complex calculus on the part of UNHCR staff in which they try to predict the policy future, anticipate the number of spots that will be open, and determine which profile of refugees will be eligible for those slots. All of this is made far more complex by the fact that each country has different resettlement priorities, criteria, and limitations that can, and do, change. At the time of our research, the shifting American policy field and the Muslim and refugee bans being tied up in courts wreaked havoc on this already complicated and confusing situation. UNHCR staff tried to mitigate against this unpredictability by systematically prescreening refugees for particular host countries so that they can move as quickly as possible should spots open up (though *as quickly as possible* is never particularly fast). The strategy inevitably results in some refugees starting a process that becomes stalled, sometimes permanently. Meanwhile, refugees themselves tried to make sense of this process from their limited vantage point on the ground in Addis Ababa or in camps, and they often developed theories of how one improved one's chances of being resettled that were, in many ways, based on a kind of divination from scarce information.

Those seeking family reunification rather than resettlement might seem to have a clearer, more guaranteed, and more transparent process, but this is often not the case either. The opaque nature of communication with embassies and the lack of clarity about how to procure the needed documentation from UNHCR and ARRA made family reunification a process that was often as magical and confusing as resettlement. A UNHCR resettlement officer noted that family members often come too soon, such as when a relative is still awaiting an asylum determination in their target country. They may wait years while they see others' processes moving quickly, and this may happen for reasons that are nuanced, complex, and hard to discern. But even in the midst of this opaque situation, refugees develop evidence-based explanations for the wait.

As a result, refugees experience a profound alienation from their own processes, which disempowers them and subjects them to powerful temporal discipline. Refugees are told that they can only go to the UNHCR office to inquire about their case once every two months. That means they have to order and organize their lives around those dates. However, when their turn comes, they often fail to get the information they need. Comments such as "there is no one over there," as one refugee noted about the UNHCR office in Addis Ababa, speak to what feels like an unmanned process. Another refugee noted the mysterious nature of trying to get information: "No one knows where to go or who to approach." Still another refugee described the infuriatingly mystifying nature of trying to access UNHCR officials: "When you go there [to UNHCR], if you speak to one officer, they tell you to go to Haya Hulet. You have to get to the right person, but they don't tell you what they need. You have to talk through a glass and explain your case, and they won't connect you with the person who can really help you."

Being inside a bureaucratic process is about being spun around from person to person with no one having full information that can help. Another urban refugee said he showed up at the UNHCR office every week. He talked about engaging in this ritual in the absence of being able to get any information to help him comprehend, manage, or plan for the process:

> It is about 8 months that I have been here. I needed to know what the problems of the refugees are. I searched the internet for information about education support and resettlement. Even doing so didn't give me much information. Even in the camp, so many people are going through the resettlement process. They don't know what percentage of the population is going through that. They [UNHCR staff] gather every Wednesday so you just go and get refused and simply you go every week. Finally, my wife and I got our turn and when we got our turn [to talk to someone], he didn't quite describe the process of resettlement. I didn't know what to say. This is my experience. It isn't his fault, but I didn't know how to communicate with him. This creates a barrier. What I am saying is if UNHCR could put a few guidelines about what programs are entitled to particular groups of refugees, it would create a better understanding than what is present now.

Refugees work extremely hard to decipher these mysteries and usually cannot. Without the ability to understand or plan, their engagement with the process becomes ritualized, and beliefs emerge about the capacity of arbitrary actions to influence a highly unpredictable outcome. Showing up regularly at UNHCR, even when they know that they probably will not get the information they need, is one such ritualized effort to engage with the episodic nature of these processes.

The opaqueness of living inside parentheses can lead to an intense subjection to a powerful regime of dates (Strathern 2000). When legal migration comes to fruition, it appears to drop out of nowhere, as do calls to report to an embassy or office to move one's process forward. As with resettlement, so many factors influence when this opportunity will arrive that they appear to exist in a time of their own. Refugees wait for the opportunity, engaging in ritualized activity to make these opportunities come about, but in reality, there is little they can do but wait hopefully. The time of waiting requires a ritualized disciplining of one's time, daily life, and near future. The dates of UNHCR appointments, for example, take precedence over school and other priorities. Refugees we spoke to described their rituals of showing up every Wednesday or waiting for their turn (which typically, in Addis Ababa, came every two months) to talk to a human across a thick piece of glass only to be told there was no information. Refugees seeking family reunification had similar stories to tell about life within a process as they engaged with bureaucracies at embassies as well as ARRA and UNHCR.

Processes mandate ritualized, date-driven events and have the power to hold people in particular places. In the midst of uncertain futures, refugees still had to make decisions about which future to invest the most hopes in. Doing so often determined where they would locate themselves spatially. In other words, the temporal discipline of life in parentheses, inside a process, structured choices in particular ways. There is some evidence that the mere existence of resettlement as an option, even if the chances of being resettled are very thin, makes it more likely that refugees will stay in Ethiopia (Mallett et al. 2017, 25). More specifically, both reunification and resettlement processes (and the process of waiting for the process) heavily influence refugees' decisions about where to live. While family reunification tends to draw people to the capital city so they can locate themselves near embassies, resettlement tends to bind refugees to the camp. When we first began researching the university scholarship program, we often heard rumors that people could not be resettled if they were attending a university. This was quickly corrected for us by both UNHCR and various INGO workers, yet we kept encountering refugees who would not go to a university for fear that it would hurt their chances at resettlement. One of our key participants explained that he would not attend the university in Ethiopia because he needed to stay in the camp to await his resettlement opportunities. If he were to be called to UNHCR for an interview, the first step on the long pathway toward resettlement, his name would appear on a physical list posted in the camp. He could of course ask a friend to look at the list and then contact him to return to the camp, but he did not trust anyone enough to do so. Additionally, some were told indirectly that they would have less of a chance of being resettled if they were at the university. When we asked who told them this, one person replied, "It is not done directly, speaking like, you are not having a chance. They imply it. They tell you having a university education is a great opportunity. So how could you ask again [for an opportunity to leave the camp]? They tell you resettlement is an opportunity for those who do not have access outside the camp."

This idea that staying in the camp was necessary to maximize one's chances at resettlement was commonly held. In a focus group, refugee university students described the complex relationship between resettlement and being a student in a way that clarified how resettlement processes bind refugees to the camp, at times leading members of their cohort to drop out. One noted, "They prefer to go to the camp." One of the complaints of this particular group of students was that they did not receive good information about their resettlement processes and lacked the ability to care for their processes while at school. They felt they got better care for their resettlement cases in the camps. There were also stories of university students who heard that their process was moving forward, left school, and returned to the camp only to be stuck there for years. Thus, the disciplining effect of date regimes might mean that refugees had to relinquish a scholarship and a coveted chance to study and move outside the camp; many returned to the camp to be closer to where they thought the people with power over their process were located.[15]

There is also some evidence that resettlement has the power to root refugees in Ethiopia itself and prevent illegal migration. An Overseas Development Institute

(ODI) report on resettlement and onward movement noted, "By offering the possibility of an *alternative future*, the hope of resettlement *incentivizes immobility over long periods of time*" (Mallett et al. 2017, 25, emphasis added). The report further details what we would consider the prophetic ordering of resettlement and the disciplining effects of its processes: "It is clear that our respondents are operating on a *long timeframe*, placing great value on *far-off goals* (even if highly uncertain) and *less on their present* situation. . . . Many were willing to *spend days waiting* in line, and *years waiting* for a final decision" (Mallet et al. 2017, 25, emphasis added). These findings, like our own, suggest that the prophetic temporalities of resettlement order and discipline the present by attaching it to a distant, hoped-for future. In the face of being forced to wait, it is no surprise that refugees' attempts to enact control over this future resonate with studies of magic. Resettlement is a particularly magical form of process because it is the least linear and the most opaque, and, as we noted earlier, it requires a complex temporal and demographic calculation on the part of the organizations managing the resettlement processes. UNHCR staff may barely understand their calculation of which refugees (and how many) may begin the resettlement process, let alone be able to explain it to refugees who experience this calculation through appointments held once every three months through thick glass in a UNHCR office in Addis or via a handwritten announcement posted to a bulletin board in the camp.

It is no wonder that refugees may develop their own somewhat magical practices in an attempt to divine the meaning of these opaque processes. Meaning is given to particular events, like the arrival in the camp of a white UNHCR Land Cruiser bearing the resettlement officer. Refugees keep timelines in their head and use those timelines in an attempt to divine the status of their process. They know, for example, that after their first interview with UNHCR, they are on some kind of list, but it will not be until after a second interview that their process actually moves forward. They may wait years after their first interview. A second interview indicates that their process is moving forward, and a medical examination indicates that the process may start advancing more rapidly.

The details of processes are turned over in an ongoing effort to make sense of them, and refugees attempt to distill meaning from the things that are happening to their peers. For example, if refugees watch others being called in for interviews or being resettled, they may question what has happened to their own process. The case of Trhas's family, who we met in chapter 4, is a particularly acute example of that. When we first visited Trhas, she sadly recounted how long she had been in the camp—almost since it had opened nearly a decade before. Despite the fact that she was relatively well-off (her husband had a lucrative business) and she was living with three children in a house that had been renovated on prime real estate near the main street, the length of time she had been waiting in the camp was a source of pressure. She did not want her children growing up there. One time when we visited, she told us with great happiness that she had started a process to go to

Australia. She rattled off the steps and the amount of time each should take, an attempt to ascribe predictability to an erratic process. On our next visit, however, she was no longer talking about Australia, but about Italy. She had been accepted by what turned out to be one of the relatively new "humanitarian corridor" programs that sought to relocate Eritrean refugees safely to camps in Italy; from there, they would be sent to other European countries. By our next visit several months later, she was, effectively, packing her bags. When we came back to the camp several months after that, we expected to find her gone. Instead, Trhas and her family were still there. She was confused and disappointed. Eager to have an explanation for what had happened, she suspected that someone had taken her place.

Many refugees had stories about resettlement opportunities being stolen by Ethiopians. Although we never met anyone this had happened to, these accounts showed up in the margins of our field notes and in the hissed anger of hushed conversations after focus groups ended. One man reported that someone he knew was ill and could not check his email for several months. By the time he became well enough to contact UNHCR, he was told that he was already moving forward with his process. Someone was moving forward with his process, but it was not him. Another person reported that their friend could not get information about their process for months, and when he finally did, he learned that according to UNHCR, he was already living in Minnesota. Refugees living in camps occasionally mentioned being aware of Ethiopians living in camps for a brief time prior to being resettled as Eritreans.

Allegations of resettlement fraud are clearly a sensitive issue that our research was not in any way poised to address. Osvaldo Costantini and Aurora Massa (2016) suggest that some people do manipulate social and symbolic borders to cross political ones; kinship, social, and trading networks have historically spanned either side of the border, challenging neat delineations of national identity. While we do not address the nature and extent of stolen resettlement in our research, these stories were common enough among refugees that they are important to mention, as they shed light on how refugees made sense of the impossible power dynamic surrounding processes. Regardless of whether or not these stories of stolen resettlement opportunities are true, they operated as a conspiracy theory through which people understood and engaged with the workings of the resettlement process. Conspiracy theories generate a framework for reading the workings of power in the resettlement system, one in which prophetic time holds forth transformative possibilities but portions them without predictability, clear logic, or a legible time frame. Regardless of whether or not they are true, they tell an important temporal story and reveal a great deal about refugees' faith in the process and sense of hope.

The global system of migration management is fundamentally undemocratic and violent. It incarcerates and slowly kills large populations of people even as it promises asylum and the possibilities of social, spatial, and temporal mobility. Indeed, while resettlement promises a particular kind of shape-shifting to a rights-bearing citizen, it also involves the dehumanization of entire populations into bare humanity and objects of humanitarian aid left waiting for the chance to leave. Stories of stolen identities attempt to make sense of forms of corruption that appear magical in their obscure and transformative workings of power. They are thus a by-product of the opaque, nonlinear, and unfair nature of resettlement processes—a form of theorizing about that which is hidden.

As much as they expose deep contradictions, these theories are also part of the fabric of prophetic time-making. They anticipate a distant future but reconfigure the near future as stolen rather than simply mysterious. Consequently, as much as they cast aspersions on the implementation of resettlement processes (and the role of particular Ethiopian actors), these conspiracy theories reaffirm the benevolence of the process itself, positing that resettlement processes are impossible and opaque not because there is something fundamentally wrong with a system that stingily rations much-needed resettlement opportunities and leaves many others stranded, but because individual actors with more power than refugees are stealing these opportunities. They enable people to maintain faith and hope while waiting because they obscure systemic violence.

Conspiracy theories enable refugees to maintain hope in the midst of a hopeless situation. Hope enables and embodies an attachment to a distant future that is not just imagined or imaginary—it is material. The materiality of hope is manifested when refugees discipline themselves to choose the process over other goals, aspirations, and temporalities and shape daily life in such a way that one is constantly ready should that process move forward. But legal migration processes are not the only thing that does this. In the next section, we explore how the temporality of irregular migration is structured in similarly prophetic ways, but by replacing hope with risk.

Deciding to Move On: The Temporality of Risk

Most refugees were keenly aware that they existed on the knife's edge of decision-making between staying and going. As one refugee put it, "Refugees are not stable. Everyone is changing his decision day by day." It was common for refugees to put irregular migration and resettlement in the same sentence.

Here we suggest that in many ways, both hope and thinking about the risk of irregular migration are structured prophetically with an orientation to the distant future. Both entail forms of magical thinking—leaps over the near future and leaps of faith—that are attached directly to the structuration of the everyday, particularly the rituals and sacrifices in everyday life. As we saw earlier, the rituals that refugees undergo as they wait for legal migration options are disciplining; they foreclose certain options in favor of others, determine priorities, bind refugees to certain places, and create commitments to a particular set of actions.

Deciding to move on through irregular channels is also a form of future-making structured according to the logics of prophetic time. It abandons the commitment to waiting in place and all the discipline and sacrifice that waiting requires. Moving on entails a different kind of choice, one that is only made after carefully weighing the risks and sacrifices involved in staying against the risks and sacrifices of leaving. While some might sacrifice opportunities, such as education, to wait for the possibility of resettlement, others might sacrifice their bodies and their freedom, placing themselves at great risk through irregular migration. Refugees often talked about not feeling safe in Ethiopia; though they generally felt physically safe, they were referring to the fact that their future was not guaranteed. They discussed the psychological damage caused by delays in processes that could push them toward irregular migration. As one refugee put it: "UNHCR is playing with Eritrean refugees. Resettlement to the Netherlands was canceled. Our mind is destroyed by UNHCR." Another refugee, who had been in process to reunify with his daughter for four years, noted: "The processes take so long that a lot of people get frustrated and leave." And still another refugee clearly and succinctly articulated the relationship between staying and deciding to leave: "If I lose hope, I will turn to irregular migration." This was a common sentiment; irregular migration was what refugees turned to when they could not hang onto hope. When seen from a temporal perspective, this exchange of hope for risk is not surprising because in many ways, the temporality of hope and risk are similarly structured.

Refugees knew that any of them might reach a point where they would exchange hope for risk. Both require a leap of faith, and they seem logical when the near future is not viable. By exchanging hope for risk, refugees trade one present for another: a present structured by waiting faithfully for a future that may never come, for a present full of risk in which one is moving toward a future that they may never reach. Both are unpredictable. Both require a remarkably similar vision of the distant future and a willingness to make sacrifices in the present. Both involve an abdication of control over the near future. One requires deciding to wait (to do nothing); the other requires deciding to move (to do something).

The risks of irregular movement are well known to most, if not all, refugees, as the following story told by someone who had attempted to migrate indicates:

> Most of the Eritreans do not want to live in Addis Ababa.[16] This is simply because there is no opportunity here. They cannot work. This is legally prohibited for refugees. They cannot continue with friends or family support for fifty or sixty years. They can't continue for longer and longer period of time. So, they risk moving out from Ethiopia and try their chance to reach Europe. I tried the chance to go out from Ethiopia and finally I was caught by Bedouin smugglers and paid 32,000 USD ransom and was released back to Ethiopia. I witnessed 42 people who died at the hands of the Bedouin. . . . In Eritrea there is no opportunity and here in Ethiopia there is no opportunity so that is why refugees try their chance through the oceans. Even if I reach Europe, there are problems there. There are people who commit suicide. But even with all this knowledge Eritreans prefer to move out of Ethiopia.

Why would someone who had experienced the brutality of the irregular migration route firsthand express understanding and empathy for refugees who choose to move on? This quotation powerfully links refugees' willingness to knowingly take risks in the hope of creating a better future with the impossibility of the near future in Ethiopia. To make this decision, refugees must suspend their thinking about the risks involved in the near future of migration and instead focus on the impossibility of the near future in Ethiopia. To make this decision, the dangers of staying must come to seem heavier than the dangers of leaving, as articulated here: "The Ethiopian government has been generous enough to let us stay here and we sleep safely with a roof over our heads, but that is not enough. Eritrean children are following dangerous routes. They don't want us to face danger, but they don't have alternatives here. However hard we try to settle here, Ethiopia has 100 million people to give jobs to and then they can help others. I have young kids and they will go through the dangerous route unless they see a change here."

Refugees also turn to the past—previous experiences and earlier histories of instability in Eritrea and Ethiopia—as evidence of the unreliable nature of the near future. Eritrean refugees have already become conditioned for sacrifice. Many commented that experiencing ongoing military service in Eritrea (or *Sawa*, as it is termed) actually conditions refugees to face the hardships of migration, as it includes training to make arduous journeys on foot through challenging arid terrain, all while rationing supplies.

Similarly, waves of displacement make refugees feel like Ethiopia is not a stable place in which they can stay. The following quotation describes the instability and uncertainty that one refugee felt after being deported from Ethiopia and then returning as a refugee:

> When the war broke out with Eritrea and Ethiopia, we were deported for no reason. My parents are traders. They are not spies. They were deported. When we went there [to Eritrea] we had to start our life from zero. In this situation I lost my father, brother, and friends. Life in Eritrea is so hard, so now I had to start my life again in Eritrea. It is so hard. I am Ethiopian by birth. There is a saying in Tigrigna. Today is OK, but we don't know about tomorrow. So, I choose to leave this country if I get any opportunity. I need a country to call it a country. To call it mine. To marry. To have kids. I don't have a guarantee here. I am not Ethiopian or Eritrean.

Effectively, his previous experience of deportation served as a constant reminder of the lack of trust he had in Ethiopia and the sense that the near future in that country would always be uncertain. In choosing to move on, refugees take agency over not only moving their bodies through space but also making time move toward a better future. The future cannot exist in Ethiopia; thus, to make the future, one must move on. This is one of the most profound forms of future-making. If prophetic time entails an abandonment of the near future in favor of the distant future, and if this distant future then serves as a modality to structure the present in ways that refugees have agency over, it is perhaps not surprising that hope (and the waiting it enables) and risk (and the movement it enables) occupy the same temporal field.

Although not explicitly a temporal analysis, Belloni's discussion of refugees as gamblers is useful in illuminating the temporality of risk. As Belloni (2019) points out, migrants know about risks, but ultimately, the "jackpot" of reaching an imagined good life takes precedence over the fear of risks. She argues that as refugees progress along their rather episodic migration journeys, their willingness to take risks increases. This is in no small part because they have already invested a great deal financially and emotionally in the journey. They have also invested a great deal temporally, as migration trajectories may be long and entail multiple stages of waiting. Rather than deterring migrants, this arduous process makes them more determined, something noted in Ruben Andersson's analysis of the temporality of migration and migration controls (Andersson 2014). Migrants are "all in" and, like gamblers, cannot divest of the risks they have taken once they have invested so much and are compelled to risk more. Theirs is a distant future–oriented strategy that is prophetic rather than teleological.

Like legal resettlement, irregular migration requires a suspension of thinking in step-by-step terms about how and when the ultimate destination will be reached. Irregular migration demands a suspension of disbelief about the actual risks; it involves not a rejection of their existence but a mental leap over them. In numerous interviews and focus groups, we heard refugees put the pain of the present with its interminable waiting on the same plane as the risks of migration. For many, there was a willingness to imaginatively leap over those risks in the interest of getting to a new place, as is evidenced by the thousands who routinely migrate onward. The sign on the wall of a small roadside restaurant in Mai Aini camp speaks to this importance of choosing movement over stasis: "I don't know where I'm going, but I'm on my way."

Refugees do prepare themselves for the perils of irregular migration, but given its utterly unpredictable nature, their preparation serves as more of a ritual talisman than as an actual risk mitigation measure. For example, knowing how high the likelihood of their experiencing sexual violence is, women often take birth control as a precaution. There is a network of brokers and smugglers to guide and help refugees with their preparations. Some refugees engage in extensive preparations for the journey, while others make rather spontaneous decisions (Mengiste 2018, 2019). Although every journey involves risk, it is generally believed that the more planful one is (and the more money one has to invest), the safer the journey. Tekalign Ayalew Mengiste (2018) skillfully details in his research the social networks through which Eritrean migrants share information, plan their journeys, and build a community of knowledge. The horrifying risks of the migrant network, particularly for refugees who lack social and financial support, mean there is no assurance of progress or a desired outcome from one's actions in the present; what is required

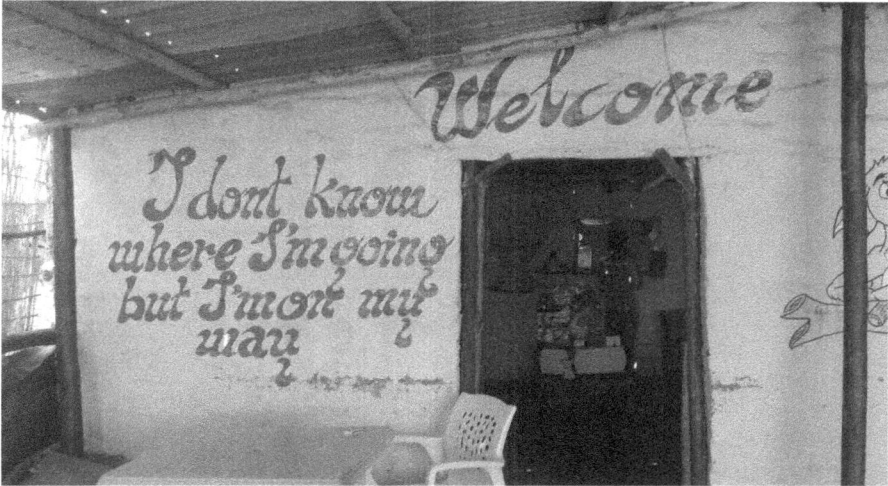

Fig. 5.1. A popular Mai Aini camp bar. Photo by Amanda Poole.

is a leap of faith. Moving from the unpleasant place of the refugee camp to the un-known place at the end of the journey involves willingly and willfully erasing the space in between—but also the *time*. Brokers and smugglers play a key role here.

In many ways, just as low-level administrative functionaries behind glass windows in the UNHCR offices served as sorcerers in legal migration processes, brokers were the sorcerers of irregular migration. Both were actors who wielded power by virtue of having more knowledge about legal processes and migration routes, but neither had full control over these highly opaque, mysterious, and magical paths. Thus, there were always risks. On a visit to the Hitsats camp, Yirga, an Ethiopian man who works with an NGO, briefed us on the smugglers—or, as he called them, the "brokers." He noted, "We are always fighting with the brokers. They lure young people away from the camp. People who have stayed in the camps for years will go abroad by any means." The brokers are depicted as wielding a sort of dark magic and preying on the particularly weak and vulnerable.

We then asked Yirga about Habtom, whose story we shared at the beginning of this chapter. He had recently migrated. "Habtom went to Sudan," he told us. "The brokers make attempts to lure people even in the universities. Habtom was lured away by brokers. They told him he didn't have to pay. He came to Hitsats from university because he heard that his family in Eritrea had a financial crisis. Then the brokers lured him away." We were then told that Habtom was arrested on his first attempt to leave and was returned to the camp, but when we last heard, Habtom was gone again. Yirga looked sad and said, "Eritreans are very attached to their families. If their family has a problem, they have to do something. If they get a call from their mother saying 'I am in this situation,' then they do something."

This was not the first time we had heard about the predatory attempts of the brokers to lure young people away from the camp and the pressures that family crises back home in Eritrea placed on refugees. Residents of Hitsats camp were particularly familiar with the temptation of brokers. The camp was reputed to be a revolving door of sorts, where refugees were placed only to leave again. Concerns about brokers were addressed by the ARRA camp coordinator and members of the Refugee Coordinating Committee (RCC). As the RCC head told us:

> Traffickers are seductive. They use beautiful words, like when someone is talking to a beautiful woman. They say nice things. They tell people they have a brother in Belgium or Germany and describe how nice it is. It is not true. Traffickers cannot enter the camp, but there are people who are like "tributaries" to the traffickers. They tend to talk with people who are from the same zone [region of origin in Eritrea]. . . . The tributary then feeds to a trafficker who is also from that zone. Known traffickers can't enter the camp, but they'll have a sort of broker or recruiter who will enter the camp or lives there and will try to seduce people. These people won't report the traffickers to authorities because they come from Eritrea where no one trusts each other. This is the legacy of the Eritrean police state. Eritreans abroad pay their two percent tax, but don't inform young people about what is going on or the dangers of trafficking. The traffickers themselves seduce young people telling them that if they can get their relative to pay half of the cost, they [the trafficker] will pay the other half. This is a lie. These recruiters never tell of the risks of this. Only the good things.

Commentary on the predatory attempts of the brokers and the traffickers to lure refugees out of the camp was widespread. Their presence was described as pervasive. If needing to be available to attend appointments with UNHCR or to check for names on lists for resettlement disciplined the present of refugees waiting for legal resettlement, it would seem that the constant, nagging, seductive presence of brokers structured their present as well, particularly as they contemplated an irregular migration decision.

While brokers were described as persistent and relentless, what many migrants said had pushed them toward irregular migration was a much more acute sense of temporality—an emergency back home. Refugees often told us that a relative was facing a financial or health crisis at home, which led to a migration decision or a sort of intense temporal trauma if they decided to wait and not to migrate. One of the reasons for the acuteness of this crisis was that refugees left Eritrea in no small part to be able to help their families. They were fleeing political circumstances that were often experienced collectively, at the family and the community levels, meaning that by leaving, refugees felt they could alleviate not only their own suffering, but that of their family.

We would argue that this is not just a communal phenomenon but a temporal one as well. Being able to care for and safeguard the stability and security of one's extended family is a central part of growing up in the Eritrean context. As families are largely hierarchically organized, with members ranked in status based on a combination of age and wealth, older siblings often feel a deep sense of obligation to care for the entire family, while the rest of the members may try to improve their position in the hierarchy by seeking out channels through which to acquire wealth. This is a central part of the cosmologies that order Eritrean migration (Belloni 2019; see also Bernal 2014; Hepner 2009; Riggan 2013). Temporally, what this means is that familial pressures and expectations that Eritreans become members of the diaspora to care for the family push them to toward irregular migration. Thus, fleeing Eritrea and migrating onward become core strategies of making the future.

Migration in many ways is teleologically oriented, but not in the same way schools are; the ends of migration are located at a distant place and a distant future. As we noted earlier, the condition of refuge in a hosting state in the Global South, such as Ethiopia, creates a temporal paradox. A place like Ethiopia is a way station, and although it is a temporary stop, it may last indefinitely. This temporal paradox makes it futile to focus on the near future and adopt its teleological orientation— one that links the present to the near future in linear, planful ways. The distant future is far more logical. The refugees who were willing to wait in Ethiopia were the ones who seemed to be able to maintain hope for this distant future and to feel like they were actively taking steps to move toward it. However, the same logic that led them to stay could also turn on itself and push them to take risks and leave.

Prophetic future-making, whether through hope or risk, enables refugees to index the present to the distant future. Some were able to do so in a way that allowed them to wait hopefully. Others felt compelled to move riskily. The choice between legal and irregular migration was ever present and brought these two variants of future-making into a constant, tense relationship with each other. But choice also gave refugees a sense of agency over time. Perhaps ironically, choice enabled hope even though it also sometimes led to risk. A sense of urgency, such as that created by a crisis at home, could tip the balance from waiting hopefully to moving riskily. But the ongoing temporal trauma of waiting with little information about one's process could also shift unpredictably, leading a refugee to suddenly choose to migrate. These, however, were not the only two choices available to refugees. There were other ways of making the future.

Creativity and Future-Making

Many refugees dreamed big—or, perhaps more accurately, dreamed *long*. As researchers, we were frequently awed by the inventiveness and boldness of these dreams. Refugees not only knew a great deal more about various manifestations of the distant future than we did but believed in its tangibility and ordered their everyday lives to work toward it. They were not merely struggling to survive, a point many scholars of refugees have made; they were actively engaged in making their future regardless of whether they had decided to wait for it, to take risks for it, or to engage in a number of other future-making projects. While thinking about futures that involved migration or waiting for resettlement involved risks and suffering, attachments to the distant future in other spheres were often a source of joy, pleasure, and hope. Most importantly, a telos located in the near future did not figure significantly in the way they forged their futures. Refugees were making their future in a fundamentally different way.

At the end of chapter 3, we discussed the formation of ERUSA, the Eritrean Refugee University Student Association. We might argue that ERUSA was a bold attempt at future-making that rejected the failed teleologies imposed on refugees. ERUSA members had the audacity to imagine a very different kind of future for refugees in Ethiopia and behaved in ways that assumed that future already existed. For example, unlike many refugees in both camps and urban areas who believed they should be silent and thankful, ERUSA leaders never considered themselves to be docile guests, instead representing themselves as equals who could walk into the offices of ARRA officials and university administrators to boldly advocate for refugee university student needs. ERUSA was logical, strategic, tenacious. It was also keenly aware of the barriers and impediments in its way and did not assume its own success. In that sense ERUSA members had faith that by ordering their present as if it were already part of a particular future, that future would come to be.

Similarly, many refugees had creative entrepreneurial ideas for businesses and the arts. In addition to their many other ideas, Tesfay and Haile had a vision for a take-out coffee place that would serve cappuccinos in creatively shaped recyclable cones. This was visionary in a couple of ways, as it recognized that increasingly busy Addis Ababa residents might not have time (and often the means) to sit at a café and drink a cappuccino nor could Addis Ababa sustain the levels of pollution that plastic cups would bring. Gerie also had a vision; he hoped to build an internet café near a housing condominium where refugees resided. All the internet cafés were in the center of town, but refugees likely had greater need for them. Another refugee, a filmmaker, had dropped out of the university to move to Addis and pursue filmmaking, something he had done in Eritrea. He spent well over two hours with us one day detailing the complex and riveting plot of the film he hoped to make, a love story about shifting identities that are concealed and revealed in the context of flight and refuge. Another refugee discussed how migrants could use their phones to generate revenue in ways that bypassed the Ethiopian legal prohibition on refugees working or owning businesses. At first glance, these strategies might seem more pragmatic, planful, and oriented to the near future than the phenomena we discussed earlier. Indeed, these plans, which were developed by university students, are in many ways teleological. And yet they reject the teleological chronotope of education, calling its bluff, refusing to submit to its discipline and violence, instead daring to imagine a different, more inventive future. In this way, they attach the present to the distant future. The examples below illustrate even more pointedly how the distant future becomes a "phenomenological existential position" (Brun 2016, 401) as refugees work to move toward it even in the absence of knowing exactly how to get there.

Prophetic Time, Literally

In the school closing ceremony at the Mai Aini camp discussed in chapter 3 parents, staff, and students were given the chance to make comments. Most of them lauded the value of education and expressed concerns about the vast number of refugees who did not attend school. Many people noted that education was everything and was far more important than fleeing through irregular migration. One of the last speakers was a young woman who said she had stopped coming to school because of some problems. Iyob, who was sitting next to us, leaned over and whispered that her "problem" was that she had joined the followers of a local monk, and when her family was resettled, she chose to stay behind. She continued: "This year there were some good and bad students, some happy and some not happy. Some passed and some didn't. The students should come to school, just playing is not good. I dropped out because of my problem, but students should come to school. I felt bad to stop. Why did I stop? I have my own aim for the future. For the others they live in their houses. It's better to be in school because it's better to not be idle. It's better to create something for the future. This is the base of your life." At first, her words sounded like the typical "education talk" of disciplined teleological time—creating the future, avoiding idleness. We later realized this woman's story revealed a commentary on future-making rather than teleological time.

According to Iyob, there were about three or four hundred children who had begun to follow a radical Orthodox Christian monk in the camp who was convincing children to not be resettled in the United States. This monk himself was supposed to be resettled with his family as a child, but he had refused to go, fearing America to be the land of the devil. He remained in the camp and continued to frighten children about America by telling them that what violent movies portray is real, that gang hand signs are the devil's sign, and that the devil's number is in America. We wondered why anyone would forgo the highly coveted opportunity for resettlement. It turned out it was not just about fear but about the kind of future envisioned as an alternative. Iyob told us, "She didn't go with her family for resettlement because she thinks Jesus is coming."

Jennifer, trying to grasp the temporality of this choice, asked, "When?"

Iyob's answer revealed the logics of prophetic time: "I do not know the date." It is hard to think of a more ap illustration of the nature of prophetic time than waiting for the Second Coming of Christ. For these young followers of the monk, a point in distant future when Christ would return had become more tangible than the coveted distant future of resettlement. But more importantly, despite their locus in the distant future, resettlement and the Second Coming occupy a similar temporal position that is tangible, orders everyday life, and pressures important choices. This shows that refugees are faced with making choices not only between empty time, teleological time, waiting, and risk-taking but also between an array of distant futures, all of which order the present in very different ways.

Followers of this monk were dedicated to a pious present. They walked bare-foot, dressed simply, and lived together. There is a long tradition in Eritrean and Ethiopian Orthodox Christianity of including young people in the work of the church and of people abandoning the world to live piously and ascetically within the walls of the church or monastery, relying on alms and spending their days pray-ing. But in this case, the nearby orthodox monastery refused to support this monk, considering him too radical. Most of the people who followed the monk were boys, and there was nowhere to house girls, which was part of the problem for the young woman who spoke at the school closing ceremony. The present was oriented toward piety and simplicity and was disciplined not by date regimes of resettlement, the temptations of brokers, or the crises back home but by a rejection of immorality and a distant future oriented toward religious salvation.

The effects of choosing to wait for the Second Coming were powerful, material, and far-reaching. In the middle of this conversation, Berhane arrived and added to our understanding of this issue: "It is worse even than refusing to be resettled, because if the child is a minor, it messes up the whole family's resettlement case." He knew of several other specific cases where this had happened. In one case, a relative came from abroad to convince the child to do a resettlement interview, but the child refused to go. The relative tried to force the child to do the interview, and the child had the relative arrested after accusing him of kidnapping. In the end, the relative was released from jail, and the child was finally convinced to do the inter-view. "But I don't think the story is over," Berhane added. "He could refuse later in the process."

This is literally prophetic time in which the near future is abandoned for the distant prophesized future—in this case, the Second Coming. With both migration and its millenarian disavowal, the mundane world of incremental progress exists in a suspended state as a false promise. For millenarian followers, it is a spiritu-ally dangerous promise. Ironically, the prophetic time-making of millenarianism may be more successful than education in generating the desire among refugees to remain in Ethiopia. Its promises, after all, rest in the distant future and therefore parallel other forms of prophetic time-making. There is agency in deciding to reject something that others covet so much and in choosing a different prophecy—one that is biblical—over the prophecy of life in an evil land.

Material Fantasies: Futurism and Cryptocurrency

Before we conclude this chapter, we would like to return to our discussions with Tesfay and Haile. The two took us on a tour of the department where Tesfay was studying. Earlier, when Tesfay had shocked and awed us—and, frankly, talked way over our heads about his futuristic inventions—he shaped our imaginaries of glass-plated labs and scientists scurrying about with tablets and spotless white lab coats, like something from one of the science fiction movies that he had referenced. In re-ality the lab he had been allocated was a machine shop, and the materials he hoped to experiment with were in a scrap heap in one corner, seemingly discarded and uncared for. The disjuncture between the aspirations he had evoked and the space he had to work in was enormous. It was easy to see why he felt that the university was not the right home for his ambitions. As we toured the facility, Tesfay greeted everyone and was greeted warmly. Clearly, he was well liked. Toward the end of our tour, we visited the dean's office, where the sample of the plastic he had made was being held. He approached a secretary and asked if he could take it. He asked if the dean had had time to look at it yet, to which she replied that he had not. The plastic was a solid square, approximately one foot by one foot. He said he had tested its strength and endurance.

This square of plastic was the material embodiment of Tesfay's vision of the future. For Tesfay, it was a tangible representation that that future was possible, germinating possibilities for bulletproof fabric and circular, transparent bulletproof motorcycles. Far from the high-tech laboratories of Elon Musk—and perhaps as far from there as from the fictional laboratories of Stark Industries—Tesfay tinkered away at his inventions in a forgotten, dusty, and disheveled corner of the faculty of engineering at Addis Ababa University, producing a square of plastic on which he did not so much pin his hopes as he tried to create his own evidence that his vision of the future was not as fantastical as it might have seemed.

It would be easy to dismiss Tesfay's vision of the future as far-fetched. Instead, we suggest that in a world in which a near-future-oriented telos is out of reach and teleological time does harm, this kind of "fantasy" futurism is not only logical, it is the only way to remain hopeful and, therefore, sane. Tesfay's dreams of future inventions were a phenomenological strategy to claim control over time and to order the present toward the future in a particular way.

Throughout this chapter, we have shown that both legal resettlement and irregular migration are structured temporally as prophecies. The prophetic future is one in which the near future is irrelevant, and the distant future becomes a tangible thing to be worked toward as if it were a certainty, even though the materiality of when it will occur is never known.

When Tesfay was not busy tinkering with his inventions, he and Haile were deeply engaged in discussions with other refugees and students about Bitcoin. Indeed, when we saw him a few months later, he had not dropped out of school but he also did not want to talk about school. What he was really excited about was his cryptocurrency business, which seemed to be booming. They had to explain cryptocurrency sales to us several times. The dots did not quite add up, but in some ways, that was the point.

Bitcoin emerged in 2008 as one of several electronic currencies in circulation. It is "a system that uses a decentralized, peer-to-peer network to produce and transmit value tokens" (Swartz 2018, 6). Bitcoin can be acquired in exchange for goods, services, or other currency, much as most conventional currency is acquired. It can also be electronically mined. A limited number of minable Bitcoin mimics "the increasing scarcity of commodity mining" (Swartz 2018, 7) and therefore controls the value.

But in our conversation with Tesfay and Haile, the question we kept coming back to was where the immediate value came from—the kind of value that they seemed to derive from Bitcoin to be able to pay their rent. Tesfay and Haile attempted to explain to us how value transferred from Bitcoin to material goods and back to birr (Ethiopian currency), noting that in other countries, you could actually withdraw your Bitcoin from ATMs, but that was not yet possible in Ethiopia. The trajectory through which Bitcoin was transformed into value that Tesfay and Haile could actually make use of leapt over space and traveled from electronic symbol, to material goods, to paper symbol, following pathways that currency itself often traveled. For example, when Eritreans send remittances to relatives in Eritrea or elsewhere, hawala agents often make use of the same kinds of pathways that use currency in country A to purchase valuable material goods in country B that are exported and sold in country C, where the value transfers to local currency. This system is well understood, and its existence enabled brokers to transfer funds between people instantaneously at favorable rates, subverting banks and, in the case of Eritrea, the government. What we could not understand vis-à-vis Bitcoin was where the equivalent transfer of value in material goods was occurring. To the best of our understanding, unlike cash transfers through the hawala system, there was no import-export business to which it was attached. When we pushed on this point, Tesfay and Haile shifted to talk about how the mining of Bitcoin and the fact that only a limited number could be mined ensured that they would increase in value.

The "techno-economic imaginaries" of Bitcoin have been described as both prophetic and linked to precarity (Swartz 2018). As Lana Swartz notes, money is "always hypothesizing and projecting a particular future," but Bitcoin does this in a certain way that creates value by speculating on its own future value on the basis of a utopian vision of that future (2018, 2). It is also key that it emerged during a financial crisis and thus was arguably born of precarity, "distrust in institutions" (Swartz 2018, 2), and distrust in the teleological pathways through the near future that we had been told for so long were reliable. In other words, Bitcoin fundamentally relies on trust—in mathematics, in the community that mines them, and in a particular vision of the future. Swartz's analysis of Bitcoin also points out that it will create a new financial system that is anarchic, flattens access to wealth, and evades surveillance, but there are many critiques, and Bitcoin has strayed from its original vision. On one hand, high-tech "factory" mining of Bitcoin has changed the community on which it is based. Meanwhile, others say that the immediate value given to Bitcoin constitutes a Ponzi scheme (Swartz 2018).

Opinions about cryptocurrency vary wildly depending on the temporal frame through which one looks at it. Viewed teleologically through the lens of the near future, cryptocurrency may look like a giant pyramid scheme. Viewed prophetically, cryptocurrency looks like a revolution in the future tense, a way to wrest financial power from banks and the linear control over currency and value that powerful bankers have created simply by making rules and holding us all to them.

So, in selling shares in cryptocurrency, were our friends engaging others in a giant pyramid scheme? Or were they helping them get in on a new form of value that was more egalitarian, flatter, and more accessible to a population that had been systematically denied access to every other modality of increasing their income and creating stability? Answering this question is far beyond the scope of our research. But the Bitcoin investments were perhaps the most material of all of our examples of prophetic future-making based on a faith in a particular future—a future that refugees would typically not have access to.

Conclusion

For refugees in camps and in Addis Ababa, decisions about migration populated both the present and the future. By the time they arrive in a hosting state like Ethiopia, refugees are already "on their way." Migration decisions are hierarchically ordered as a "cosmology of destinations," with Ethiopia ranked low on the desirability of destinations (Belloni 2019). Whether refugees had an immediate or a distant plan to leave, the future was almost never imagined in Ethiopia. Understanding how refugees think of the relationship between present, near future, and distant future and how they hinge relationships with place to those different futurescapes illuminates the complex conditions that facilitate, inspire, shape, or forestall migration decisions. But to equate migration and places "out there" with the future would be an oversimplification of refugee future-making projects.

Desires to live elsewhere are not only about place-making; they are also a response to particular temporalities—specifically the temporality of progress. We would argue that for refugees, this is less about achieving a settled *end* than it is about wanting to be in a place where there is a possibility for time to move and progress toward something better.

Here we have explored various future-making projects and why some refugees are willing to wait indefinitely for resettlement or family reunification while others feel pressured to risk irregular migration. The orientation toward the distant future explains why Habtom chose the dangers of migration over a full university scholarship, why Tesfay and Haile thought they had more of a future in Bitcoin than at the university, and why some chose to wait in the camps for the Second Coming. These choices are framed by refugees' understanding of the relationship between an indeterminate and open-ended *end* in the distant future and life in the pause, or parentheses, of the present. Caught between the trauma of empty time and the violence of modernist teleological time, many refugees abandoned the near future in favor of the distant future, which can be the object of hope. As the near future has become evacuated in favor of a distant one, the idea that one can rationally plan for progress or have much control or power over the future is abandoned.

As with the caretaking activities we discussed in the last chapter, the kinds of future-making we have examined here are forms of care. More precisely, they emerge from a need to care for the future. They might be thought of as an effort to safeguard one's "capacity to aspire" (Appadurai 2004), to nurture "radical hope" (Kallio et al. 2021), and to enact "existential mobility" (Hage 2005) by "expecting to have expectations" (Bryant and Knight 2019).

But these methods of future-pointing caretaking are also always intertwined with forms of temporal violence and are thus risky. The future will always be, in large part, unknowable and outside of refugees' capacity to control. Prophetic time entails a radical temporal reorientation—"living in the present with the knowledge that what it means will only become clear in the millennial future" (Guyer 2007, 415). It entails living with a distant end point in mind and living in a way that both holds that end point open and connects with it somehow—magically, ritually, or hopefully—on a daily basis. For refugees, these efforts at making the future will seldom be effective at "tricking" the future (Ringel 2016; Moroşanu and Ringel 2016). The dots that we were desperately trying to connect in our conversation with Haile and Tesfay about Bitcoin value are never going to fully connect. Refugees know this, which is why hope is such a necessity. When hope fails, there is a risk of falling into stasis with "ruptures of process, demanding extraordinary effort to counteract and regain any sense of momentum" (Guyer 2007, 418). This is one of the reasons why many refugees choose the risks of irregular migration. It is also why the distant future keeps showing up in extremely creative and innovative ways. It shows up not only in dreams of migration but in faith in the Second Coming, the solvency of cryptocurrencies, or plans to invent something that is not yet technologically possible. While stuck in parentheses where time does not move and where one is subject to endless waiting and the incessant discipline of date regimes, it is easier to care for those points in the distant future than it is to care for the near future, where the evidence of teleological violence can be experienced daily. It is easier to have hope for those points on the horizon. Doing so enables living with the kind of inventiveness and creativity born of believing in a future that you cannot completely understand but are compelled to work toward. The dots may never connect, but there is evidence that for some, that distant future eventually arrives.

Notes

1. We derive our distinction between near future and distant future from Jane Guyer's 2007 work.

2. There is an increasingly vast literature on future-making (see, for example, Ringel 2016, 2021; Jansen 2008, 2014; Bryant and Knight 2019; Appadurai 2004). Our use of the term *future-making* is limited to a focus on making the distant future. In this way, we distinguish it from the near-future-oriented activities and the present-oriented activities discussed in earlier chapters.

3. Our thinking here again resonates with Felix Ringel's notion of tricking the future, which we mentioned earlier. According to Ringel (2016, 2021; see also Moroşanu and Ringel

2016), planning is a component of "tricking" the future. Although Ringel acknowledges that the capacity to trick time is not equally distributed, less attention is paid to how the future is tricked by those who have been deprived of the capacity to make plans that will be viable. In many ways, we are putting Ringel and Arjun Appadurai in conversation here by asking how the future gets "tricked" by people who lack the "capacity to aspire" (Appadurai 2004). Refugees have minimal likelihood of succeeding in tricking the future in terms of actually affecting outcomes, but the attempt to do so is an essential antidote against the suffering of camp time and the teleological violence inherent in linear, progress-oriented activities, such as schooling.

4. In a somewhat similar vein, Helga Nowotny (2018) argues that progress—with its linear temporal formulations—is dead. Nowotny and Guyer (2007) both call our attention to how the contemporary era has fundamentally altered the way we temporalize in general and think about the future in particular. They both note profound shifts as a result of the cyclical nature of late capitalism, the sense of simultaneity, and the pressure to innovate, which forestall the linear planning so prevalent in temporalities that emerged as a result of industrialization. However, where Guyer emphasizes the differences in the apprehension of the future, Nowotny emphasizes the increased cyclicality of the present.

5. Our notion of hegemonic temporalities comes from Paul Stubbs, who develops this Gramscian concept based on Michele Filippini's work (2017): "the notion of 'hegemonic temporality' [is] found in a re-reading of 'time' in Gramsci's work. 'Hegemonic temporality,' according to Filippini, is a force which prevails over other temporalities, overdetermining 'the rules of the struggle' (Filippini 2017, 106) while never managing to assimilate other temporalities completely" (Stubbs 2018).

6. For an exception, see Jansen (2008, 2014). Drawing on Guyer and others, Stef Jansen explores how the reconceptualization of the distant future reframes the present.

7. Increasingly, work on refugees and time has taken up this precise issue. Brun (2015) argues that there is agency in waiting. Kallio, Meier, and Häkli's (2021) notion of radical hope is another reframing of the phenomenologies of present and future.

8. The pressure that the near future places on the present is the kind of teleological violence we described earlier. Schools are adept at producing these pressures but are certainly not the only institution to do so. In contrast, the kinds of caretaking activities we discussed in the previous chapter enable the present to be bearable.

9. Hope, in the way we use it, is fundamentally agentive. There is a good deal of debate in the literature about hope as emotional disposition or affect versus hope as a way of framing agency, action, or choice. Hope has traditionally been thought of as an affect or emotion, as in a *feeling* of hopefulness (Bloch et al. 1986). Building on this, Hirokazu Miyazaki (2006) describes hope as a method, a way of being that points toward an indeterminate future. Moving away from the distinction between hope as affect versus action, Jansen (2016) usefully differentiates between intransitive hope, which is both a state of being and an affective feeling of hopefulness, and transitive hope, which has an object and is oriented toward a particular end or ends. This is the difference between "being hopeful" and hoping for something specific. The intransitive form of hope is more akin to Miyazaki "hope as method" or hope as a way of being. However, when scholars talk about the unequal distribution of hope (Hage 2016; Appadurai 2004), it is not completely clear whether they are speaking about hope in its intransitive form or its transitive form. We are mostly thinking of hope in its transitive form—for example, the hope for life in another place, the hope for resettlement, the hope for policies that would allow refugee graduates to work. While we did not find that refugees had an abundance of hopefulness (intransitive), we did observe that they were actively engaged in the act of hoping for something.

10. Felix Ringel (2016) notes that "By predicting, forecasting, prophesising, conjuring, pro- and evoking, adumbrating, dreading, hoping, planning, projecting, envisioning, arranging, intending, designing, budgeting, aligning, organizing, coordinating, we attempt to subject the future content of the progression of time to our agency" (2016, 8). We note that many of these modes of "tricking" (or enacting agency over) the future are products of modernist teleology. For example, predicting and forecasting are practices that often require forms of knowledge and technology only available to elites. Meanwhile, planning, budgeting, organizing, and coordinating are all technologies of modern forms of organization, bureaucracy, and institutions. They are modalities associated with modernist teleological time. They are also the types of temporal agency that students are expected to master in the process of schooling but that refugees find will not—and cannot—bring about their desired future.

11. There is some debate on whether hope is damaging or helpful. Lauren Berlant's (2011) notion of cruel optimism suggests that hope is damaging, as it encourages people to engage in actions that are not in their interest. Meanwhile, other scholars see hope as a critical form of agency that endows us with the imaginative and agentive capacity to bring future potentialities into the present in meaningful ways (see Bryant and Knight 2019). When we think about the function of hope in our field site, we find ourselves wanting to view it as neither a bane nor a boon but as a social fact, an unavoidable necessity. While cruel optimism forms a central component of our discussion of teleological violence and hopes invested in education were certainly damaging, we see the kinds of distant-future-oriented hopes that we are discussing in this chapter as distinct. At the same time, we do not think that hope is always rooted in things that can potentially come to pass.

12. We turn to studies of magic, in part, as an alternative form of "time tricking." As stated in an earlier note, many of the modalities of time tricking discussed by Ringel are unavailable to refugees. We find that studies of magic, particularly those that put magic in conversation with modern institutions (Geschiere 1997; Whitehead and Finnström 2013), highlight other modalities of tricking the future. Anthropological theories of magic are fundamental to understanding how people confront unpredictable and high-stakes circumstances (Malinowski [1925] 1954), interpret the workings of power in the world, and exert agency (Geschiere 1997; West 2008; Whitehead and Finnström 2013).

13. Drawing on the broad literature on the anthropology of magic, Neal Whitehead and Sverker Finnström (2013) apply the framework of magic to modern, high-tech warfare, using it to explore an array of phenomena including drone warfare, video games, forecasting, and the role of cultural expertise in the military. We adapt and adopt their perspective on magic to suggest that processes of legal resettlement appear similarly magical.

14. For example, Peter Geschiere (1997) uses magic to make sense of politics that are profoundly disempowering, David Price (2013) and Jeffrey Sluka (2013) use it to explain drone warfare, and Roberto J. González uses it to explore military forecasting (2013).

15. Relinquishing a scholarship might also be thought of as a necessary sacrifice, part of the "global rule of magic" in which the possibility of future reward is proportional to sacrifices made (Stroeken 2013).

16. This was an urban refugee, so his orientation was toward the capital city of Ethiopia. Suffice it to say that the camps were even less desirable to live in. Indeed, after study of both urban and rural refugees, it would seem that most urban refugees felt just as unsettled as camp refugees.

Conclusion

In October 2019, a year after our last research trip to the refugee camps in northern Ethiopia, Berihu sent us pictures of his newborn son. He had recently married an old friend who arrived during the brief window when the border between Ethiopia and Eritrea was open. When we last spoke in person, marriage and having a child had not entered into Berihu's thinking.

Berihu's story reflects the oscillations between the creative agency of time-making and the temporal suffering that we have explored throughout this book. He had recently graduated when we met him and had hopes for progress through further study or some form of professional employment; however, he lacked the connections needed to navigate the prohibitions on refugees working in the formal sector and wound up stuck in the camp, where he took a teaching job for incentive pay. Although he believed in the work, he quickly became disillusioned and sank into despair. He pulled himself out of it with meaningful caretaking work. He taught in the local elementary school, tutored youth through the Save Eritrean Seeds program that we discussed in chapter 4, started his first business (a bar), and began to farm (illicitly) on the rocky land behind it. He was simultaneously caring for the earth, the youth, his community, and himself.

Caretaking kept Berihu going but did not fulfill his aspirations, particularly as structural barriers to success repeatedly got the better of him. His business failed. He was repeatedly told that he could not pursue higher education. He moved his business to a different part of town, abandoning his efforts at farming. He still held out hopes for a life where he could progress.

Having a child and investing that child with hopes and dreams is, in many ways, an example of both caretaking and future-making. "I just live for today. I wish my son will get a better life for the future. I stopped wishing for myself to be successful. Maybe my son will hope for that. Maybe this is my last stage, my last place. The condition I am living in will be my last, with poverty and stress. But maybe my son will have hope for a different future," Berihu wrote to Amanda. His hopes hinged on the distant future, as he appeared to be accepting life in parentheses, in the pause, in the empty present.

Like running a shop, completing a vocational training course, or any one of a number of other forms of caretaking, caring for a child structures daily life around meaningful work. Starting a family enables refugees like Berihu to imagine a future that goes beyond the bleak near term and is more distant and expansive than the bounds of an individual life. But unlike these other forms of caretaking, raising a child is a constant source of temporal suffering—a reminder of time moving forward, the stuckness and profound precarity of the near future in refugee camps, and the impossibility of linear, incremental progress. Starting a family and raising a child with care, love, and hope infuses meaning into the chronic present but also requires brutal honesty about the suffering inherent in the indefinite temporariness of that present and in the risky and unpredictable nature of the future.

But Berihu, it turned out, had not sacrificed hope for himself. He continued to talk about resettlement and worked extremely hard to seek scholarships abroad. He never abandoned his aspirations and goals, which were, in no small part, put in place by and through his education. And yet, he was constantly reminded of the limitations of his life in the camp. Even amid the foreclosure of options, refugees like Berihu are tenacious and insist on having choices.

Throughout this book, we have explored a variety of temporalities: 1) the complex and paradoxical temporalities of humanitarianism; 2) the utopian teleologies of developmentalism; 3) the temporalities of hospitality; 4) the condition of temporal suffering found in the stasis and stuckness of waiting in both the camp and cities; 5) the teleological orientation toward near future progress found in education; and 6) the orientation toward hopeful points in the distant future.[1] Some of these temporalities are explicitly teleological, while others are not necessarily so, and some are forms of time stripped of telos, such as empty time in the camp. Teleologies themselves may vary. They may be linked with modernist notions of progress or be indeterminate and open-ended. They may focus on the near future with its spaces of temporal discipline and planfulness or on the distant future, imagination, creativity, hope, and risk.

We conclude by bringing home several central assertions of our book. First, teleological time operates hegemonically to simultaneously frame both policy mandates and refugee desires for progress.[2] Notions of teleological progress wend their way through humanitarian policy and practice as well as refugees' strategies of time-making. Second, even amid great constraints and violence, refugees *make time*. They make time meaningful and make choices based on their assessment of the balance of different temporalities. The policy frameworks that form the context of this book do not leave space for this kind of decision-making or for an understanding of future-making strategies that simultaneously hold open the possibility of multiple futures. Even though understanding how refugees make temporal choices will not resolve the vast problem of teleological violence, there are lessons to be learned from observing their strategies of time-making. Finally, refugee hosting in countries in the Global South, such as Ethiopia, is profoundly precarious and unstable. Refugees know this, but policy directions are often premised on the assumption that these large hosting states are and will remain stable. The kinds of places that refugees are relegated to in the name of progress may be the most profound form of teleological violence. These understandings of the way refugees make sense of and choose between temporalities amidst precarity and teleological violence can and should inform local policy and refugee management practices.

Choice and Time-Making

Teleological time and notions of progress are prevalent in the multiplicity of temporalities that refugees and policy actors are engaged with. These teleologies are hegemonic, but this does not mean that they deprive people of agency. Refugees retain the capacity to make choices about how they think about, plan for, fill up, or abandon time in the present, near future, and distant future, even as their choices are constrained and influenced by teleological notions of progress.

Throughout this book, we have centered refugees awareness of their lack of power over time and their efforts to maintain a semblance of choice amid that lack of power. Time-making reveals the delicate balance of laying claim to teleological time and making meaning out of time without telos. This delicate balance framed the present, the future, and the relationship between them. Refugees continued to care for the present and make their lives as meaningful as possible, despite constantly being pushed back into the "enforced presentism" (Guyer 2007) of the "chronic present" (Dunn 2017). If refugees' focus on the present was on making life bearable and more livable through acts of caretaking, their focus on the future was on advocating for the right to progress—in other words, the right to have a future where they can "expect to have expectations" (Hage 2009) and exercise the "capacity to aspire" (Appadurai 2004). Refugees struggled because of the teleological violence and false hopes offered by education but did not give up on education; rather, they organized and advocated for their right to progress and to achieve "existential mobility" (Hage 2009).

Still, teleological violence is painful and dangerous. Refugees are stuck in a time where they often feel deprived of telos, even when there is the appearance of it being offered to them. Furthermore, the stuckness of the camp appears more sticky given the prevalence of teleological ideals that constantly assert the promise of progress. Under these conditions, refugees do more than merely survive but are a long way off from thriving.

Caretaking in the present is not a replacement for having a future in which time appears to move and refugees have the capacity to progress. For this reason, future-making, as another form of time-making, is a companion to caretaking. Future-making enables care for the future by allowing refugees to cultivate and protect, or at times, invent and act on, alternative futures. This sometimes leads to the abandonment of the kind of near-future plans that are often associated with teleological activities, such as schooling, and instead makes the future a site of creativity and inventiveness.

The orientation to the distant future, along with caretaking in and for the present, is a double-edged sword. It makes indefinite periods of waiting possible, but it also creates pressures that lead to migration. When does caretaking for the present and the future lead to waiting, and when does it lead to migration? How does it frame refugees' choices? To understand what enables refugees to choose to wait in the present rather than to leave requires us to explore the forces that place pressure on the present.

One factor that makes waiting more tenable is the meaning refugees are able to derive from their caretaking activities. This is why vocational education and recreational programming such as sports, art, and small business development programs were important to refugees. It was not that refugees had any illusions that these programs would produce a better future, but they did serve to fill the present meaningfully. Hope makes waiting bearable and meaningful, and the loss of hope can make migration seem like the only option. Education, with its disciplined orientation toward the near future and its constant markers of time moving forward, was one such thing that could pressure the present and make it less bearable.

Conversely, waiting became untenable when caretaking activities failed, were not supported, or were undermined. Caretaking initiatives were essential to making the permanent temporariness of the present bearable but were always at risk of being forestalled. The closure of the International Rescue Committee (IRC) youth center in the Mai Aini camp was often talked about as a great loss, for example. Failing businesses were a lingering reminder of a stalled future. And refugee university students felt tremendously frustrated when they faced bureaucratic barriers to offering enrichment programming in the camps. The precariousness of caretaking meant that it was intertwined with temporal suffering.

What also enabled refugees to wait was making the future meaningful through future-making. As we detailed in the last chapter, successful cases of resettlement coupled with concrete indications that a *process* was moving forward made waiting less painful. Although resettlement remained an elusive point in the distant future, that future came to feel more tangible if there were indications that it might come to pass one day or that there were specific, meaningful actions refugees could take to influence that future. However, the distance that refugees felt from resettlement processes—a distance that was reinforced by physical barriers, such as talking to UNHCR representatives through glass plates, and temporal ones, such as being rationed a certain amount of time per quarter with a representative—sometimes led to an abandonment of hope and its replacement with the equally prophetic temporalities of risk.

Knowledge about the dangers of the migration route, constricting border control policies in Europe, and the difficulties faced once migrants arrive in their "target" countries—all components of many migration-deterrence campaigns—did not seem to have much impact on refugees' sense of their choices. We found that refugees were well aware of these dangers. Knowledge of the risks of migration was present alongside awareness of its possibilities. There were always options. It might seem counterintuitive that anyone would take these incredible risks knowingly, and indeed, before deciding to migrate, refugees tend to plan intensively for months in advance. Their willingness to risk life, liberty, and safety may not make sense if we are thinking teleologically and see the refugee journey as a series of incremental steps toward something better. But if we understand that many refugees perceive time as having stopped moving, we can make sense of the decision to migrate as a means to make time move again. Temporally this decision is structured similarly to the decision to wait for resettlement. Both are end points that sit prophetically outside of the linear timeline, outside one's immediate control. They are both arrived at through faith and hope and not consistent durational activity.

In contrast, one thing that pressures the present is a sense of personal or family crisis. Crises may create an acute pressure on the timeline, pushing refugees to exchange the temporality of hopeful waiting for risky movement (Belloni 2019). What ultimately pressured Habtom to move on was word that his parents back home in Eritrea were facing difficulties and needed money. This is not uncommon. Milena Belloni discusses this phenomenon in detail, noting that pressures from home and acute family crises frequently drove migrants to take risks. We often heard that refugees were pressured to migrate because they had heard that a family member was sick or financially in need. Alternately, refugees who heard that their families needed them and chose not to migrate often faced severe distress, succumbing to periods of depression, malaise, and drinking. Waiting became untenable when refugees faced news of a crisis at home. The stress of waiting then pressured them to choose either the temporality of hope or that of risk, both of which are prophetically oriented toward the distant future, but require very different actions.

Teleological time also pressures the present by setting expectations for the near future—particularly expectations about its alignment with the distant future. These thwarted expectations can result in refugees choosing risk over hope or despair. Being stuck back in the camp after graduation involves the steady erosion of possibility and the fading of credentials that were obtained through the discipline and hard work of schooling. These unfulfilled aspirations, along with an awareness of one's unmet potential, press painfully on the present.

What Can We Learn from the Creativity of Time-Making?

One of our favorite places to visit in the Mai Aini refugee camp was the Jesuit Refugee Services (JRS) compound. It was a cacophony of noise and sound. A basketball game was always going on outside. In one room, students learned to play keyboards and guitars. In another room, a boom box played loud music while a dance troop rehearsed. Next door, children took an art class in a room covered with drawings. Around back, a dozen or so women sewed handmade reusable sanitary napkins, an entrepreneurial project that they hoped would become self-sustaining.

What was striking about the JRS compound, in addition to the noise and the obvious joy, was the absence of alienating humanitarian bureaucracy. There was little waiting and lots of activity. The mood was also decidedly different than it was in schools where refugees and Ethiopian national students alike were disciplined by the teleological ordering of the daily schedule, the school week, the academic year, and beyond. In the JRS compound, refugees were actively creating—sewing, learning an instrument, dancing, drawing. They were making things, not just filling time, and in doing so, they were making time meaningful.

We could make a compelling argument that far too little attention is paid to the vastly creative and inventive elements of the refugee experience. Indeed, scholars such as Oliver Shao have demonstrated that an attention to dancing and making music can complicate the image of the refugee as a burden or icon of crisis, importantly shifting research toward a social justice lens by shedding light on and potentially rectifying "the oppressive forces that shape our shared world" (2017). In the course of our fieldwork, we observed a handful of NGOs that were precisely concerned with supporting and encouraging refugee creativity—and therefore humanity. JRS was known for doing this kind of work. Similarly, the Danish Refugee Council supported musicians and held weekly cultural sessions in the Hitsats camp. Vocational education programming run by the Norwegian Refugee Council (NRC) often focused on creativity. As we were conducting an interview with a program coordinator at NRC, we became aware of the delicious smell of fried fish wafting into the room and the sound of laughter and talking. When we finished our interview, we walked past a room full of refugees who were enrolled in a culinary training program enjoying the food they had prepared. Another day, we stumbled on a graduation ceremony for an International Rescue Committee beautician training program. We were instantly swept up in the joy of the moment and asked to pose for pictures with the robe-clad graduates. We posit that the joy in these events had nothing to do with teleological time or the near future. Refugees were well aware that there were no job prospects in the camp for them as beauticians or chefs (although, interestingly, musicians could get work playing at events like weddings and the JRS dance troop did tour in other parts of the country at times). The joy derived from these activities came from the way they filled the present and attached to a distant future. Refugees also noted that these vocational programs might give them skills they could use when they left Ethiopia, but they did not expect them to be useful while they still lived there. In contrast, this programming had to be rationalized to funders as meeting a larger objective—providing protection, education, or supporting livelihoods. These policy priorities did not support refugees' creative endeavors, their efforts to fill the present meaningfully, or their dreams of a distant future elsewhere. Refugee and policy priorities seemed to make sense of the same activities in very different ways.

We considered including a list of policy recommendations in this conclusion to highlight the essential nature of the kind of programming that supports refugees' efforts to care for the present and formulate a future; however, such a policy framing would itself be taken as a teleological tool to suggest that the refugee condition can be fixed or improved somehow in order to bring their suffering to an end. We believe the refugee condition is fundamentally flawed and cannot be ended without a radical reorientation of the global system of migration management and humanitarianism. We add our voices to the compelling critiques by the many scholars who have argued that the humanitarian system will never be able to deliver the kinds of lives that refugees need and deserve. We return to that discussion in the next section.

Having acknowledged that no policy recommendation is capable of "fixing" the global humanitarian system, engaging with a list of what-if measures is still a useful exercise. Such what-if exercises illuminate our flawed assumptions about refugees and how to "help" them and also give us a mechanism to shift our paradigms in how we think about them. What would happen if we shifted the paradigm with which we think about refugees as temporal agents and biographical subjects rather than biopolitical objects of humanitarian intervention (Brun 2016)? What if we—researchers, policy makers, and humanitarian workers—embraced the ambiguity of the refugee condition? What if we named the impossibilities of that condition and its vast injustices and still thought creatively and respectfully about how refugees rise to the challenge of living that life every day? What if we followed refugees' lead by attending to and supporting their efforts and aspirations rather than imposing our own teleologically derived frameworks on them?

We suggest that a list of policy recommendations based on this kind of paradigm shift would encourage ongoing support for the kinds of programming that we described at the beginning of this section as well as for the provision of spaces for leisure and community gatherings, such as the closed IRC youth club. Given that refugees work very hard to ameliorate the pain of the endless present and that doing so often makes the long period of waiting and uncertainty tenable, any activity or space that supports their efforts by filling the present in meaningful ways is essential to staving off temporal suffering and stemming the flow of onward migration. These kinds of programming do not necessarily have to yield future results to be successful. Indeed, the imagined futures posited by vocational training are impossible. What would happen if the explicit policy goals of such programming better enabled refugees to care for the present?

Even more importantly, to support caretaking, it is essential for NGOs to learn about and support refugees' own grassroots efforts to care for their community. Efforts by such organizations as the Eritrean Refugee University Student Association (ERUSA) and Hawat fill an essential gap, making camp life modestly safer and better. These kinds of initiatives make refugees feel that they have agency over their own lives and communities.

Attention to the future is also vital. We were repeatedly told of the hardships that a life of stuckness entails. Again and again, we were exposed to refugees' dismay, anger, and suffering on realizing that there was no reliable, legal way out of Ethiopia that did not involve interminable waiting for something that may never come to pass. In a focus group with urban refugees, we spoke with Dawit, a talented refugee who had fled Eritrea with his son and wife. He was highly educated, was fluent in English, and had good family connections in Ethiopia. In other words, he was doing better than most. An NGO employed him to do interviews with Eritrean refugees in Addis Ababa. He was not paid for this work because refugees were not allowed to be employed by the NGOs that were there to assist them. However, he and the others working on this project were given a transportation stipend, which proved to be vital income for many. Dawit was not desperate for money and was mainly doing this work to remain professionally and personally active. He had been in Ethiopia for only eight months when I interviewed him to learn about his research findings. His concerns were familiar:

> As a refugee I haven't stayed long. What I learned is that some of the legal processes that should take a few years or months, take longer than you can believe. Some have stayed for 12 years and some for 6 years. This gave me a scare. As a refugee I don't have a permanent status here. I don't have a sustainable future for my kid. This makes you question whether your decision to come to Ethiopia was correct. This was quite frightening for me. You could see refugees that could go in [thinking they will stay for] two or three years tops and they stay for 7 or 8 years. This is quite a heavy thing.

Dawit continued, articulating the frustrations with the lack of clear information from UNHCR and the difficulties with getting an appointment and communicating with resettlement officers. He clearly noted what was needed to make this process less frustrating and more dignified: "What I am saying is if UNHCR could put a few guidelines about what programs are entitled to particular groups of refugees, it would create a better understanding than what is present now. . . . *UNHCR needs to get to the level of the refugees.* Most refugees aren't even at a basic education level. They can read and write, but they don't understand policies. Some refugees don't even understand that they are refugees with no rights. They don't understand what they are getting here in Ethiopia" (emphasis added).

Dawit was asking organizations such as UNHCR to figure out how to communicate clearly with refugees. Resettlement processes are notoriously opaque, leading refugees to theorize about them through accounts of corruption and stolen resettlement opportunities. Repeatedly, we heard refugees explain that there was no clarity about these policies. Repeatedly, we heard humanitarian workers say that they were being as clear as they could be and that refugees' expectations were unrealistic. "They think that they have the right to be resettled," one humanitarian worker told us. "They are very entitled."

What accounts for this discrepancy between the assertion by humanitarian workers and resettlement staff that they are being clear and the confusion and complaints about a lack of clarity among refugees? This question was beyond the scope of our research but is something that humanitarian organizations need to address.

What if resettlement officers and humanitarian workers made it a priority to be on the same level as refugees? What if they took it on themselves to understand why there are such vast misunderstandings between refugees and resettlement staff? What if, instead of labeling refugees as "entitled," they tried to understand what resettlement means to refugees and how it functions as a temporal choice?

Ultimately, the refugees who populate these pages want a future that will lead somewhere—not necessarily to a particular location but toward the possibility of progress. We are accustomed to thinking about the choices that refugees make as choices between places—the choice of whether to go or to stay. Refugee policies, particularly this new wave of policies, reify the spatiality of this choice and ignore the temporal dimensions of refugees' decision-making. Other studies have emphasized the agency that refugees and other displaced people exert through place-making, which pushes us beyond the purely biological emphasis of humanitarian biopolitics (Hammond 2004; Rishbeth and Powell 2013; Vasey 2011). We have suggested throughout this book that exploring refugee agency and choice through the lens of time allows us to see a much more volatile and fluid field—an alternate logic in which safety and danger, need and the satisfaction of those needs, look very different than they do if we focus narrowly on the biological being of the refugee or on the places where those biological beings reside and might be incentivized to make a life.

If place-making is about making space—including spaces in which one is forced to live—into a place endowed with meaning and relationships, then time-making is about laying a similar claim to time. Just as refugees make undesirable places bearable by infusing them with sociality and relationships, so too do they inhabit (and creatively make) particular points in time—the present, the near future, the distant future, and the past—crafting them and imbuing them with particular meanings. Just as place-making for refugees is an enactment of agency amid severe spatial constraints, time-making is an enactment of agency amidst temporal constraints. The present is rife with limited possibilities and elongated in painful ways. The near future, often teleologically ordered, is painful because what it promises— and the expectations it engenders—more often than not, turns out to be myths. It takes little effort to reveal that the promises of teleological time and the incremental way that it aligns the present with the near future will never come to pass for refugees who are ultimately thrust back into a subject position that demands gratitude and punishes those who are too demanding.

Time-making in this sense is a political project. It is an act of care that evades the politics of care with which humanitarian biopolitics is imbued. It is a politics that asserts that every human life has the right to progress and the capacity to imagine a future that is not stuck in the interminable present. What if policy makers, researchers, and humanitarian actors of all kinds engaged with refugees in this politics of time-making?

Earlier, we noted how understanding refugees' temporal priorities might enable solidarities to form that could make the present better and the distant future more hopeful. It is important to focus on the everyday lived realities refugees face and refugee aspirations to appreciate how they open the world with creative future-work and care. But that is not enough. We also have to understand the profound damage done by global forms of teleological violence at work within these new incarnations of humanitarian and migration management policy.

The Teleological Violence of the Humanitarian-Security-Development Nexus

What we have called the *humanitarian-security-development nexus* is a form of borderwork intended to safeguard the borders of Europe through stringent forms of migration management and deterrence that simultaneously appear compassionate while also constraining migration. This concept derives from notions of compassionate borderwork (Little and Vaughn-Williams 2016) and the ideal of a humanitarian-security nexus that patrols the borders in the Global North in an ostensibly humane way while masking the overarching goal of securing borders (Rumford 2008; Jones et al. 2017; Pallister-Wilkins 2017). We have argued that setting up hosting states in the Global South as viable long-term refugee hosts is a component of these broader, global processes of borderwork and humanitarian security. The humanitarian-development-security nexus shifts the locus of European border protection southward while also layering the temporality of development onto the already contradictory temporalities of humanitarianism.

More specifically, the policy approaches driven by influential scholarly works (such as Betts and Collier 2017) and introduced in Ethiopia (and elsewhere) at the time of our fieldwork function as a component of humanitarian security, bordering, and migration deterrence. Here we would like to build on arguments made in chapter 1 to explore the way this particular form of transnational migration-deterrence functions to reinforce a racialized, global form of teleological violence.

What we have termed *teleological violence* is the systematic inculcation of a specific set of beliefs about progress and the equally systematic deprivation of the capacity to move toward those notions of progress. In chapter 1, we argued that the emphasis on local integration and developmentalism is a form of teleological violence because it pushes refugees toward a particular *end* by holding open the possibility that they can have a permanent, viable life in the host state but does not address the structural barriers (such as land, labor, and citizenship laws) to that life. The policy shift that formed the context for our fieldwork proposed to resolve the problem of the durable solutions through long-term hosting of refugees in the Global South and a revamped version of local integration. The merger of humanitarian and development efforts was central to this approach. Development and local integration were bundled with migration deterrence. This was problematic for a number of reasons. It neglected the fact that the success of the proposed development initiatives had not yet been demonstrated. It also neglected the very different temporalities of development and humanitarianism.

The complex and paradoxical temporalities of humanitarianism are at once slow and urgent, terminal and interminable, yet they are constantly (if futilely) seeking an end point to crises. As a crisis response mechanism, we might think of the temporality of humanitarianism as urgent, fast-paced, and responsive. And indeed, the humanitarian apparatus is designed to function this way. However, for the people *in* crisis, humanitarianism is always too slow, and the experience of being under the care of this apparatus is the experience of having to wait for bureaucracies that are always sluggish.

Protracted refugee situations only exacerbate this paradox. The urgency of the immediate crisis fades, but the crisis never reaches an end. As such, refugees are subject to the slow bureaucratic time of humanitarianism and the emptiness of the endless present. The sluggishness of humanitarianism is full of risks. These include boredom, the temporal suffering of waiting, and mental and physical health risks associated with what Peter Redfield calls "minimalist biopolitics" (2005). The biopolitical apparatus of humanitarianism may keep the largest number of refugees possible alive, but just barely. Food and medical care may be scarce, and preventable disease is prevalent.

The durable solutions promise an *end* to protracted refugee situations through three channels: repatriation, resettlement, and local integration. There has been much critique of these so-called solutions. Scholars argue that the global refugee regime has been an utter failure at providing any sort of durability and has only created a state of limbo and protracted precarity for refugees (Betts and Collier 2017; Long 2014). Local integration, in particular, while appearing to provide an end, often results in a series of partial, rather than permanent, statuses (Hovil 2014).

The policy clusters we have written about here were called on not only to address the crisis of humanitarianism but also to deter northward migration and thereby move toward an *end* to the so-called refugee crisis. But for whom or what entity did these new policies propose this end? The durable solutions are arguably more focused on absolving the humanitarian apparatus of responsibility than on caring for refugees, on providing an *end* to the organizational responsibility of humanitarian organizations rather than for refugees. At the same time, emphasizing local integration as *the* preferred durable solution promises an *end* to northward migration. By simultaneously absolving the humanitarian apparatus from this responsibility for protection and positing local integration as a viable end to migration, these policies become a component of what Tricia Redeker Hepner and Magnus Treiber refer to as a globally emerging "anti-refugee machine" that erodes rights to claim asylum in the Global North while relegating refugees to the Global South (2021). These policies seemed to signal the end of (or at least a rolling back of) internationally mandated care.

The focus on a revamped form of local integration in these new policy directions leans heavily on the teleology of development, but these are problematic. They assert the hegemony of teleological notions of progress. Even if they fail to make good on their promised progress, they function as a powerful engine to shape desires and aspirations (Ferguson 1999; Katz 2004; Mains 2011). Development is adept at creating beliefs about progress, but actual development projects and policies often fail to bring about progress.[3] These failures to change people's lives materially and the successful promotion of the idea that things should be improving create a sensation of time being stuck or even moving backward. James Ferguson notes how the failures of modernization combined with neoliberal policies and structural adjustment, which were "so long narrated in terms of linear progressions and optimistic teleologies," came to be seen as a "slipping backward: history, as it were, running in reverse" (1999, 13).[4]

This combined assertion of the hegemony of teleological progress and its failure to yield actual progress has been felt throughout the postcolonial world. Studies of education and the failure of degrees to bring about promised progress are a particularly acute site of time appearing to move backward (Jeffrey et al. 2004, 2005, 2008). Specific to Ethiopia, neoliberal approaches to economic development and state formation shape Ethiopian developmentalism where high modernist teleologies still promise a trajectory toward progress in spite of producing high levels of inequality and declining wealth for the poorest (DiNunzio 2019; Mains 2011).

The teleology of development promotes spatial assumptions as well temporal ones. Progress, or the capacity to make time move meaningfully, is often posited as being located in a specific place or places, as we noted earlier (Dick 2010, 2018; Belloni 2019). Useful here to capture this relationship between time and space is Mikhail Mikhaïlovich Bakhtin's notion of the chronotope (2010).[5] Hilary Parsons Dick helps us track linkages between broader, national, transnational, or globally circulating imaginaries of time and temporality and the ways individuals talk about the effects of time and space in everyday lives (2010).[6] Chronotopes of progress and development are teleological in the sense that they assume movement toward a particular end. But they also fundamentally constitute some as farther back in time and lower in status, poised at an early stage of advancement, making marginalization seem natural and the scarcity of resources legitimate. Modernist teleologies thus promote particular notions of progress and produce desires for particular places because only particular places are posited as spaces where time can move.

Notions of progress that refugees and migrants carry with them are also spatialized in particular ways. Migration destinations are hierarchically organized in what Belloni calls "cosmologies of migration" (2019). These cosmologies, while bound up with a distinctly Eritrean political economy of migration, are ordered by teleological assumptions about the trajectory of progress. Countries that are less valued destinations of migration are places where progress is less possible, while the more "desirable" countries are spaces where progress is imagined to be more possible. Belloni's notion of cosmologies of destinations thus points to a migrational telos. This cosmological, hierarchical ordering of destinations is temporal, placing some places ahead and some behind (Dick 2018). Because no one wants to be stuck in a place that is behind, these hierarchies can lead to greater risk-taking (Belloni 2019) and dedication to repeated attempts at border crossing (Andersson 2017), particularly when other options are foreclosed. Migration trajectories are thus a product of the broader global temporalizations that posit the "north" as a viable location where one can progress and the "south" as a precarious place of stuckness and danger.

Refugees' spatialization of progress is disjunctive from the spatialization of progress inherent in the policy initiatives we have discussed here. In other words, refugees and migrants tend to locate progress in the Global North, while policy initiatives seek to relegate those from the Global South to developmental spaces within the Global South. The ends of both are ordered by global spatial and temporal teleologies of progress.

These global teleologies also relegate racialized subjects to spaces and temporalities where progress either moves ahead or is stalled. Shahram Khosravi, drawing on Frantz Fanon, notes the colonial racialization of time, which relegates non-Europeans to a space of "belatedness":

> Colonial racism is built on the idea of the belatedness of non-Europeans. A black person, a non-European, a colonized person arrives to white time, and it is already too late. She arrives to a pre-existing world of meanings, a world already shaped, in which a non-European is not a subject with a history and agency but is only an object, fixed as a category and imagined in a different temporality.
>
> Part of the colonial condition is the racialization of time. Racialization of time means *the other* arrives to a world in which bodies are already divided. A world where access to resources and power is allocated according to this logic of belatedness. To a white time that is assumed and presented as secular, civilized, modern, progressive, neutral, the racialized other always arrives too late. (Khosravi 2021, 66)

The logic of belatedness casts the non-European as an object belonging to a different temporality, a temporality where access to progress and what Arjun Appadurai terms "the capacity to aspire" (2004) need not exist because those are not expected in places that are behind or belated; they are expected in places where time moves toward progress. We consider the colonial and racialized logic of belatedness as a form of teleological violence because it simultaneously relegates non-Europeans to times and spaces where progress is not possible and reifies the hegemony—and superiority—of the time-spaces where progress is thought to exist.

The teleology that simultaneously makes migration seem like the only way to create a future while blocking the possibility of safe and legal migration is a violent one that begins with the psychological and cultural violence of colonialism pointed to by Khosravi and Fanon. It is bound up with the idea that places "out there" are better than "here," casting one part of the world as progressing and others as stuck or moving backward (Dick 2010, 2018; Ferguson 1999). Simultaneously, the vast machinery of white supremacist capitalism has created material realities that mean that some non-European time-spaces are neither safe nor viable places to live. In many ways, teleological violence writ globally is a double-edged sword that mirrors and scales up the kind of teleological violence we described as a product of education; it is a racialized global order that creates desires, establishes economic and political systems and patterns that produce the need for that desire, and then enables those same systems to deny—and block—that desire.

The violence of teleologies is in the holding up of an end and then foreclosing the possibility of reaching that end. The locus of the power to enact teleological violence resides with those policies, practices, institutions, and ideologies that may be intentionally or unintentionally in collaboration with each other to set and shift the ends. The move to emphasize what some would term local integration creates an end that relegates refugees to a time-space that they have already decided is not viable. Who is this an end for? It is hardly the end that refugees imagined for themselves.

The policies that provided the context for this book attempted to reorient refugee ends by supplanting the (already paradoxical) temporalities of humanitarianism with the teleological ideals of development and proposing this new temporal dispensation to disincentivize irregular migration and thereby secure the borders of the north. They problematize the teleology of humanitarianism by noting the impossibility of the durable solutions (particularly resettlement and repatriation) while shifting the locus of the end southward. In doing so, they relegate refugees to developmentalist teleologies that have previously failed to bring about their promises and that posit the Global South as a place that has not yet arrived, a place that is backward or unmoving, a place that is "belated." Relocating the end to the Global South and relegating refugees to these spaces imagined as backward while simultaneously curtailing opportunities—both legal and illegal—for northward migration is the epitome of teleological violence. The violence of containing refugees in the Global South becomes particularly extreme given the inherent instability of many host states there—instability that refugees know can always erupt into political violence or war.

Notes

1. Paul Stubbs's notion of heterotemporalities (2018) is useful to understand the overlapping forms of temporalizing at play in refugees' lives.
2. As we have noted elsewhere, we see teleological time, particularly teleologies oriented toward modernist progress, as a "hegemonic temporality" (Stubbs 2018). Although there are alternatives that subvert teleological notions of progress, it is always that temporality that is being responded to, evaded, or averted.

3. See, for example, Ferguson's assertion that urbanization in the Copperbelt was "a teleological process, a movement toward a known end point that would be nothing less than Western-style modernity" (1999, 5).

4. Ferguson poses a question: "Given the tropes of development, progress, emergence and advance," how do scholars make sense of the "teleological metanarrative of modernization?" (15). We might think of our study as addressing the question of how people living with the effects of decline and stasis make sense of this metanarrative. Even for refugees, the metanarratives of modernization, development, and progress have staying power, so that as modernization, development, and progress fail to bring about their promises, the ideas and temporalities that undergird them are resilient.

5. Chronotopes highlight the socially imbued relationships between place and time and have been described as narrative "time-space envelopes" that draw time and space into a particular storyline.

6. Dick notes that modernist chronotopes shape relationships between place and time, positing Mexico and the United States as not only different places but on different temporal trajectories (2010, 2018). Dick states that while Mexico is the space of "tradition" and thus is rooted in the unmoving timeless past, the United States is the space of modernization, movement, and progress. We might think of this trajectory from tradition to modernity as teleological (although Dick argues that the spaces of tradition and modernity are contrapuntal, constantly informing and inflecting each other).

Epilogue

Unfreezing the Ethnographic Present

WHEN WE WROTE this book, Hitsats, like the other camps, seemed frozen in time. Our writing reinforced this as we slipped into the ethnographic present to describe what life there was like, the cartography of the camp, wandering along the hard-baked ravines between housing zones, and stopping to talk with shop owners taking shelter from the sun in doorways and under makeshift porches. Hitsats, we wrote, was this place where people made do in the context of teleological violence and temporal harm. It was a place where, as people insisted on each return visit, nothing happened.

The ethnographic present can deny coevalness to people; it can misrepresent culture as frozen and bounded in time and space, the very things we are working against. When we wrote this book, however, we slipped into the ethnographic present as a way to describe and generate a sense of connection to lived time, a recognition and witnessing of how people cope by caretaking the present and holding open the possibilities of better, if distant, futures.

Hitsats camp no longer exists. People living there faced unspeakable violence and were displaced yet again; many did not survive. As we began drafting this epilogue, Mai Aini and Adi Harush were on the front lines of a war that was nearing its second anniversary. The stories of violence were chilling. Throughout this book, we have focused on various forms of temporal harm, but as a result of the war, refugees became victims of physical violence that far exceeded anything we have written about here. We feel it is important to detail the events that occurred in and around the refugee camps in northern Ethiopia following our fieldwork and to acknowledge how they profoundly ruptured refugees' already precarious lives.

From the outset of our project, we, as researchers, wanted to be hopeful about the new role that Ethiopia was carving for itself as a refugee host and what appeared to be magnanimous gestures of hospitality. Refugees thought otherwise, and we listened. Early on in our fieldwork, an old friend of Jennifer's from Eritrea noted that the only people who would even consider staying in Ethiopia long term were those who had family there, and even those people would prefer to move on. Eritreans in Ethiopia recalled the past as a reason to not stay in Ethiopia. They talked about the border war and the animosity against Eritreans that arose with the deportations. As we have written about elsewhere, Eritrea has been imagined and reimagined in the Ethiopian political landscape many times (Poole and Riggan 2022). Ethiopia has never fully let go of Eritrea. This creates a highly unstable situation for Eritreans in Ethiopia, something they are keenly aware of. Their understanding of Ethiopian hospitality was thus based not on a linear trajectory toward progress and improvement in relations and circumstances but rather on a cyclical one in which they were constantly aware of the possibility that the political circumstances could loop back to the past, with its conflicts and animosities. Things could always get worse again.

Although temporal violence cannot be equated with the horrific brutality brought on by the war in northern Ethiopia, there is a link between the physical violence of war and the teleological violence of policies that posit places like Ethiopia as a viable—and safe—end point for refugees. Somehow the promotion of Ethiopia as an end point seems particularly egregious given that refugees understood that waves of war, expulsion, and ethnic targeting had occurred repeatedly throughout the long history of Ethiopian-Eritrean relations. They did not trust Ethiopia's assertion of its own stability and their safety. They often stated that they felt unsafe and precariously situated in Ethiopia because history might repeat itself. In short, refugees knew that this could happen again.

This assumption that Ethiopia is a safe, stable place fundamentally misreads and misrepresents the history of political violence there and the violence that was occurring in various parts of the country even at the time of our fieldwork. More specifically, it ignores the ongoing instability of being an Eritrean in Ethiopia (Poole and Riggan 2022). Ethiopia has worked hard to project an image of itself as politically stable despite waves of political violence throughout the country in recent years (Tronvoll 2022). Ethiopia's projection of itself as a stable, reliable place was necessary in order for the country to posit itself as a long-term home for refugees and was central to the role the country seemed to be carving out for itself on the international stage as a leader in what were then new refugee and migration management initiatives. As we noted earlier, refugees were constantly calling our attention to how Ethiopia was not stable, even if it was relatively safe at the time. Needless to say, Ethiopian stability turned out to be as illusory as refugees asserted that it was. Refugees suffered tremendously when this illusion dissipated.

In 2018, a series of seismic political changes swept through Ethiopia. Abiy Ahmed came to power as prime minister in April 2018, overturning decades of rule by the Ethiopian People's Revolutionary Democratic Front (EPRDF), which was dominated by the Tigrayan People's Liberation Front (TPLF). The decentering of Tigrayan power would turn out to have substantial implications for Ethiopia's relationship with Eritrean refugees, the majority of whom were located in Tigray, on the Eritrean-Ethiopian border. As the field of power began to shift, both in Tigray and in Ethiopia as a whole, the categorization of Eritreans in Ethiopia would continue to be a volatile and unpredictable process.

We arrived for a period of fieldwork in June 2018 to find Addis Ababa filled with images and talk of the new prime minister. Abiy had come to power that spring against a backdrop of government protests that led to the resignation of the former prime minister and EPRDF chair, Hailemariam Desalegn. An ethnic Oromo leader, Abiy promised sweeping reforms and an era of peace and unity to confront the ethnic divisions that fueled the recent protests. He moved quickly to release political prisoners and lift media restrictions.

Abiy also had plans with regard to Eritrea and Eritreans in Ethiopia. He declared peace with Eritrea in July 2018, ending a twenty-year standoff that had followed a three-year border conflict—an act that earned him the Nobel Peace Prize in 2019. The news on the day of our arrival featured Abiy's declaration that people should pack their bags, as flights to Asmara were poised to resume for the first time in two decades. Main city thoroughfares flew Ethiopian and Eritrean flags side by side for the arrival of a high-level delegation from Asmara. Less than two weeks later, Abiy and Isaias Afwerki, the president of Eritrea, met in Asmara to declare the end of the war and "a new era of peace and friendship." As events unfolded and phone lines opened up, the mood in Addis was euphoric. It even looked like the pledges that had been made would finally be passed into legislation.

We encountered a starkly different atmosphere when we visited the Mai Aini refugee camp in northern Ethiopia only days after peace was declared. Despite the celebratory tone of national and international reporting, Eritrean refugees were worried about the implications of peace, which they believed would destabilize the Tigray region. They expressed concern that a new alliance between the Ethiopian federal government and Eritrea would create a profoundly unsafe situation for them. This alliance might result in the rollback of Eritreans' refugee status, compromising their chances at resettlement and endangering their long-term stability and safety in the region (Riggan and Poole 2018). Furthermore, should the border be opened, some worried that Eritrean security forces would have access to refugees, many of whom were regarded as political dissidents. In short, they began to think that Ethiopia was no longer a safe place for them. When we raised refugees' concerns with officials at ARRA and UNHCR, we were assured that the border would not open quickly, that the process of border opening would be slow and deliberative, and that protection of the refugees living near the border would be a high priority.

As it turned out, the refugees were right about the pace of the border opening. Shortly after the peace agreement was signed, the border opened on September 11, 2018, for a brief period, making travel, family reunions, and widespread trade possible (*BBC News* 2019). For Eritreans in Eritrea, the border opening meant that for the first time since the border war, they could leave the country without undergoing a grueling (and seldom successful) process of acquiring a passport and exit visa to leave the country legally or risking prison and torture or death at the border if they crossed it illegally.

Not surprisingly, the opening of the border led to an influx of Eritrean refugees into Ethiopia. In the first two weeks that the border was open, UNHCR reported that ten thousand Eritrean refugees were either registered or awaiting registration

(UNHCR 2018e; Gardner 2018). UNHCR estimated that around six thousand Eritreans arrived in Ethiopia every month in 2019 (UNHCR 2019).

Somewhat mysteriously, formal border crossing points closed almost as quickly as they opened. By March 2019, all but one crossing point had been officially closed. A few months later, by April 2019, all the official border crossings were closed (Belloni and Jeffrey 2019). On Riggan's last visit to Ethiopia, she heard accounts that it was possible to cross the border, but unofficially. "The guards just look the other way," one interlocutor told her. "You can't take your car, but there are porters waiting to take your belongings across the border," another noted. It seemed that the leadership of both countries had agreed to informal border traffic while formally maintaining a closed border. This was a vast improvement over Eritrea's decades-long reputed shoot-to-kill policy that put many refugees fleeing Eritrea in grave danger when they attempted to cross into Ethiopia. But while many appreciated this opening and relished being reunited with family members, the lack of clarity about the terms of peace, the delineation of the border, and the creation of border protocols did nothing to reassure refugees about the stability of the situation.

In January 2019, the long-awaited refugee proclamation was voted into law, but as we have noted elsewhere, many of the key details remained unaddressed, such as the specifics of whether refugees could legally work, making the proclamation feel a bit anticlimactic. A year later, in January 2020, Ethiopia quietly began to roll back the long-awarded *prima facie* status to Eritrean refugees, noting that only certain categories of Eritreans merited this status. They also announced the planned closure of the Hitsats camp. Closing a camp is conveniently in keeping with the trend toward local integration made in the 2016 pledges, but the closure was not accompanied by other components of the pledges that would enable refugees to establish secure livelihoods outside of the camps. Refugee leaders and the humanitarian community raised concerns about forced relocation to the older, more crowded camps during the pandemic (Creta 2020).

In November 2019, one month after Abiy was awarded the Nobel Peace Prize, he disbanded the former ruling political party, the EPRDF, and formed the Prosperity Party. The Tigrayans refused to join, indicating further tensions to come. Meanwhile, it was unclear whether Ethiopia would have the same commitment to refugees—and to Eritrean refugees in particular—under Abiy's leadership as it previously had. Abiy's new alliance with Eritrean leadership, coupled with the fact that Eritrea considers those who flee to be criminals who have unlawfully defected from national service, led Eritreans to worry about whether their refugee status in Ethiopia would continue to be honored and if they would still be protected.

Meanwhile, Ethiopia descended into political chaos. In the summer of 2020, political uprisings following the assassination of popular singer Hachalu Hundessa resulted in the death of over two hundred people, the arrest of nearly five thousand people, and a military clampdown. But with the whole world focused on the outbreak of COVID-19 in the first half of 2020, little attention was paid to

Ethiopia. Tensions between Tigrayan leadership and Abiy's government continued to worsen, escalating sharply when Abiy postponed the elections slated to be held that summer and Tigray held its own elections (Paravicini 2020). In October of that year, the federal government withheld funding from Tigray, leading to both sides issuing "dueling statements of denunciation and derecognition" (Tronvoll 2022).

In early November, war broke out and escalated quickly. Each side differed in their interpretation of events that triggered the war. The federal government cited a Tigrayan attack on federal military installations in Tigray (the so-called Northern Command), and Tigrayan leadership claimed the attack was self-defense against an operation launched by the federal government that same day (Weldemichael et al. 2022; Tronvoll 2022).

A media and internet blackout made it almost impossible to know precisely what was happening in Tigray. It was well known that Eritrea was almost immediately embroiled in the war, although they denied involvement repeatedly. In retaliation for Eritrea's involvement, Tigray launched missiles at Asmara in mid-November. In late November 2020, Ethiopian federal forces captured Mekelle and declared victory, but the war was far from over (Anna 2020).

There was little information available about what was happening in refugee camps during the blackout. Still, stories of atrocious violence against civilians and refugees, including attacks in the historic town of Axum, ethnic massacres, and the use of rape as a weapon of war, began to trickle out, although these would not be fully reported on until early 2021 (Human Rights Watch 2021a). Anthropologist Natalia Paszkiewicz, who had worked with an INGO in the Hitsats camp, began receiving phone calls with details of the atrocities occurring in the camps, which she published on social media and later assembled into one of the first reports on what happened there (Paszkiewicz 2021). It became clear that refugees were being brutalized by all sides—first by the Eritrean forces, later by Tigrayans. Poole also received calls from an interlocutor in the Adi Harush camp who was desperately trying to get his family away from what had become a front line in the fighting. Along with the atrocities committed against the civilian population in Tigray, there were horror stories in the camps of forced returns to Eritrea, rape, indiscriminate killing, and torture, but a full picture did not emerge until the blackout was lifted in late January 2021.

Eventually, published reports assembled and detailed an account of what had transpired in the camps during the early months of the war, and satellite images showed that the Hitsats and Shimelba camps had been destroyed (Mersie et al. 2021; EHRC/OHCHR 2021; Human Rights Watch 2021b; Miller 2022; Weldemichael et al. 2022). UNHCR staff left the camps as soon as the war began. After that, refugees were repeatedly targeted by several different actors in the conflict—Eritreans, Tigrayan militia, and possibly Tigrayan government forces and Ethiopian federal forces. Between November 2020 and January 2021, the Eritrean army and Tigrayan militia alternately occupied the Hitsats and Shimelba camps, which housed approximately twenty thousand Eritrean refugees at the start of the conflict. Eritrean forces were targeting refugees, many of whom were regarded as political dissidents. By many accounts, the Eritrean forces had lists of names of people in both Hitsats and Shimelba. People who were able to escape told stories of forced return to Eritrea and destruction of houses and humanitarian infrastructure in the two camps.

When Eritrean forces withdrew from the camps, Tigrayan militias forcibly returned refugees who had fled Hitsats back to the camp. In the process, refugees reported killings, sexual assault, looting, and arbitrary detention without food during the occupation of the area by Tigrayan militias, who also sought out and punished refugees, possibly because they suspected them of participating in looting the local town and likely also because they were Eritreans and, ironically, were blamed for the atrocities committed against the civilian population by the Eritrean army in Tigray.

Like the refugees in Hitsats, those in Shimelba, many of whom are ethnic Kunama, were forced to flee due to heavy fighting around the camp, intimidation by both sides, and concerns about possible revenge attacks by the host community for the reportedly widespread killings and rapes of Tigrayan civilians committed by Eritrean forces (EHRC/OHCHR 2021). When UNHCR and other humanitarian agencies were finally able to visit the camps in late March 2021, after a protracted news blackout, they found them empty and destroyed, with many of the shelters and aid offices burned to the ground (Human Rights Watch 2021a).

Because of these dangers, many refugees struggled to find somewhere to go. Some of the refugees displaced from Hitsats and Shimelba arrived at the older camps of Mai Aini and Adi Harush. There, they faced crowded conditions, dwindling water supplies, a lack of health services, and violence and looting from armed militias. Some refugees fled to Addis Ababa early in the war, but they faced hardships there as well. Assistance from UNHCR and ARRA was initially not forthcoming for refugees who self-relocated to Addis Ababa, meaning those who had fled to the capital city had no way to live. There were accounts of refugees being returned to the camps by ARRA officials who told them it was safe. In December 2020, for example, Reuters reported that a busload of Eritreans were forcibly returned to Tigray from Addis with military escort (Reuters 2020). A handful of diaspora-sponsored GoFundMe initiatives cropped up to fill the gap that the humanitarian apparatus left open, but the reach of these initiatives was limited to the immediate networks of those sponsoring them, and refugees who were not connected with these particular networks still lacked resources to live. Refugees staged a protest supported by a Twitter storm to demand assistance (Endeshaw 2021), which they eventually received from UNHCR (2021a).

Impeding the flow of aid to both refugee and civilian populations has been a tactic deployed primarily by the Ethiopian government throughout the war, leaving refugees with no good options. Throughout the course of the war, blockades against humanitarian convoys were deployed, stopping much-needed aid from reaching displaced civilian populations and Eritrean refugees. When aid workers were able to access refugees and civilian populations, they found people in desperate need and food sources deliberately targeted (Anna 2021). Refugees who tried to escape the region on foot through the mountains did not fare much better, as they found themselves caught in the cross fire between warring sides. They were targeted by Tigrayans because they were Eritrean (and therefore associated with the invading Eritrean army) *and* by Amharic- and Oromo-speaking troops who associated anyone who spoke Tigrigna with Tigrayans (Rudolf 2022).

No one was surprised that fighting continued following Ethiopia's declaration of victory in November 2020. In June of the next year, the same month that Ethiopia held delayed elections and formally elected Abiy, the tide of the war shifted again. Tigrayans regained control over their region and by late June had retaken the capital, Mekelle (Walsh 2021). They continued to push into the Amhara region, eventually capturing several key towns, including the symbolically important UNESCO World Heritage Site, Lalibela, in late August (Reuters 2021). In November 2021, roughly a year after they declared victory, the Ethiopian government declared a state of emergency and "called on its citizens to pick up arms to defend the capital" as Tigrayan forces advanced southward toward the capital after capturing the key towns of Dessie and Kombolcha, which lie only 160 miles from Addis Ababa (Walsh and Marks 2021).

The war altered course several times, but one consistency was the extreme vulnerability of both refugees and the civilian population, particularly given the limited and fluctuating access to the region by both reporters and the humanitarian community. Aid agencies reported being repeatedly blocked from accessing camps (Miller 2022). There were accounts of Eritreans trapped in Mai Aini and Adi Harush camps in Tigray as fighting escalated in June 2021 (Schlein 2021), and food shortages and overall animosities created by the war may have triggered tensions between refugees and local populations. In July 2021, UNHCR issued a statement of concern that refugees were being intimidated in the camps (UNHCR 2021b). In June 2021, the Alemwach camp for Eritreans was set up in the Amhara region. It has been similarly difficult to ascertain the status of refugees there, but personal communications with interlocutors and social media have revealed atrocious conditions, attacks on refugees, and profound insecurity in Alemwach. Additionally, the camp was located close to the front lines and was likely unsafe (Weldemichael et al. 2022).

In October 2021, Abiy was formally sworn in as prime minister, and two weeks later, Ethiopian defense forces launched a new round of strikes in Tigray. By the end of December, the Ethiopian forces had begun using drone strikes, resulting in a retreat of the Tigrayans to Tigray (they were either driven back or they strategically withdrew, depending on one's news source). Ethiopian air strikes continued, worsening in January 2022 and leading aid agencies to suspend operations again

(UNHCR 2022a). On January 7, Reuters reported that three people were killed in an air strike on Mai Aini camp, two of them children. It was suspected that these were Ethiopian government air strikes because they were the only actor with this capacity in the region (Reuters 2022). On January 21, 2022, UNHCR issued a statement saying that they had not been able to reach the camp for three weeks, and when they did, they found refugees struggling to access food, water, and basic medical care (Miller 2022). Additionally, the spread of the war into the Afar region meant that Eritrean Afar refugees in the Berhale camp faced similar shortages of food and supplies and also experienced the territory on which the camp is located changing hands multiple times (Weldemichael et al. 2022; Miller 2022).

The government declared an indefinite humanitarian truce in March 2022, and the first international aid convoy to arrive by land since December reached Mekelle on April 1 (Al Jazeera 2022). Still, Tigrayans complained that the government had limited the flow of aid to a trickle. The government denied this and in turn blamed the Tigrayans (Mwai 2022). Angered by Western allegations of a government-sponsored blockade of Tigray, Abiy accused international aid agencies of collaborating with terrorists (*Africa Confidential* 2022). Some aid eventually reached civilians and refugees during the humanitarian truce, which lasted roughly five months, but the situation remained tense. In July, there were accounts of the arbitrary detention of Eritreans in Ethiopia. A group of Tigrigna speakers including Eritreans, Tigrayans, Eritrean refugees, and Eritreans with foreign passports were detained near Debark, in the Amhara region, in harsh conditions (Kassa 2022).

The humanitarian truce broke down in late August 2022, when all parties to the conflict moved to solid war footing. The renewed fighting was preceded by mass mobilizations and conscription in Tigray and the Amhara region (De Waal 2022a). In Eritrea, a country in which forcible conscription of civilians, even in peacetime, is one of the main drivers of refugee flight, coercive conscription has gone to unprecedented lengths to boost the country's military capacity (*BBC News Tigrinya* 2022). It has been argued that the Eritrean president had been calling the shots in this war and that his personal desire to obliterate the Tigrayan leadership once and for all was the driving force behind the resumption of fighting (De Waal 2022b).

According to UNHCR's flash update in late September 2022, fighting occurred on multiple fronts in the Tigray, Afar, and Amhara regions. The Ethiopian government announced that aid organizations should cease work in certain areas in Tigray, leading UNHCR to suspend field missions there. They once more lost access to several refugee camps and sites for internally displaced persons. Additionally, authorities in the town of Shire advised humanitarian agencies not to travel to or from Adi Harush or Mai Aini; however, UNHCR and the World Food Program (WFP) were able to distribute food and other staples to 9,800 refugees before ceasing operations (UNHCR 2022b).

The scale of humanitarian emergency and human suffering due to the war in Ethiopia was staggering. Although difficult to estimate the human cost of the war, experts say that half a million people probably died—fifty thousand to a hundred thousand due to being casualties of fighting, a hundred and fifty thousand to two hundred thousand due to starvation, and another hundred thousand from the absence of medical care (Ghosh 2022). Prior to the humanitarian truce, 9.4 million people were in need of assistance, an estimated 425 to 1,201 people were dying of starvation per day, and displaced people had resorted to eating leaves (Miller 2022). As of late August 2022, the WFP estimated that thirteen million people in the Tigray, Amhara, and Afar regions could be severely food insecure, including nearly half (47 percent) of Tigray's six million residents and large numbers of people in the Afar and Amhara regions (WFP and FAO 2022).

On November 2, 2022, the TPLF and the Ethiopia government signed a cessation of hostilities agreement which "promised to disarm Tigrayan troops, return control of Tigray to the Ethiopian government, end the Mekelle Offensive, and permit full humanitarian aid access to Tigray" (Council on Foreign Relations 2023). Although the war seemed to be over at the time of this writing, the situation in Tigray was still tense and Eritrean refugees were unsafe in Ethiopia.

Meanwhile, migration northward has also grown more dangerous as European countries seek to put an end to irregular migration. Even as Ukrainian refugees are welcomed in Europe and North America, the migration of Africans is being actively deterred through measures that make their journeys more dangerous. The United States is still detaining migrants to await asylum processing in Mexico, where there is concern for their human rights. Although these are predominantly migrants from South and Central America and the Caribbean, African migrants, including Eritreans, do routinely find their way to the US-Mexico border. Controversially, Britain has recently attempted to relocate asylum seekers whose cases are pending to Rwanda. African and other migrants who are fleeing horrifying circumstances are systematically denied the ability to receive refugee protections in the name of migration deterrence.

The central Mediterranean route, most commonly used by Eritrean migrants, is a particularly deadly and torturous route that has been made more dangerous due to migration-deterrence policies. Twenty-three thousand people are estimated to have died crossing the Mediterranean since 2014, and sixteen hundred people are estimated to have died making the journey in 2021 alone (Ritter 2021). Meanwhile, Italy has struck various deals with Libya to avoid doing some of the less legal and more unsavory parts of migration deterrence (Vari 2020). Italy's 2017 Memorandum of Understanding (MOU) with Libya gives Libya greater tools to intercept boats crossing the Mediterranean as well as to detain migrants and return them to their country of origin regardless of protected status. This MOU effectively relocates migrant detention to a highly unstable state, making migrants vulnerable to trafficking, extortion, and torture and making Mediterranean crossings more dangerous (Vari 2020). As a result of the memorandum, the rollback of search and rescue operations in the Mediterranean, and the rise of border protection activities by Frontex, conditions in Libya and on the Mediterranean crossing have deteriorated steadily.

Describing the horrifying conditions in Libya, an Eritrean quoted in a report by *Médecins Sans Frontières* noted, "Trying to cross the sea is facing death, but staying in Libya is facing death too" (2022). We would emphasize that staying in (or returning to) Eritrea is also facing death, particularly in the face of new waves of far more stringent mass conscription. And staying in Ethiopia means facing the risk of death, both because of insufficient food supplies and medical care and because all actors in this particular war have targeted Eritreans with egregious and punishing violence. It seems that they have run out of choices.

Eritrean refugees in Ethiopia are caught between a war that seems to have no end and laws and practices that effectively end their ability to seek safety. The policies of local integration that we analyze and discuss in this book appear to be a more benign companion to these deadly migration measures, but they have always also been about securitizing the racialized borders of the Global North. Local integration, as we have argued in these pages, sought to locate an end to Eritrean migration in Ethiopia in a broader policy setting that emphasized an end of migration in other large hosting states in the Global South. These policies are about the desire of countries in the Global North to find an *end* to what is depicted as an *endless* flow of irregular migrants, predominantly black and brown people, regardless of the dangers that they are fleeing from. The desired *end* to migration trumps the profound need among refugees for safety and protection. In the service of seeking that end—an end to migration—those who are already safe and settled (in predominantly and historically white countries) determine who will belong to a class of people relegated to endless suffering.

What kinds of temporality relegate places like the Hitsats camp to the permanent ethnographic present, while in reality, they are vulnerable to obliteration? We would argue that this is the ultimate teleological violence—the assertion that places like Ethiopia will guarantee not only progress but also safety and stability for refugees, while those places are far from stable, safe, and capable of promising progress. Indeed, those places subject refugees to the worst excesses of violence.

Changing these passages to past tense felt like its own version of teleological violence, generating distance from our lives now, or from a common future, by sticking things back in time and doing nothing to fix the lack of coevalness attributed to migrants and refugees. Weeding out the ethnographic present in this book and rendering descriptions of people's lives in past tense have involved the pain of coming to terms with the horrors facing people throughout the Tigray region. They have also meant coming to terms with how small these ethnographic efforts to generate empathetic connection feel in the face of the immediate brutality of war and the chronic brutality of global migration deterrence.

Bibliography

Abbink, Jon. 2005. *Vanguard or Vandals: Youth, Politics and Conflict in Africa*. Leiden: Brill.

Abebe, Tsion. 2017. "As Doors Close to Refugees, Ethiopia's Stay Open." *ISS Today*, June 19, 2017. https://www.dailymaverick.co.za/article/2017-06-19-iss-today-as-doors-close-to -refugees-ethiopias-stay-open/#.WXdEWWLys2x.

Abramovitz, Mimi, and Jennifer Zelnick. 2010. "Double Jeopardy: The Impact of Neoliberalism on Care Workers in the United States and South Africa." *International Journal of Health Services* 40, no. 1: 97–117.

Africa Confidential. 2022. "Abiy's War Aims Meet Geopolitics." May 26, 2022. https://www .africa-confidential.com/article/id/13958/Abiy%E2%80%99s_war_aims_meet_geopolitics.

Agamben, Giorgio. 2005. *The Time That Remains: A Commentary on the Letter to the Romans*. Stanford, CA: Stanford University Press.

Agier, Michel. 2002. "Between War and City: Towards an Urban Anthropology of Refugee Camps." *Ethnography* 3, no. 3: 317–341.

———. 2011. *Managing the Undesirables*. New York: Polity.

———. 2021. *The Stranger as My Guest: A Critical Anthropology of Hospitality*. Hoboken, NJ: John Wiley & Sons.

Al Jazeera. 2022. "Ethiopia Declares Unilateral Truce to Allow Aid into Tigray." March 24, 2022. https://www.aljazeera.com/news/2022/3/24/ethiopia-declares-truce-to-allow-aid-into -tigray.

Allan, Diana. 2013. *Refugees of the Revolution: Experiences of Palestinian Exile*. Stanford, CA: Stanford University Press.

Allison, Anne. 2016. "Precarity: Commentary by Anne Allison." *Curated Collections, Cultural Anthropology*. https://journal.culanth.org/index.php/ca/precarity-commentary-by-anne -allison.

Altman, Irwin, and Setha M. Low, eds. 2012. *Place Attachment (Human Behavior and Environment Book 12)*. New York: Springer Science & Business Media.

Amnesty International. 1999. "Ethiopia and Eritrea: Human Rights Issues in a Year of Armed Conflict." May 20, 1999. https://www.amnesty.org/en/documents/afr04/003/1999 /en/#:~:text=It%20covers%20indiscriminate%20or%20deliberate,removal%20of%20 their%20Ethiopian%20citizenship.

Andersson, Ruben. 2014. "Time and the Migrant Other: European Border Controls and the Temporal Economics of Illegality." *American Anthropologist* 116, no. 4: 795–809.

———. 2016a. "Europe's Failed 'Fight' against Irregular Migration: Ethnographic Notes on a Counterproductive Industry." *Journal of Ethnic and Migration Studies* 42, no. 7: 1055– 1075.

———. 2016b. "Why Europe's Border Security Approach Has Failed and How to Replace It." International Migration Institute. https://www.migrationinstitute.org/publications/why -europes-border-security-approach-has-failed-and-how-to-replace-it.

———. 2017. "Rescued and Caught: The Humanitarian-Security Nexus at Europe's Frontiers." In *The Borders of Europe*, edited by Nicholas De Degenova, 64–94. Durham, NC: Duke University Press.

Anna, Cara. 2020. "Ethiopia's Tigray Leader Confirms Firing Missiles at Eritrea." Associated Press, November 15, 2020. https://apnews.com/article/international-news-eritrea -ethiopia-asmara-kenya-33b9aea59b4c984562eaa86d8547c6dd.

———. 2021. "'Extreme Urgent Need': Starvation Haunts Ethiopia's Tigray." Associated Press, January 17, 2021. https://apnews.com/article/ethiopia-united-nations-kenya -efob6b2db2994d4c3042cf19f3d92a2a.

Appadurai, Arjun. 2004. "The Capacity to Aspire: Culture and the Terms of Recognition." In *Culture and Public Action*, edited by Vijayendra Rao and Michael Walton, 59–84. Stanford, CA: Stanford University Press.

———. 2019. "Traumatic Exit, Identity Narratives, and the Ethics of Hospitality." *Television & New Media* 20, no. 6: 558–565.

Auyero, Javier. 2012. *Patients of the State: The Politics of Waiting in Argentina*. Durham, NC: Duke University Press.

Bailey, Adrian J., Richard Wright, Alison Mountz, and Ines M. Miyares. 2002. "(Re)producing Salvadoran Transnational Geographies." *Annals of the Association of American Geographers* 921:125–144.

Bakhtin, Mikhail Mikhaïlovich. 1981. *The Dialogic Imagination: Four Essays*. Austin: University of Texas Press.

Barakat, Sultan, and Sansom Milton. 2020. "Localisation across the Humanitarian-Development-Peace Nexus." *Journal of Peacebuilding & Development* 15, no. 2: 147–163.

Bardelli, Nora. 2018. "The Shortcomings of Employment as a Durable Solution." *Forced Migration Review* 58:54–56.

BBC News. 2016. "Refugee Crisis: Plan to Create 100,000 Jobs in Ethiopia." September 21, 2016. http://www.bbc.com/news/world-africa-37433085.

———. 2019 "Ethiopia-Eritrea Border Boom as Peace Takes Hold." January 9, 2019. https://www .bbc.com/news/world-africa-46794296.

BBC News Tigrinya. 2022. "Eritrea's Mass Mobilization amid Ethiopia Civil War." September 16, 2022. https://www.bbc.com/news/world-africa-62927781.

Bell, Sarah L., Ronan Foley, Frank Houghton, Avril Maddrell, and Allison M. Williams. 2018. "From Therapeutic Landscapes to Healthy Spaces, Places and Practices: A Scoping Review." *Social Science & Medicine* 196:123–130.

Bellino, Michelle. 2018. "Youth Aspirations in Kakuma Refugee Camp: Education as a Means for Social, Spatial, and Economic (Im)mobility." *Globalisation, Societies and Education* 16, no. 4: 541–556.

Belloni, Milena. 2019. *The Big Gamble: The Migration of Eritreans to Europe*. Berkeley: University of California Press.

Belloni, Milena, and James Jeffrey. 2019. "Eritrea: Amid Border Wrangles, Eritreans Wrestle with Staying or Going." *The New Humanitarian*, April 30, 2019. https://www .thenewhumanitarian.org/feature/2019/04/30/amid-border-wrangles-eritreans-wrestle -staying-or-going.

Bennett, Anna, and Penny Jane Burke. 2018. "Re/conceptualising Time and Temporality: An Exploration of Time in Higher Education." *Discourse: Studies in the Cultural Politics of Education* 39, no. 6: 913–925.

Berlant, Lauren. 2011. *Cruel Optimism*. Durham, NC: Duke University Press.

Bernal, Victoria. 2000. "Equality to Die For? Women Guerrilla Fighters and Eritrea's Cultural Revolution." *Political and Legal Anthropology Review* 23, no. 2: 61–76.

———. 2014. *Nation as Network: Diaspora, Cyberspace, and Citizenship*. Chicago: University of Chicago Press.

Besteman, Catherine L. 2019. "Militarized Global Apartheid." *Current Anthropology* 6, no. 19: 26–38.

Betts, Alexander, and Paul Collier. 2017. *Refuge: Transforming a Broken Refugee System*. Oxford: Oxford University Press.

Biesta, Gert. 2013. "Time Out: Can Education Do and Be Done Without Time?" In *Education and the Political: New Theoretical Orientations*, edited by Thomas Szkudlarek, 75–88. Leiden: Brill.

Black, Steven P. 2018. "The Ethics and Aesthetics of Care." *Annual Review of Anthropology* 47:79–95.

Bloch, Ernst, Neville Plaice, Stephen Plaice, and Paul Knight. 1986. *The Principle of Hope*. Cambridge, MA: MIT Press.

Boğaç, Ceren. 2009. "Place Attachment in a Foreign Settlement." *Journal of Environmental Psychology* 29, no. 2: 267–278.

Bourdieu, Pierre. 1977. *Outline of a Theory of Practice*. Cambridge: Cambridge University Press.

———. 2000. *Pascalian Meditations*. Translated by Nice Richard. Cambridge: Polity Press.

Bourdieu, Pierre, and Jean-Claude Passeron. 1990. *Reproduction in Education, Society and Culture*. London: Sage.

Bowles, Samuel, and Herbert Gintis. 1976. *Schooling in Capitalist America: Educational Reform and the Contradictions of Economic Life*. New York: Basic Books.

Brooks, Aaron. 2017. "Will Jobs for Eritrean Refugees in Ethiopia Stop the Influx to Europe?" East Africa Monitor, July 14, 2017. http://eastafricamonitor.com/will-job-eritrean -refugees-ethiopia-stop-influx-europe/.

Brun, Catherine. 2001. "Reterritorializing the Relationship between People and Place in Refugee Studies." *Geografiska Annaler. Series B, Human Geography* 83, no. 1: 15–25.

———. 2015. "Active Waiting and Changing Hopes: Toward a Time Perspective on Protracted Displacement." *Social Analysis: The International Journal of Social and Cultural Practice* 59, no. 1: 19–37.

———. 2016. "There Is No Future in Humanitarianism: Emergency, Temporality and Protracted Displacement." *History and Anthropology* 27, no. 4: 393–410.

Bryant, Rebecca, and Daniel Knight. 2019. *The Anthropology of the Future*. Cambridge: Cambridge University Press.

Çağlar, Ayse. 2016. "Still 'Migrants' after All Those Years: Foundational Mobilities, Temporal Frames and Emplacement of Migrants." *Journal of Ethnic and Migration Studies* 42, no. 6: 952–969.

Campbell, John R. 2013. *Nationalism, Law and Statelessness: Grand Illusions in the Horn of Africa*. New York: Routledge.

Candea, Matei, and Giovanni da Col. 2012. "The Return to Hospitality." *Journal of the Royal Anthropological Institute* 18: S1–S19.

Carruth, Lauren. 2021. *Love and Liberation: Humanitarian Work in Ethiopia's Somali Region*. Ithaca, NY: Cornell University Press.

Center for Preventative Action. 2023. "Conflict in Ethiopia" Council on Foreign Relations Global Conflict Tracker. April 25, 2023. https://www.cfr.org/global-conflict-tracker /conflict/conflict-ethiopia.

Chandler, Caitlin L. 2018. "How Far Will the EU Go to Seal Its Borders?" Dissent. https://www .dissentmagazine.org/article/how-far-eu-seal-borders-khartoum-process-central -mediterranean-migration.

Cliggett, Lisa. 2003. "Gift Remitting and Alliance Building in Zambian Modernity: Old Answers to Modern Problems." *American Anthropologist* 105, no. 3: 543–552.

Collyer, Michael. 2019. "From Preventive to Repressive: The Changing Use of Development and Humanitarianism to Control Migration." In *Handbook of Critical Geographies of Migration*, edited by Katharyne Mitchell, Reece Jones, and Jennifer L. Fluri, 170–181. Northampton, MA: Edward Edgar.

Connell, Dan. 2012. "Escaping Eritrea: Why They Flee and What They Face." *Middle East Report* 264:2–9.

Costantini, Osvaldo, and Aurora Massa. 2016. "'So, Now I Am Eritrean': Mobility Strategies and Multiple Senses of Belonging between Local Complexity and Global Immobility." In *Bounded Mobilities: Ethnographic Perspectives on Social Hierarchies and Global Inequalities*, edited by Miriam Gutekunst, Andreas Hackl, Sabina Leoncini, Julia Sophia Schwarz, and Irene Götz, 34–40. Bielefeld: transcript.

Crapanzano, Vincent. 1985. *Waiting: The Whites of South Africa*. New York: Random House.

———. 2003. "Reflections on Hope as a Category of Social and Psychological Analysis." *Cultural Anthropology* 18, no. 1: 3–32.

Creta, Sara. 2020. "Ethiopia Plans to Close Eritrean Refugee Camp Despite Concerns." Al Jazeera, April 19, 2020. https://www.aljazeera.com/author/sara_creta_190319062551452.

De Haas, Hein. 2007. "Turning the Tide? Why Development Will Not Stop Migration." *Development and Change* 38, no. 5: 819–841.

———. 2019. "Migration and Development: A Theoretical Perspective." *International Migration Review* 44, no. 1: 227–264.

Denov, Myriam, and Bree Akesson. 2013. "Neither Here Nor There? Place and Placemaking in the Lives of Separated Children." *International Journal of Migration, Health and Social Care* 9, no. 2: 56–70.

Derluguian, Georgi M. 2005. *Bourdieu's Secret Admirer in the Caucasus: A World-System Biography*. Chicago: University of Chicago Press.

Derrida, Jacques. 2005. "The Principle of Hospitality." *Parallax* 11, no. 1: 6–9.

Desjarlais, Robert, and C. Jason Throop. 2011. "Phenomenological Approaches in Anthropology." *Annual Review of Anthropology* 40:87–102.

De Waal, Alex. 2022a. "Ethiopian Civil War: Why Fighting Has Resumed in Tigray and Amhara." *BBC News*, September 1, 2022. https://www.bbc.com/news/world-africa-62717070.

———. 2022b. "Why Are Ethiopians Dying in Isaias' War?" The Elephant, October 7, 2022. https://www.theelephant.info/op-eds/2022/10/07/why-are-ethiopians-dying-in-isaias-war/.

Dick, Hilary Parsons. 2010. "Imagined Lives and Modernist Chronotopes in Mexican Nonmigrant Discourse." *American Ethnologist* 37, no. 2: 275–290.

———. 2018. *Words of Passage: National Longing and the Imagined Lives of Mexican Migrants*. Austin: University of Texas.

Dikeç, Mustafa, Nigel Clark, and Clive Barnett. 2009. "Extending Hospitality: Giving Space, Taking Time." *Paragraph* 32, no. 1: 1–14.

DiNunzio, Marco. 2019. *The Act of Living: Street Life, Marginality, and Development in Urban Ethiopia*. Ithaca, NY: Cornell University Press.

Doughty, Karolina. 2018. "Therapeutic Landscapes." In *The Routledge Companion to Landscape Studies*, edited by Peter Howard, Ian Thompson, Emma Waterton, and Mick Atha, 341–353. London: Routledge.

Drangsland, Kari Anne. 2020. "Mo's Challenge. Waiting and the Question of Methodological Nationalism." In *Waiting and the Temporalities of Irregular Migration*, edited by

Christine Jacobsen, Marry-Anne Karlsen, and Shahram Khosravi, 75–95. London: Routledge.

Dryden-Peterson, Sarah. 2017. "Refugee Education: Education for an Unknowable Future." *Curriculum Inquiry* 47, no. 1: 14–24.

Dryden-Peterson, Sarah, Elizabeth Adelman, Michelle J. Bellino, and Vidur Chopra. 2019. "The Purposes of Refugee Education: Policy and Practice of Including Refugees in National Education Systems." *Sociology of Education* 92, no. 4: 346–366.

Dunn, Elizabeth Cullen. 2017. *No Path Home: Humanitarian Camps and the Grief of Displacement*. Ithaca, NY: Cornell University Press.

Durkheim, Émile. (1912) 1965. *The Elementary Forms of the Religious Life*. New York: Collier.

Dyck, Isabel, and Parin Dossa. 2007. "Place, Health and Home: Gender and Migration in the Constitution of Healthy Space." *Health & Place* 13, no. 6: 91–701.

Eckenwiler, Lisa A. 2016. "Defining Ethical Placemaking for Place-Based Interventions." *American Journal of Public Health* 106, no. 11: 1944–1946.

EHRC (Ethiopian Human Rights Commission)/OHCHR (Office of the United Nations High Commissioner). 2021. "Report of the Ethiopian Human Rights Commission/Office of the United Nations High Commissioner for Human Rights Joint Investigation into Alleged Violations of International Human Rights, Humanitarian and Refugee Law Committed by All Parties." Office of High Commissioner of Human Rights, November 3, 2021. https://www.ohchr.org/sites/default/files/2021-11/OHCHR-EHRC-Tigray-Report.pdf.

El-Shaarawi, Nadia. 2015. "Living an Uncertain Future: Temporality, Uncertainty, and Well-Being among Iraqi Refugees in Egypt." *Social Analysis* 59, no. 1: 38–56.

Emirbayer, Mustafa, and Ann Mische. 1998."What Is Agency?" *American Journal of Sociology* 103, no. 4: 962–1023.

Endeshaw, Dawit. 2021. "Eritrean Refugees in Ethiopian Capital Protest Insecurity at Tigray Camps." Reuters, July 30, 2021. https://www.euronews.com/2021/07/30/us-ethiopia-conflict.

Ethiopian News Agency. 2016. "WB Funds 100 Mln USD for Refugee Project in Ethiopia." December 29, 2016.

Evans-Pritchard, Edward Evan. 1939. "Nuer Time-Reckoning." *Africa: Journal of the International African Institute* 12, no. 2: 189–216.

Farwell, Nancy. 2001. "'Onward Through Strength': Coping and Psychological Support among Refugee Youth Returning to Eritrea from Sudan." *Journal of Refugee Studies* 14, no. 1: 43–69.

Fassin, Didier. 2012. *Humanitarian Reason: A Moral History of the Present*. Berkeley: University of California Press.

Feldman, Ilana. 2018. *Life Lived in Relief*. Berkeley: University of California Press.

Feldman, Ilana, and Miriam Ticktin, eds. 2010. *In the Name of Humanity: The Government of Threat and Care*. Durham, NC: Duke University Press.

Ferguson, James. 1994. *The Anti-Politics Machine: Development, Depoliticization and Bureaucratic Power in Lesotho*. Minneapolis: University of Minnesota Press.

———. 1999. *Expectations of Modernity: Myths and Meanings of Urban Life on the Zambian Copperbelt*. Los Angeles: University of California Press.

Filippini, Michele. 2017. *Using Gramsci: A New Approach*. London: Pluto.

Foucault, Michel. 1978. *Discipline and Punish: The Birth of the Prison*. New York: Vintage.

Friese, Heidrun. 2010. "The Limits of Hospitality: Political Philosophy, Undocumented Migration and the Local Arena." *European Journal of Social Theory* 13, no. 3: 323–341.

Fuller, Bruce. 1991. *Growing-Up Modern: The Western State Builds Third-World Schools.* Vol. 59. London: Routledge.

Gardner, Tom. 2018. "'I Was Euphoric': Eritrea's Joy Becomes Ethiopia's Burden amid Huge Exodus." *Guardian*, October 12, 2018. https://www.theguardian.com/global-development/2018/oct/12/eritrea-joy-becomes-ethiopia-burden-huge-exodus-refugees.

Gebru, Bereket. 2017. "Ethiopia: The Two Faces of Migration." *Ethiopian Herald*, June 30, 2017. https://allafrica.com/stories/201706300894.html.

Geschiere, Peter. 1997. *The Modernity of Witchcraft: Politics and the Occult in Postcolonial Africa.* Charlottesville: University of Virginia Press.

Gesler, Wilber M. 1992. "Therapeutic Landscapes: Medical Issues in Light of the New Cultural Geography." *Social Science & Medicine* 34, no. 7: 735–746.

Getnet, Berhanie, Girmay Medhin, and Ataley Alem. 2019. "Symptoms of Post-traumatic Stress Disorder and Depression among Eritrean Refugees in Ethiopia: Identifying Direct, Meditating and Moderating Predictors from Path Analysis." *BMJ Open* 9, no. 1: 1–12.

Gettleman, Jeffrey. 2016. "Africa Rising? African Reeling May Be More Fitting Now." *New York Times*, October 17, 2016. https://www.nytimes.com/2016/10/18/world/africa/africa-rising-africa-reeling-may-be-more-fitting-now.html.

Ghosh, Bobby. 2022. "The World's Deadliest War Isn't in Ukraine, But in Ethiopia." *Washington Post*, March 23, 2022. https://www.washingtonpost.com/business/the-worlds-deadliest-war-isnt-in-ukraine-but-in-ethiopia/2022/03/22/eaf4b83c-a9b6-11ec-8a8e-9c6e9fc7a0de_story.html.

Giuliani, Maria Vittoria. 2017. "Theory of Attachment and Place Attachment." In *Psychological Theories for Environmental Issues*, edited by M. Bonnes, 137–170. London: Routledge.

González, Roberto J. 2013. "Cybernetic Crystal Ball: 'Forecasting' Insurgency in Iraq and Afghanistan." In *Virtual War and Magical Death: Technologies and Imaginaries for Terror and Killing*, edited by Neal Whitehead and Sverker Finnström, 65–84. Durham, NC: Duke University Press.

Greenhouse, Carol J., Elizabeth Mertz, and Kay B. Warren, eds. 2002. *Ethnography in Unstable Places: Everyday Lives in Contexts of Dramatic Political Change.* Durham, NC: Duke University Press.

Gupta, Akhil, and James Ferguson. 1997. *Anthropological Locations: Boundaries and Grounds of a Field Science.* Berkeley: University of California Press.

Guyer, Jane I. 2007. "Prophecy and the Near Future: Thoughts on Macroeconomic, Evangelical, and Punctuated Time." *American Ethnologist* 34, no. 3: 409–421.

Habtom, GebreMichael Kibreab, and Pieter Ruys. 2007. "Traditional Risk-Sharing Arrangements and Informal Social Insurance in Eritrea." *Health Policy* 80, no. 1: 218–235.

Hage, Ghassan. 2005. "A Not So Multi-sited Ethnography of a Not So Imagined Community." *Anthropological Theory* 5, no. 4: 463–475.

———. 2009. *Waiting.* Carlton: Melbourne University Press.

———. 2016. "Questions Concerning a Future-Politics." *History and Anthropology* 27, no. 4: 465–467.

Hall, Stuart. 1997. "The Centrality of Culture: Notes on the Cultural Revolutions of Our Times." In *Media and Cultural Regulations*, edited by K. Thompson, 208–238. Thousand Oaks, CA: Sage.

Hammond, Laura C. 2004. *This Place Will Become Home: Refugee Repatriation to Ethiopia.* Ithaca, NY: Cornell University Press.

Hardy, Vincent and Hauge, Jostein. 2019. "Labour Challenges in Ethiopia's Textile and Leather Industries: No Voice, No Loyalty, No Exit?" *African Affairs* 118, no. 473: 712-736.

Harrell-Bond, Barbara, Eftihia Voutira, and Mark Leopold. 1992. "Counting the Refugees: Gifts, Givers, Patrons and Clients." *Journal of Refugee Studies* 5, no. 3–4: 205–225.

Hepner, Tricia Redeker. 2009. *Soldiers, Martyrs, Traitors, and Exiles: Political Conflict in Eritrea and the Diaspora*. Philadelphia: University of Pennsylvania Press.

Hepner, Tricia Redeker, and Magnus Treiber. 2017. "Economic Migrants, Terrorists, and Illegals: Transnational State Collusion in the Creation of a Post-Refugee World." Paper presented at the 2017 meeting of the American Anthropological Association, Washington, DC, November 29–December 3, 2017.

———. 2021. "Discussion Paper. The Anti-Refugee Machine: A Draft Framework for Migration Studies." *Sociologus* 71, no. 2: 175–189.

Hermez, Sami. 2017. *War Is Coming: Between Past and Future Violence in Lebanon*. Philadelphia: University of Pennsylvania Press.

Hoffman, Daniel. 2011. "Violence, Just in Time: War and Work in Contemporary West Africa." *Cultural Anthropology* 26, no. 1: 34–57.

Hoffstaedter, Gerhard. 2019. "Arrested Refugee Mobilities." *Sojourn: Journal of Social Issues in Southeast Asia* 34, no. 3: 521–546.

Honwana, Alcinda, and Filip De Boeck. 2005. *Makers & Breakers: Children and Youth in Postcolonial Africa*. Oxford: James Currey.

———, eds. 2012. *The Time of Youth: Work, Social Change, and Politics in Africa*. Sterling: Kumarian.

Horst, Cindy. 2006. "Buufis amongst Somalis in Dadaab: The Transnational and Historical Logics behind Resettlement Dreams." *Journal of Refugee Studies* 19, no. 2: 143–157.

Horst, Cindy, and Katarzyna Grabska. 2015. "Flight and Exile—Uncertainty in the Context of Conflict-Induced Displacement." *Social Analysis* 59, no. 1: 1–18.

Hovil, Lucy. 2014. "Local Integration." In *The Oxford Handbook of Refugee and Forced Migration Studies*, edited by Elena Fiddian-Qasmiyeh, 488–498. Oxford: Oxford University Press.

———. 2016. *Refugees, Conflict, and the Search for Belonging*. London: Palgrave Macmillan.

Hovil, Lucy, and Lutz Oette. 2017. "Tackling the Root Causes of Human Trafficking and Smuggling from Eritrea: The Need for an Empirically Grounded EU Policy on Mixed Migration in the Horn of Africa." International Refugee Rights Initiative. https://reliefweb.int/report/eritrea/tackling-root-causes-human-trafficking-and-smuggling-eritrea-need-empirically.

Human Rights Watch. 2003. "The Horn of Africa War: Mass Expulsions and the Nationality Issue." https://www.hrw.org/sites/default/files/reports/ethioerito103.pdf.

———. 2016. "Ethiopia: State of Emergency Risks New Abuses." https://www.hrw.org/news/2016/10/31/ethiopia-state-emergency-risks-new-abuses#.

———. 2021a. "Ethiopia: Eritrean Forces Massacre Tigray Civilians." https://www.hrw.org/news/2021/03/05/ethiopia-eritrean-forces-massacre-tigray-civilians.

———. 2021b. "Ethiopia: Eritrean Refugees Targeted in Tigray." https://www.hrw.org/news/2021/09/16/ethiopia-eritrean-refugees-targeted-tigray.

Hyndman, Jennifer, and Wenona Giles. 2016. *Refugees in Extended Exile: Living on the Edge*. London: Routledge.

Igunza, Emmanuel. 2017. "Can Jobs in Ethiopia Keep Eritrean Refugees Out of Europe?" *BBC News*, July 5, 2017. http://www.bbc.com/news/world-africa-40479530.

IOM (International Organization for Migration). 2018. "Humanitarian Situation Worsens as Over 800,000 Displaced People Face Cold Heavy Rains in Ethiopia." July 13, 2018. https://www.iom.int/news/humanitarian-situation-worsens-over-800000-displaced-people-face-cold-and-heavy-rains-ethiopia.

Jacobsen, Christine M., Marry-Anne Karlsen, and Shahram Khosravi, eds. 2021. *Waiting and the Temporalities of Irregular Migration*. London: Taylor & Francis.

Janeja, Manpreet K., and Andreas Bandak, eds. 2018. *Ethnographies of Waiting: Doubt, Hope and Uncertainty*. London: Bloomsbury.

Jansen, Stef. 2008. "Hope and the State in the Anthropology of Home: Preliminary Notes." *Ethnologia Europaea* 39, no. 1: 54–60.

———. 2014. "On Not Moving Well Enough: Temporal Reasoning in Sarajevo Yearnings for 'Normal Lives.'" *Current Anthropology* 55, no. 9: S74–S84.

———. 2016. "For a Relational, Historical Ethnography of Hope: Indeterminacy and Determination in the Bosnian Herzegovinian Meantime." *History and Anthropology* 27, no. 4: 447–464.

Jean, Melissa. 2015. "The Role of Farming in Place-Making Processes of Resettled Refugees." *Refugee Survey Quarterly* 34, no. 3: 46–69.

Jeffrey, Craig. 2010. *Timepass: Youth, Class, and the Politics of Waiting in India*. Stanford, CA: Stanford University Press.

Jeffrey, Craig, Patricia Jeffery, and Roger Jeffery. 2004. "Degrees without Freedom: The Impact of Formal Education on Dalit Young Men in North India." *Development and Change* 35, no. 5: 963–986.

———. 2005. "When Schooling Fails: Young Men, Education and Low–Caste Politics in Rural North India." *Contributions to Indian Sociology* 39, no. 1: 1–38.

———. 2008. *Degrees without Freedom? Education, Masculinities and Unemployment in North India*. Stanford, CA: Stanford University Press.

Jones, Reese, Corey Johnson, Wendy Brown, Gabriel Popescu, Polly Pallister-Wilkins, Alison P. Mountz, and Emily Gilbert. 2017. "Interventions of State Sovereignty at the Border." *Political Geography* 59:1–10.

Kallio, K. P., I. Meier, and J. Häkli. 2021. "Radical Hope in Asylum Seeking: Political Agency beyond Linear Temporality." *Journal of Ethnic and Migration Studies* 47, no. 17: 4006–4022.

Kassa, Lucy. 2022. "Eritrean Refugees Say They Are Being Arbitrarily Detained in Ethiopian Camps." *Guardian*, July 28, 2022. https://www.theguardian.com/global-development /2022/jul/28/eritrean-refugees-claim-arbitrarily-arrested-beaten-detained-in-ethiopian -camps-unhcr.

Katz, Cindi. 2004. *Growing Up Global: Economic Restructuring and Children's Everyday Lives*. Minneapolis: University of Minnesota Press.

Kawano, Masaharu. 2020. "An Anthropology of Hospitality." *Japanese Review of Cultural Anthropology* 21, no. 1: 509–513.

Haybano, Alebachew Kemisso. 2016. *Integration and Identity among Refugee Children in Ethiopia: Dilemmas of Eritrean and Somali Students in Selected Primary Schools of Addis Ababa*. PhD diss., Addis Ababa University, April 2016. http://etd.aau.edu.et/handle /123456789/3499.

Keunen, Bart. 2011. *Time and Imagination: Chronotopes in Western Narrative Culture*. Evanston, IL: Northwest University Press.

Khosravi, Shahram. 2017. *Precarious Lives: Waiting and Hope in Iran*. Philadelphia: University of Pennsylvania Press.

———. 2019. "What Do We See if We Look at the Border from the Other Side?" *Social Anthropology* 27, no. 3: 409–424.

———. 2021. "Stolen Time." In *Waiting: A Project in Conversation*, edited by Shahram Khosravi, 65–71. Bielefeld: transcript.

Kibreab, Gaim. 1996. *People on the Edge in the Horn: Displacement, Land Use & the Environment in the Gedaref Region, Sudan.* Trenton, NJ: Red Sea Press.

Klein, Natalie. 1998. *Mass Expulsion from Ethiopia: Report on the Deportations of Eritreans and Ethiopians of Eritrean Origin from Ethiopia June–August 1998.* New Haven, CT: Yale School of Law. http://www.dehai.org/conflict/deportees/Klein.html.

Lavers, Tom. 2012. "'Land Grab as Development Strategy? The Political Economy of Agricultural Investment in Ethiopia." *Journal of Peasant Studies* 39, no. 1: 105–132.

Legesse, Asmarom. 1998. *The Uprooted: Case Material of Ethnic Eritrean Deportees from Ethiopia Concerning Human Rights Violations.* Eritrean Human Rights Task Force.https://www.ehrea.org/The%20Uprooted1.htm.

Lems, Annika. 2016. "Placing Displacement: Place-Making in a World of Movement." *Ethnos* 81, no. 2: 315–337.

Lenner, Katharina, and Lewis Turner. 2018. "Making Refugees Work? The Politics of Integrating Syrian Refugees into the Labor Market in Jordan." *Middle East Critique* 28, no. 1: 65–95.

Lester, Rebecca. 2013. "Back from the Edge of Existence: A Critical Anthropology of Trauma." *Transcultural Psychiatry* 50, no. 5: 753–762.

Levinson, Bradley. 2001. *We Are All Equal: Student Culture and Identity at a Mexican Secondary School, 1988–1998.* Durham, NC: Duke University Press.

Levinson, Bradley A., Douglas E. Foley, and Dorothy C. Holland. 1996. *The Cultural Production of the Educated Person: Critical Ethnographies of Schooling and Local Practice.* Albany: State University of New York Press.

Lie, Jon Harald Sande. 2020. "The Humanitarian-Development Nexus: Humanitarian Principles, Practice, and Pragmatics." *Journal of International Humanitarian Action* 5, no. 18: 1–13.

Little, Adrian, and Nick Vaughn-Williams. 2016. "Stopping Boats, Saving Lives, Securing Subjects: Humanitarian Borders in Europe and Australia." *European Journal of International Relations* 23, no. 3: 1–24.

Long, Katy. 2014. "Rethinking 'Durable' Solutions." In *The Oxford Handbook of Refugee and Forced Migration Studies*, edited by Elena Fiddian-Qasmiyeh, 475–487. Oxford: Oxford University Press.

López-Sala, Ana. 2015. "Exploring Dissuasion as a (Geo)Political Instrument in Irregular Migration Control at the Southern Spanish Maritime Border." *Geopolitics* 20, no. 3: 512–534.

Lynch, Paul, Jennie Germann Molz, Alison McIntosh, Peter Lugosi, and Conrad Lashley. 2011. "Theorizing Hospitality." *Hospitality & Society* 1, no. 1: 3–24.

MacLeod, Jay. 2008. *Ain't No Makin' It: Aspirations and Attainment in a Low-Income Neighborhood.* Boulder, CO: Westview.

Mains, Daniel. 2007. "Neoliberal Times: Progress, Boredom, and Shame among Young Men in Urban Ethiopia." *American Ethnologist* 34, no. 4: 659–673.

———. 2011. *Hope Is Cut: Youth, Unemployment, and the Future in Urban Ethiopia.* Philadelphia: Temple University Press.

Makki, Fouad. 2012. "Power and Property: Commercialization, Enclosures, and the Transformation of Agrarian Relations in Ethiopia." *Journal of Peasant Studies* 39, no. 1: 81–104.

Malinowski, Bronislaw. 1927. "Lunar and Seasonal Calendar in the Trobriands." *Journal of the Royal Anthropological Institute of Great Britain and Ireland* 57:203–215.

———. (1925) 1954. *Magic, Science, and Religion, and Other Essays.* New York: Doubleday.

Malkki, Liisa H. 1995a. *Purity and Exile: Violence, Memory, and National Cosmology among Hutu Refugees in Tanzania.* Chicago: University of Chicago Press.

———. 1995b. "Refugees and Exile: From 'Refugee Studies' to the National Order of Things." *Annual Review of Anthropology* 24, no. 1: 495–523.

———. 1996. "Speechless Emissaries: Refugees, Humanitarianism, and Dehistoricization." *Cultural Anthropology* 11, no. 3: 377–404.

Mallett, Richard, Jessica Hagen-Zanker, Nassim Majidi, and Clare Cummings. 2017. "Journeys on Hold: How Policy Influences the Migration Decisions of Eritreans in Ethiopia." Working Paper No. 506, Overseas Development Institute. https://www.odi.org/features /journeys-on-hold.

Mathur, Nayanika. 2014. "The Reign of Terror of the Big Cat: Bureaucracy and the Mediation of Social Times in the Indian Himalaya." *Journal of the Royal Anthropological Institute* 20:148–165.

Matsumura, Keiichiro. 2008. "Moral Economy as Emotional Interaction: Food Sharing and Reciprocity in Highland Ethiopia." In *Contemporary Perspectives on African Moral Economy*, edited by Isaria Kimambo, 139–152. Oxford: African Books Collective.

Mattingly, Cheryl. 2014. *Moral Laboratories: Family Peril and the Struggle for a Good Life.* Berkeley: University of California Press.

Mauss, Marcel. 1990. *The Gift: The Form and Reason for Exchange in Archaic Societies.* London: Routledge.

McClaren, Peter. 1986. *Schooling as a Ritual Performance.* London: Routledge & Kegan Paul.

Médecins Sans Frontières. 2022. "Trying to Cross the Sea Is Facing Death, but Staying in Libya Is Facing Death Too." June 17, 2022. https://www.doctorswithoutborders.org/latest /trying-cross-sea-facing-death-staying-libya-facing-death-too.

Megento, Tebarek Lika. 2013. "Inner City Housing and Urban Development-Induced Displacement: Impact on Poor Female-Headed Households in Arada Sub City of Addis Ababa, Ethiopia." *Journal of Sustainable Development in Africa* 15, no. 2: 131–141.

Mehari, Getaneh, Mesfin Bogale, Lakew Regassa, and Tewodros Mekonnen. 2002a. *Civics and Ethical Education Student Textbook Grade 10.* Addis Ababa: Federal Democratic Republic of Ethiopia Ministry of Education; New Delhi: Laxmi Publications.

Mehari, Getaneh, Mesfin Bogale, Lakew Regassa, and Tewodros Mekonnen. 2002b. *Civics and Ethical Education Student Textbook Grade 11.* Addis Ababa: Federal Democratic Republic of Ethiopia Ministry of Education; New Delhi: Laxmi Publications.

Mengiste, Tekalign Ayalew. 2018. "Refugee Protections from Below: Smuggling in the Eritrea-Ethiopia Context." *The ANNALS of the American Academy of Political and Social Science* 676, no. 1: 57–76.

———. 2019. "Precarious Mobility: Infrastructures of Eritrean Migration through the Sudan and the Sahara Desert." *African Human Mobility Review* 5, no. 1: 1482–1509.

Mersie, Ayenat, Giulia Paravicini, and Katharine Houreld. 2021. "Dual Agenda: In Ethiopia's Civil War, Eritrea's Army Exacted Deadly Vengeance on Old Foes." Reuters Special Report, November 1, 2021. https://www.reuters.com/investigates/special-report/ethiopia -conflict-eritrea/.

Miller, Kenneth E., and Andrew Rasmussen. 2017. "The Mental Health of Civilians Displaced by Armed Conflict: An Ecological Model of Refugee Distress." *Epidemiology and Psychiatric Sciences* 26, no. 2: 129–138.

Miller, Sarah. 2022. "Nowhere to Run: Eritrean Refugees in Tigray: Brief, March 2022." Refugees International, March 3, 2022. https://www.refugeesinternational.org /reports/2022/3/1/nowhere-to-run-eritrean-refugees-in-tigray.

Miyazaki, Hirokazu. 2006. "Economy of Dreams: Hope in Global Capitalism and Its Critiques." *Cultural Anthropology* 21, no. 2: 147–172.

Moroşanu, Roxana, and Felix Ringel. 2016. "Time-Tricking: A General Introduction." *Cambridge Journal of Anthropology* 34, no. 1: 17–21.

Mwai, Peter. 2022. "Ethiopia's Tigray Crisis: Why It's Hard Getting Aid into the Region." *BBC News*, April 7, 2022. https://www.bbc.com/news/57929853.

Nowotny, Helga. 2018. *Time: The Modern and Postmodern Experience*. Hoboken, NJ: John Wiley & Sons.

Olwig, Karen Fog. 2021. "The End and Ends of Flight. Temporariness, Uncertainty and Meaning in Refugee Life." *Ethnos* 2021:1–17. https://doi.org/10.1080/00141844.2020.1867606.

O'Neill, Bruce. 2014. "Cast Aside: Boredom, Downward Mobility, and Homelessness in Post-Communist Bucharest." *Cultural Anthropology* 29, no. 1: 8–31.

Ortner, Sherry B. 2006. *Anthropology and Social Theory: Culture, Power, and the Acting Subject*. Durham, NC: Duke University Press.

Oxfam. 2017. "The Commitment to Reducing Inequality Index 2018: A Global Ranking of Governments Based on What They Are Doing to Tackle the Gap between Rich and Poor." https://policy-practice.oxfam.org/resources/the-commitment-to-reducing-inequality -index-2018-a-global-ranking-of-government-620553/.

Pallister-Wilkins, Polly. 2015. "The Humanitarian Politics of European Border Policing: Frontex and Border Police in Evros." *International Political Sociology* 9, no. 1: 53–69.

———. 2017. "Humanitarian Borderwork." In *Border Politics: Defining Spaces of Governance and Transgressions*, edited by Cengiz Gunay and Nina Witjes, 84–103. Berlin: Springer.

Pankhurst, Alula, and François Piguet, eds. 2009. *Moving People in Ethiopia: Development, Displacement and the State*. Woodbridge: James Currey.

Papademetriou, Demetrios, and Susan Fratzke. 2016. "Beyond Care and Maintenance: Rebuilding Hope and Opportunity for Refugees, Council Statement." Transatlantic Council on Migration, a Project of the Migration Policy Institute. https://www .migrationpolicy.org/research/beyond-care-and-maintenance-rebuilding-hope-and -opportunity-refugees-transatlantic-council.

Paravicini, Giulia. 2020. "Ethiopia's Tigray Holds Regional Election in Defiance of Federal Government." Reuters, September 8, 2020. https://www.reuters.com/article/us-ethiopia -politics/ethiopias-tigray-holds-regional-election-in-defiance-of-federal-government -idUSKBN25Z35S.

Paszkiewicz, Natalia. 2017. "'One Day, I Hope, I Will Go': How Trump's Ban Hit an Eritrean Refugee Camp in Ethiopia." Middle East Eye, March 29, 2017. https://www.middleeasteye .net/opinion/one-day-i-hope-i-will-go-how-trumps-ban-hit-eritrean-refugee-camp -ethiopia.

———. 2021. "'The Whole World Has Left Us': Eritrean Refugees Caught in Tigray Crossfire." TRT World, July 26, 2021. https://www.trtworld.com/perspectives/the-whole-world-has -left-us-eritrean-refugees-caught-in-tigray-crossfire-48675.

Perumal, Juliet. 2015. "Responding with Hospitality: Refugee Children in the South African Education System." *Education as Change* 19, no. 3: 65–90.

Pherali, Tejendra, and Mai Abu Moghli. 2021. "Higher Education in the Context of Mass Displacement: Towards Sustainable Solutions for Refugees." *Journal of Refugee Studies* 34, no. 2: 2159–2179.

Pitt-Rivers, Julian. 2012. "The Law of Hospitality." *HAU: Journal of Ethnographic Theory* 2, no. 1: 501–517.

Poole, Amanda, and Jennifer Ann Riggan. 2022. "Oscillating Imaginaries: War, Peace, and the Precarious Relations between Eritrea and Ethiopia." *Modern Africa: Politics, History and Society* 10, no. 1: 33–60.

Price, David. 2013. "The Role of Culture in Wars Waged by Robots: Connecting Drones, Anthropology, and Human Terrain Systems Prehistory." In *Virtual War and Magical Death: Technologies and Imaginaries for Terror and Killing*, edited by Neal Whitehead and Sverker Finnström, 46–64. Durham, NC: Duke University Press.

"Proclamation No. 378/2003 on Ethiopian Nationality." 2003. Citizenship Rights in Africa Initiative, December 23, 2003. https://citizenshiprightsafrica.org/proclamation-no -3782003-on-ethiopian-nationality/.

Pyle, Jean L. 2006. "Globalization, Transnational Migration, and Gendered Care Work: Introduction." *Globalizations* 3, no. 3: 283–295.

Raffles, Hugh. 2014. *In Amazonia*. Princeton, NJ: Princeton University Press.

Raghuram, Parvati, Clare Madge, and Pat Noxolo. 2009. "Rethinking Responsibility and Care for a Postcolonial World." *Geoforum* 40, no. 1: 5–13.

Ramsay, Georgina. 2018. *Impossible Refuge: The Control and Constraint of Refugee Futures*. New York: Routledge.

Ramsay, Georgina, and Hedda Haugen Askland. 2020. "Displacement as Condition: A Refugee, a Farmer and the Teleology of Life." *Ethnos* 87, no. 3: 600–621. https://doi.org/10.1080 /00141844.2020.1804971.

Redfield, Peter. 2005. "Doctors, Borders, and Life in Crisis." *Cultural Anthropology* 20, no. 3: 328–361.

Refugees International. 2019. "Ethiopia's Treatment of Its Own IDPs Making Crisis Worse." https://www.refugeesinternational.org/reports/2019/5/17/ethiopias-treatment-of-its-own -idps-making-crisis-worse.

Reno, William. 2011. *Warfare in Independent Africa*. Vol. 5. Cambridge: Cambridge University Press.

Reuters. 2020. "Ethiopia Returning Eritrean Refugees to Tigray Camps; U.N. Concerned over Move." December 11, 2020. https://www.reuters.com/article/uk-ethiopia-conflict -idUKKBN28L0X8.

———. 2021. "Tigrayan Forces Take Control of Ethiopia's Lalibela, a UN World Heritage Site— Eyewitnesses." August 5, 2021. https://www.reuters.com/world/africa/tigrayan-forces -take-control-ethiopian-town-lalibela-un-world-heritage-site-2021-08-05/.

———. 2022. "UN: Air Strike Kills Three in Eritrean Refugee Camp in Ethiopia." January 7, 2022. https://www.reuters.com/world/africa/un-ethiopian-air-strike-kills-three-camp -eritrean-refugees-2022-01-07/.

Riggan, Jennifer. 2011. "In Between Nations: Ethiopian-Born Eritreans, Liminality, and War." *Political and Legal Anthropology Review* 34, no. 1: 131–154.

———. 2013. "Imagining Emigration: Debating National Duty in Eritrean Classrooms." *Africa Today* 60, no. 2: 85–106.

———. 2016. *The Struggling State: Mass Militarization and the Education of Eritrea*. Philadelphia: Temple University Press.

Riggan, Jennifer, and Amanda Poole. 2018. "'We Can't Go Home': What Does Peace Mean for Eritrea's Refugees?" African Arguments, August 1, 2018. http://africanarguments.org /2018/08/01/cant-go-home-peace-eritrea-refugees/.

———. 2019. "The Global and Local Politics of Refugee Management in the Horn: Ethiopian Refugee Policy and Eritrean Refugee Agency." In *Refugees and Forced Migration in the Horn and Eastern Africa*, edited by Johannes Dragsbaek Schmidt, Leah Kimathi, and Michael Omondi Owiso, 155–174. Berlin: Springer.

Ringel, Felix. 2016. "Can Time Be Tricked? A Theoretical Introduction." *Cambridge Journal of Anthropology* 34, no. 1: 22–31.

———. 2021. "Hope and the Future: Temporal Agency and the Politics of Hope in Late Capitalism." *Society and Space* 39, no. 5: 880–886.

Rios, Michael, and Joshua Watkins. 2015. "Beyond 'Place': Translocal Placemaking of the Hmong Diaspora." *Journal of Planning Education and Research* 35, no. 2: 209–219.

Rishbeth, Clare, and Mark Powell. 2013. "Place Attachment and Memory: Landscapes of Belonging as Experienced Post-Migration." *Landscape Research* 38, no. 2: 160–178.

Ritter, Karl. 2021. "1,600 Migrants Lost at Sea in Mediterranean This Year." Associated Press, November 25, 2021. https://apnews.com/article/immigration-africa-migration-united -nations-mediterranean-sea-0b8f05247565648500045123e6e617717.

Robbins, Joel. 2004. *Becoming Sinners: Christianity and Moral Torment in a Papua New Guinea Society*. Berkeley: University of California Press.

Rozakou, Katerina. 2012. "The Biopolitics of Hospitality in Greece: Humanitarianism and the Management of Refugees." *American Ethnologist* 39, no. 3: 562–577.

———. 2020. "The Violence of Accelerated Time: Waiting and Hasting During 'The Long Summer of Migration' in Greece." In *Waiting and the Temporalities of Irregular Migration*, edited by Christine Jacobsen, Marry-Anne Karlsen, and Shahram Khosravi, 23–39. London: Routledge.

Rudolf, Markus. 2022. "We Live in a State of Fear: Eritrean Refugees Keep Bearing the Brunt of the Ethiopian Crisis." Ammodi: African Migration, Mobility, and Displacement, September 19, 2022. https://ammodi.com/2022/09/19/we-live-in-a-state-of-fear-eritrean -refugees-keep-bearing-the-brunt-of-the-ethiopian-crisis/.

Rumford, Chris. 2008. "Introduction: Citizenship and Borderwork in Europe." *Space and Polity* 12, no. 1: 1–12.

Sampson, Robyn, and Sandra M. Gifford. 2010. "Place-Making, Settlement and Well-Being: The Therapeutic Landscapes of Recently Arrived Youth with Refugee Backgrounds." *Health & Place* 16, no. 1: 116–131.

Schlein, Lisa. 2021. "UN Says Armed Groups Threaten Thousands of Eritrean Refugees in Tigray." Voice of America, July 27, 2021. https://www.voanews.com/a/africa_un-says -armed-groups-threaten-thousands-eritrean-refugees-tigray/6208795.html.

Scott, James C. 1998. *Seeing like a State: How Certain Schemes to Improve the Human Condition Have Failed*. New Haven, CT: Yale University Press.

Shao, Oliver. 2017. "Forced Migration and Ethnomusicology." Presentation from "President's Roundtable: Engaged Activism among Ethnomusicologists Responding to the Contemporary Dynamic of Migrants and Refugees." Chaired by Anne K. Rasmussen (College of William and Mary). Society for Ethnomusicology Annual Meeting, Denver, CO, October 27, 2017. YouTube video, 00:13:39, posted October 23, 2018. https://www .youtube.com/watch?v=FRUrbb5cuk4.

Shryock, Andrew. 2012. "Breaking Hospitality Apart: Bad Hosts, Bad Guests, and the Problem of Sovereignty." *Journal of the Royal Anthropological Institute* 18:S20–S33.

Sluka, Jeffrey. 2013. "Virtual War in the Tribal Zone: Air Strikes, Drones, Civilian Casualties, and Losing Hearts and Minds in Afghanistan and Pakistan." In *Virtual War and Magical Death: Technologies and Imaginaries for Terror and Killing*, edited by Neal Whitehead and Sverker Finnström, 171–193. Durham, NC: Duke University Press.

Smith, Lahra. 2013. *Making Citizens in Africa: Ethnicity, Gender and National Identity in Ethiopia*. Cambridge: Cambridge University Press.

Stambach, Amy. 2000. *Lessons from Mount Kilimanjaro: Schooling, Community, and Gender in East Africa*. New York: Routledge.

Stambach, Amy, and Kathleen Hall, eds. 2016. *Anthropological Perspectives on Student Futures: Youth and the Politics of Possibility.* New York: Palgrave Macmillan.

Stern, Maximilian. 2015. "The Khartoum Process: Critical Assessment and Policy Recommendations." Working papers, Istituto Affari Internazionali, Rome. https://www.files.ethz.ch/isn/195645/iaiwp1549.pdf.

Stevenson, Jacqueline, and Sally Baker. 2018. *Refugees in Higher Education: Debate, Discourse and Practice.* Bingley: Emerald Group.

Strand, Arne. 2020. "Humanitarian–Development Nexus." In *Humanitarianism: Keywords,* edited by Antonio De Lauri, 104–106. Leiden: Brill.

Strathern, Marilyn. 2000. *Audit Cultures: Anthropological Studies in Accountability, Ethics and the Academy.* London: Routledge.

Stroeken, Koen. 2013. "War at Large: Miner Magic and the Carrion System." In *Virtual War and Magical Death: Technologies and Imaginaries for Terror and Killing,* edited by Neal Whitehead and Sverker Finnström, 234–250. Durham, NC: Duke University Press.

Stubbs, Paul. 2018. "Slow, Slow, Quick, Quick, Slow: Power, Expertise and the Hegemonic Temporalities of Austerity." *Innovation: The European Journal of Social Science Research* 31, no. 1: 25–39.

Swartz, Lana. 2018. "What Was Bitcoin, What Will It Be? The Techno-economic Imaginaries of a New Money Technology." *Cultural Studies* 32, no. 4: 623–650.

Tesfa-Alem, Tekle. 2016. "Ethiopia Wins Seat on UN Security Council." Sudan Tribune, June 30, 2016. https://sudantribune.com/article57748/.

Tesfay, Sába. 2016. "Gift-Giving and Hospitality in Eritrean Tigrinya Society." *Acta Ethnographica Hungarica* 61, no. 1: 117–133.

Ticktin, Miriam. 2011. *Casualties of Care: Immigration and the Politics of Humanitarianism in France.* Oakland: University of California Press.

Townsend, Robert Allan, and Janice Pascal. 2012. "Therapeutic Landscapes: Understanding Migration to Australian Regional and Rural Communities." *Rural Society* 22, no. 1: 59–66.

Treiber, Magnus. 2014. "Grasping Kiflu's Fear—Informality and Existentialism in Migration from North-East Africa." *Modern Africa: Politics, History and Society* 1, no. 2: 111–141.

———. 2019. "Informality and Informalization among Eritrean Refugees: Why Migration Does Not Provide a Lesson in Democracy." In *Immigration and the Current Social, Political, and Economic Climate: Breakthroughs in Research and Practice,* edited by Information Resources Management Association, 644–668. Hershey, PA: IGI Global.

Tronvoll, Kjetil. 2022. "The Anatomy of Ethiopia's Civil War." *Current History* 121, no. 835: 163–169. https://online.ucpress.edu/currenthistory/article/121/835/163/124577/The-Anatomy-of-Ethiopia-s-Civil-War.

UNHCR (UN High Commissioner for Refugees). 2014. "Which Side Are You On? Discussion Paper on UNHCR's Policy and Practice of Incentive Payments to Refugees." December 2014. https://www.refworld.org/docid/549951ec4.html.

———. 2016. "Global Focus: 2016 Year End Report: Operation: Ethiopia." November 6, 2017. https://reporting.unhcr.org/sites/default/files/pdfsummaries/GR2016-Ethiopia-eng.pdf.

———. 2017a. "Ethiopia: Applying the Comprehensive Refugee Response Framework (CRRF)." https://data.unhcr.org/en/documents/download/65916.

———. 2017b. "Global Focus: 2017 Year End Report: Operation: Ethiopia." July 7, 2018. https://reporting.unhcr.org/sites/default/files/pdfsummaries/GR2017-Ethiopia-eng.pdf.

———. 2017c. "Oral Update on the Comprehensive Refugee Response, 16 March 2017." 68th Meeting of the Standing Committee, Palais des Nations. http://www.unhcr.org/58cfa1d97.pdf.

———. 2017d. "Refugees and Asylum Seekers from Eritrea in Ethiopia." https://reporting.unhcr .org/node/15848.

———. 2018a. "Camp Profile—Mai Aini." https://data2.unhcr.org/ar/documents/download /62694.

———. 2018b. "Country Data Ethiopia—UNHCR Data Portal." https://data2.unhcr.org/en /country/eth/160.

———. 2018c. "Ethiopia." March 2018. https://www.unhcr.org/en-us/ethiopia.html.

———. 2018d. "From Commitment to Action: Highlights of Progress towards Comprehensive Refugee Responses Since the Adoption of the New York Declaration." https://www.unhcr .org/events/conferences/5b8d1ad34/commitment-action-highlights-progress-towards -comprehensive-refugee-responses.html.

———. 2018e. "Update #2 on New Arrivals from Eritrea." https://reliefweb.int/sites/reliefweb .int/files/resources/66202.pdf.

———. 2019. "Ethiopia: An Overview of How the Global Compact on Refugees Is Being Turned into Action in Ethiopia." https://globalcompactrefugees.org/article/ethiopia.

———. 2021a. "Eritrean Refugees in Tigray Caught Up in Conflict." July 27, 2021. https://www .unhcr.org/en-us/news/briefing/2021/7/60ffc4d44/eritrean-refugees-tigray-caught -conflict.html.

———. 2021b. "UNHCR Ethiopia Operational Update (December 2021)." ReliefWeb, December 21, 2021. https://reliefweb.int/report/ethiopia/unhcr-ethiopia-operational-update -december-2021.

———. 2022a. "Deteriorating Conditions Putting Eritrean Refugees in Grave Risk in Tigray." January 21, 2022. https://www.unhcr.org/en-us/news/briefing/2022/1/61ea6fe74 /deteriorating-conditions-eritrean-refugees-grave-risk-tigray.html.

———. 2022b. "Flash Update #3—UNHCR Northern Ethiopia Emergency Situation." ReliefWeb, September 28, 2022. https://reliefweb.int/report/ethiopia/flash-update-3 -unhcr-northern-ethiopia-emergency-situation-28-september-2022.

UN OCHA (UN Office for the Coordination of Humanitarian Affairs). 2021. "Ethiopia—Tigray Region Humanitarian Update Situation Report." ReliefWeb, July 19, 2021. https:// reliefweb.int/report/ethiopia/ethiopia-tigray-region-humanitarian-update-situation -report-19-july-2021.

Valletta Summit Action Plan. 2015. "2015 Valletta Summit on Migration." Valletta Summit, November 11–12, 2015. https://www.consilium.europa.eu/media/21839/action_plan_en.pdf.

Varenne, Herve, and Ray McDermott. 1998. *Successful Failure: The School America Builds*. New York: Routledge.

Vari, Elisa. 2020. "Italy-Libya Memorandum of Understanding: Italy's International Obligations." *Hastings International and Comparative Law Review* 43, no. 1: 5. https:// repository.uchastings.edu/cgi/viewcontent.cgi?article=1844&context=hastings _international_comparative_law_review.

Vasey, Katie. 2011. "Place-Making, Provisional Return, and Well-Being: Iraqi Refugee Women in Australia." *Refuge: Canada's Journal on Refugees* 28, no. 1: 25–36.

Walsh, Declan. 2021. "Jubilant Tigray Capital Greets Insurgents after Ethiopian Retreat." *New York Times*, June 29, 2021. https://www.nytimes.com/2021/06/29/world/africa/Tigray -Ethiopia.html.

Walsh, Declan, and Simon Marks. 2021. "Ethiopia Declares State of Emergency as Rebels Advance Toward Capital." *New York Times*, November 2, 2021. https://www.nytimes .com/2021/11/02/world/africa/ethiopia-state-of-emergency.html.

Weldemichael, Awet T., Yibeyin Hagos Yohannes, Meron Estefanos, and Anonymous. 2022. "Between a Rock and a Hard Place: Eritrean Refugees in Tigray and the Ethiopian Civil War." International Peace Research Association. https://martinplaut.files.wordpress .com/2022/02/between_a_rock_and_a_hard_place-eritrean_refugees_in_tigray_and _ethiopian_civil_war_weldemichael_et._al._2022.pdf.

West, Harry. 2008. *Ethnographic Sorcery*. Chicago: University of Chicago Press.

WFP (World Food Program) and FAO (Food and Agriculture Organization). 2022. "Hunger Hotspots. FAO-WFP Early Warnings on Acute Food Insecurity: October 2022 to January 2023 Outlook." Rome. https://docs.wfp.org/api/documents/WFP-0000142656/download /?_ga=2.9888054.266458646.1665840293-1267393985.1665840293.

Whitehead, Neal, and Sverker Finnström. 2013. "Introduction: Virtual War and Magical Death." In *Virtual War and Magical Death: Technologies and Imaginaries for Terror and Killing*, edited by Neal Whitehead and Sverker Finnström, 1–25. Durham, NC: Duke University Press.

Willis, Paul E. 1977. *Learning to Labor: How Working Class Kids Get Working Class Jobs*. London: Columbia University Press.

Woldemikael, Tekle Mariam. 2018. "Introduction." In *Postliberation Eritrea*, edited by Tekle Mariam Woldemikael. Bloomington: Indiana University Press. https://iu.pressbooks.pub /postliberationeritrea/chapter/introduction-postliberation-eritrea-2/.

World Bank. 2018. "Ethiopia: Economic Opportunities Program." Report No: 126766-ET. http:// documents.worldbank.org/curated/en/226021530243071432/pdf/NEW-ETHIOPIA-PAD-06072018.pdf.

Xinhua. 2017. "UN Praises Ethiopia for its Refugee Handling." New China, June 21, 2017. http:// www.xinhuanet.com/english/2017-06/21/c_136384048.htm.

Yntiso, Gebre. 2008. "Urban Development and Displacement in Addis Ababa: The Impact of Resettlement Projects on Low-Income Households." *Eastern Africa Social Science Research Review* 24, no. 2: 53–77.

Index

Abiy Ahmed, ix, 163, 164, 165; awarded Nobel Prize, ix, 164, 165; elevation to power as Prime Minister of Ethiopia, 163

Addis Ababa, xi, 44, 51, 88, 115, 117, 141, 143, 154, 163, 167, 168; as field site, 21–22, urban development, 37, 138, urban refugees in, 62, 64, 81, 87, 100, 124–127, 132

Addis Ababa University, xi, 115, 124, 141

Adi Harush, ix, xi, 22, 60, 61, 75, 79, 162, 166, 167, 168, 169

Administration for Refugee and Returnee Affairs (ARRA), xi, 7, 27, 77, 91, 124

agency, 4, 12, 23, 26, 52, 63, 94–96, 102, 112, 122, 133–134, 137, 140, 145n7, 145n9, 146n11, 146n12, 147, 149, 153, 155, 159; economic agency, 42; temporal agency, 2, 5, 12, 16–21, 25n13, 25n19, 86, 87–89, 113, 117–119, 123, 146n10; through care practices, 103

Amhara, ix, 52, 168, 169, 170

Amharic, 92, 109, 168

Afar, ix, 10, 25n10, 169, 170

alcohol, 48

alcoholism, 70, 101, 106

Andalusia, 67n8

anthropology, 12, 24, 25n14, 49, 67n2, 73, 90n6, 103, 120, 146n13; anthropology of time, 24n8

Appadurai, Arjun, 18, 20, 66, 90n7, 145n3, 159

Asmara, 4, 5, 164, 166

aspirations, 2, 13, 18, 21, 40, 41, 69, 79, 89, 122, 131, 141, 148, 153, 156, 158; unfulfilled aspirations, 70, 147, 151

asylum, 1, 5, 10, 14, 24n2, 24n5, 25n10, 28, 30, 33, 36, 46, 47, 50, 52, 55, 94, 114n6, 126, 130, 157, 170

asylum seekers, 1, 10, 24n2, 25n10, 28, 30, 46, 47, 50, 52, 114n6, 170

Axum university, 22, 64, 65

Bakhtin, Mikhail, 74, 158

biopolitics, 103, 155, 157

bitcoin, 115, 116, 117, 141–44. *See also* cryptocurrency

borders, 1, 9, 28, 29, 39, 46, 53, 102, 130, 156, 160, 171; securing European borders, 30–34, 36, 37

Bourdieu, Pierre, 14, 19, 70, 89n2, 90n4

bureaucracy, 12, 25n11, 63, 64, 66, 71, 73, 75, 77, 79, 89, 97, 107, 111, 146n10, 151; bureaucratic processes, 85, 97, 120; bureaucratized care, 85, 105; bureaucratized hospitality, 65, 66, 79

businesses, 3, 4, 8, 20, 42, 60, 62, 64, 82, 92, 94, 96, 99, 100, 101, 103, 104, 107–112, 114n5, 129, 138, 141, 142, 147, 150

care, caretaking, 6, 18, 19, 29, 22, 27, 36, 40, 48, 65, 76, 77, 79, 81, 94–109, 111–113, 116, 118, 120, 122, 128, 143–144, 147–150, 152, 153, 155, 156, 162; care for family, 136–137; care of refugees by aid workers, 103; caretaking as time-making, 19, 21; cartography of care, 58–59; medical care, 157, 169–171; temporal caretaking, 20, 94, 96, 102, 107, 109. *See also* hospitality

chronotope, 74, 138, 158

citizens, citizenship, 8, 10, 27, 38, 39, 44, 47, 52–54, 64, 66, 74, 78, 97, 98, 115, 121, 156; status of Eritreans in Ethiopia, 55–57; second-class citizenship, 64, 78

Civic and Ethical Education (CEE) curriculum, 72

civics, 62, 72

Collier, Paul, and Betts, Alexandra, 6, 28, 45n4

colonialism, 97, 159

colonial racism, 114n3, 159

Communist. *See* Derg

Comprehensive Refugee Response Framework (CRRF), 34, 38, 44, 46, 60

conscription. *See* national service

conspiracy theories, 130, 131

Copperbelt (Zambia), 161n3

cosmology, cosmologies, 24n8, 119–124, 137, 143, 158, 159
COVID-19, ix, xii, 88, 165
crisis, 2, 12, 23, 25n13, 28, 30–31, 40, 54, 70, 102, 110, 121, 142, 152; cosmology in crisis, 121; crisis of hope, 102; crisis of teleology, 70; family crisis 135–136, 151; financial crisis, 135, 136, 142; humanitarian crisis, 54; refugee crisis, ix, 9, 28, 37, 46, 157
cryptocurrency, 140, 141, 142, 143. *See also* Bitcoin
culture, 4, 11, 48, 49, 50, 51, 52, 96, 121, 162
cultural production, 75, 76, 90n4

dance, 3, 151, 152. *See also* music
Danish Refugee Council, xi, 105, 152
death, 1, 2, 8, 29, 54, 85, 86, 102, 124, 164, 165, 172. *See also* life, suffering
deportations, 56, 57, 63, 92, 114n4, 133, 162
Derg, 53
Dessie, 168
development, 1, 9, 19, 44, 45n3, 45n6, 53, 54, 60, 66, 68, 72, 74, 104, 105, 107, 128, 150, 156–158, 160, 161n4; approach to refugee management 27–38; temporality of development 40–43. *See also* economic development
Development and Inter-Church Aid Commission (DICAC), xi, 105
Dick, Hilary Parsons, xii, 158, 161n6
displacement, 4–5, 12, 16, 18–19, 23, 25n14, 33, 37, 50, 54, 101, 103, 112, 120, 122, 133
distimement, 4
durable solutions, 2, 24n5, 27–29, 34–35, 43, 156–157, 160
Durkheim, Emil, 24n8

economic actors, 6, 28, 38, 41–42
economic development, 29, 44, 60, 158
education, 11, 14–15, 19, 20, 21–22, 26n15, 35, 55, 62, 64, 78, 80–88, 89n2, 90n4, 91, 92, 104, 105, 107, 116–118, 120, 127, 128, 132, 138–140, 146n11, 147–150, 152, 154, 160; as local integration 6–8, 37–38; as deterrent to migration, 1–3; as a strategy of time-making 19–20; as teleological 70–75; primary school, 21, 91, 106, 107; secondary school, 21, 22, 61, 68–69, *69*, 75, 77, 84,

115; tertiary education, 78; university education, 1, 14, 78, 128; vocational education, 42, 104, 120, 150, 152. *See also* civic and ethical education (CEE), schooling, universities
Enlightenment, the, 12
Ethiopian Orthodox Tewahedo Church Development and Inter-Church Aid Commission (DICAC). *See* Development and Inter-Church Aid Commission (DICAC)
Eritrea, Eritreans, 1, 2, 6, 7, 16, 24n2, 37, 76, 78, 81, 86, 87, 89, 92, 95, 98, 100, 101, 102, 106, 107, 108, 114n1, 115, 121, 122, 124, 130, 132–138, 140, 142, 147, 151, 153, 154, 158; displacement from Eritrea 4–5; hospitality by and towards 47–60, 62–66; status in Ethiopia 9–11, 25n10, 42; research with, 21–23; in Tigray conflict 162–171
Eritrean People's Liberation Front (EPLF), 101
Eritrean Refugee University Student Association (ERUSA), 87, 138, 153. *See also* future-making
Ethiopia, ix, x, xi, xii, 1, 2, 3, 5–12, 13, 14, 16, 20, 22, 23, 24n2, 25n10, 27–30, 32, 34–37, 38, 39–43, 45n6, 46, 47, 48, 50–58, 62–66, 70, 74, 76, 81, 83–87, 92, 95, 99, 100–102, 104, 105, 106, 112, 113, 116, 118, 122, 125, 126, 128, 132, 133, 137, 138, 140, 142, 143, 146, 147, 148, 152, 153, 154, 156, 158, 162–166, 168–171; Eritreans, threat of deportation from Ethiopia of, 92, 133, 164; Ethiopian government, 7, 25n10, 53, 54, 56, 57, 62, 65, 86, 87, 88, 133, 164, 166, 167, 168, 169, 170; Ethiopian hospitality to refugees, 46, 52, 54, 163; Ethiopian Nationality Law Proclamation, 57; Ethiopian Pledges 1, 6, 7, 8, 9, 11, 38, 39, 40, 41, 42, 43, 44, 54, 164, 165; Ethiopian Refugee Proclamation, 7, 8, 39, 44, 165. *See also* Tigray
Ethiopian People's Revolutionary Democratic Front (EPRDF), 163
ethnographic methods, 21–22
ethnographic present, 162, 171
Europe, 1, 2, 6, 9, 10, 23, 24n4, 28–35, 46, 65, 72, 116, 132, 150, 156, 170; growing restrictiveness of migration management paradigms in Europe, 28

JENNIFER RIGGAN is Professor and Director of International Studies in the Department of Historical and Political Studies at Arcadia University. She is author of *The Struggling State: Nationalism, Mass Militarization, and the Education of Eritrea.*

AMANDA POOLE is Professor of Anthropology at Indiana University of Pennsylvania.

For Indiana University Press

Lesley Bolton, Project Manager/Editor
Brian Carroll, Rights Manager
Allison Chaplin, Acquisitions Editor
Sophia Hebert, Assistant Acquisitions Editor
Samantha Heffner, Marketing and Publicity Manager
Brenna Hosman, Production Coordinator
Katie Huggins, Production Manager
Dan Pyle, Online Publishing Manager
Jennifer Witzke, Senior Artist and Book Designer

www.ingramcontent.com/pod-product-compliance
Lightning Source LLC
Chambersburg PA
CBHW030331270326
41926CB00010B/1575